Cambridge Historical Series

EDITED BY G. W. PROTHERO, Litt.D., LL.D.

HONORARY FELLOW OF KING'S COLLEGE, CAMBRIDGE,
LATE PROFESSOR OF HISTORY IN THE UNIVERSITY OF EDINBURGH.

T0300517

WESTERN CIVILISATION

IN ITS ECONOMIC ASPECTS

(MEDIAEVAL AND MODERN TIMES)

AN ESSAY

ON

WESTERN CIVILISATION

IN ITS ECONOMIC ASPECTS

(MEDIAEVAL AND MODERN TIMES)

BY

W. CUNNINGHAM, D.D.

HON. LL.D. EDIN.; HON. FELLOW OF GONVILLE AND CAIUS COLLEGE,
FELLOW AND LECTURER OF TRINITY COLLEGE, AND
VICAR OF GREAT S. MARY'S, CAMBRIDGE.

CAMBRIDGE:
AT THE UNIVERSITY PRESS
1900

CAMBRIDGE UNIVERSITY PRESS
Cambridge, New York, Melbourne, Madrid, Cape Town,
Singapore, São Paulo, Delhi, Mexico City

Cambridge University Press
The Edinburgh Building, Cambridge CB2 8RU, UK

Published in the United States of America by Cambridge University Press, New York

www.cambridge.org
Information on this title: www.cambridge.org/9781107624146

First published 1900
First paperback edition 2013

A catalogue record for this publication is available from the British Library

ISBN 978-1-107-62414-6 Paperback

TO

PRESIDENT ELIOT

I DEDICATE THIS MEMENTO OF MY WORK

AT HARVARD UNIVERSITY.

PREFACE.

THROUGHOUT this Essay I have tried to show how the material progress of the human race has been carried on and affected by one great polity after another. Friendly critics have said that the scheme of the book brings out the organic connection between countries and between periods that seem to lie very far apart; but the selection of materials[1] and the proportion of space assigned to different topics, especially in this second volume, may prove disappointing to readers who are keenly interested in the study of the past, for its own sake. Many historical problems might doubtless be seen in clearer light if they were approached from the economic standpoint, but I have not attempted to deal with such difficulties. The definite object of my Essay has been to point out the remote and complicated causes in the past which have co-operated to mould industry and commerce into their present forms. The commercial and industrial influence of the Anglo-Saxon race is so marked and far-reaching that it has been necessary to assign great prominence to the circumstances which have rendered England paramount on the sea. On the other hand the vigorous trading life of Italian

---

[1] So much uncertainty attaches to all attempts to interpret quotations of prices and to institute comparisons on this basis between the conditions current in different periods, that I have found it impossible to make much use of evidence of this kind. Compare my article *On the Value of Money* in the Harvard *Quarterly Journal of Economics*, June 1899.

cities in the Middle Ages was not very fruitful so far as after times were concerned; and we cannot but feel that these magnificent communities have been less influential on the economic progress of the world as a whole, than might have been expected by the contemporaries who chronicled their greatness.

The difficulty of marshalling facts that are drawn from so many sources and of sketching the history of centuries on a few pages has been by no means slight; it has been my good fortune that I have had throughout my task the constant assistance of Miss Lilian Tomn; her wide reading and careful criticism have been of indispensable service to me at every stage of my work on this volume.

The completion of this Essay finishes the series of three text-books[1] on which I have been engaged since 1893. They are intended to supplement one another as aids to the equipment of the student of Modern Economics; they follow the lines of my teaching in Cambridge for many years past, and this concluding portion embodies the substance of lectures which I had the honour of delivering at Harvard University in 1899.

TRINITY COLLEGE, CAMBRIDGE,
8 *November* 1900.

[1] These text-books are as follows:

Modern Civilisation in some of its Economic Aspects. Cr. 8vo. pp. xvi + 227. 1896.

Outlines of English Industrial History, with E. A. McArthur. Cr. 8vo. pp. xii + 264. 1895.

Western Civilisation in its Economic Aspects (Ancient Times). Cr. 8vo. pp. xii + 220. 1898. (*Modern Times*). Cr. 8vo. pp. xii + 283. 1900.

TABLE OF CONTENTS.

INTRODUCTION.

BOOK IV.

CHRISTENDOM.

CHAPTER I.

THE FOUNDATIONS OF SOCIETY.

CHAPTER II.

NATURAL AND MONEY ECONOMY.

CHAPTER III.

CHRISTIAN RELATIONS WITH HEATHEN AND MOSLEMS.

BOOK V.

NATIONALITIES.

CHAPTER I.

SECULARISATION.

CHAPTER II.

THE INTERVENTION OF CAPITAL.

CHAPTER III.

RIVAL COMMERCIAL EMPIRES.

BOOK VI.

THE EXPANSION OF WESTERN CIVILISATION.

CHAPTER I.

THE INDUSTRIAL REVOLUTION.

CHAPTER II.

GENERAL TENDENCIES AND PARTICULAR CONDITIONS.

CONCLUSION.

APPENDIX.

MAPS.

The following maps are available for download in colour from
www.cambridge.org/9781107624146

The Dominion and Conquests of Charles the Great
(after Spruner and Menke)
Some important Trade Routes in the XIV. Century
(based on Goetz, *Die Verkehrswege im Dienste
des Welthandels*)
The Era of Latin Expansion

WESTERN CIVILISATION.

INTRODUCTION.

71. IN the first volume of this book an attempt has been made to trace the progress of material civili- **Mediaeval, Christendom** sation in the ancient world, from its beginnings **as an organ-** in Egypt and Phoenicia to its highest develop- **ised Society.** ment in the Roman Empire under Hadrian. The influences which sapped the vigour of this great polity and left it powerless before the attacks of the barbarians, have also been described; and we have seen that though a portion of the ancient empire maintained a successful resistance at Constantinople, the Teutonic invasion shook or destroyed the whole fabric of society in the western parts of Europe. The military organisation proved insufficient; the defenceless cities became the prey of barbarian conquerors; what had once been a well administered empire was broken into fragments, and the social order was reduced to chaos. The Norse and Danish invasions in the ninth and tenth centuries were the last of the successive inundations to which Western Europe was exposed[1]: and when they had ceased, we may note the emergence of a new civilisation which was curiously like and curiously different from the old empire that had so completely succumbed.

[1] Cunningham, *Alien Immigrants*, p. 5.

Introduction.

The very name by which we speak of this new social system calls attention to its Christianity as the trait which distinguishes it most clearly from the civilisation of the ancient world. The Roman Empire had been created by military prowess; the military organisation, with the military roads which connected its various provinces, was the effective element by which it was maintained. Christendom on the contrary, under its spiritual head the Pope, expended its material energies in the raising of magnificent churches and the endowing of religious houses; it devoted its resources to aggressive struggles with the infidel. Religious aspirations and motives found expression in the magnificent buildings of the twelfth and thirteenth centuries; these ideas and sentiments permeated all social institutions; though they lie on the surface they were not merely superficial. War was practically unintermittent in the early middle ages, but it was rarely a combining force; and however much the swords of the Franks may have contributed to the rise of the papacy, the secret of its power lay far deeper. It was not by military force, but by religious authority, that the foundations of civilised society were laid anew in the dark ages; in so far as old institutions reappear in mediaeval Christendom, they were for the most part modified or remodelled under religious influence.

In looking back from the present time, when political and religious differences have done so much to accentuate the divisions of Christendom, we are apt to forget its solidarity in bygone days. In the thirteenth century the ecclesiastical organisation gave a unity to the social structure throughout the whole of Western Europe; over the area in which the Pope was recognised as the spiritual and the Emperor as the temporal Vicar of God, political and racial differences were relatively less important. For economic purposes it is scarcely necessary to distinguish different countries from one another in the thirteenth century, for there were fewer barriers to social intercourse within the limits of Christendom than we meet to-day. Latin was the only literary language, and the student who passed from one University to another found himself everywhere at home, in the method of teaching and the course of study to be pursued. The merchant who visited a foreign port, or the artisan who sojourned in a distant town, was confronted with restrictions or aided by facilities which were familiar enough to him at home. There was little in the churches of different parts of Christendom to distract the worshipper by unaccustomed rites. Similar ecclesiastical canons, and similar law merchant prevailed over large areas, where very different admixtures of civil and barbaric laws were in vogue. Christendom, though broken into so many fragments politically, was one organised society, for all the purposes of economic life, because there was such free intercommunication between its parts. From this point of view we may treat it as a clearly marked and distinct civilisation, which succeeded to the place that the Roman Empire had occupied.

Geographically they were not coincident. Western Christendom, in the thirteenth century, contained much of the territory which had been included in the Roman Empire, as it was fortified and beautified by Hadrian; but much also had fallen away. The far East and Africa had been entirely, and Spain had been partially lost, as a result of the Mohammedan invasion; and the Greek lands maintained that independence of Rome which they had achieved when Constantine founded his capital on the shores of the Bosphorus. On the other hand, there had been some acquisitions; there had been peaceful conquests of the Cross in Ireland and Scotland, Iceland, Denmark, and the Scandinavian Peninsula; and militant Christianity had at length prevailed in Saxony and Lithuania. There had thus been an expansion of Christendom on the north beyond the limits which Roman strategy had laid down for the Empire.

There was throughout this area one social system, and

it is possible to indicate the general course of its history as a whole ; but it is obvious that the rate of economic progress has not been similar and simultaneous in all these Christian lands, especially when we take account of the differences in their physical conditions and in their inhabitants. We are not concerned with the separate industrial development of each part by itself, but only with each, in turn, in so far as it was at any moment typical of changes which have taken place in Christendom as a whole. The various countries of Christendom did not start from the same point, and did not run the same course; at one time France, at another Italy, at another Germany or Flanders took the lead ; but it is not uninteresting to note the well-marked and distinct stages to which different peoples attained at different times; some were pioneers, and some were imitators at each step in advance, but still the path of progress was similar for all.

The development of civilisation in ancient times had been carried on by a succession of races which were mutually exclusive and hostile ; while the advance in the mediaeval and modern world has been due to social elements, which though distinct yet recognised a common underlying affinity[1]. The most distant places shared more or less in the movements which were at work elsewhere ; for the magnificent churches at Kirkwall, Trondhjem and Upsala show that even the outlying districts of Christendom had their part in its artistic and industrial work in the thirteenth century; these ancient monuments testify to an intercourse which never entirely ceased. The peoples of Western Christendom have formed one civilisation,—not because their conditions and history have been identical, but because, different as they were and are, the intercourse between them has been so frequent and the

[1] Their common Christianity gave a consciousness of affinity which was not natural to the city life of the ancient world (Fustel de Coulanges, *La Cité Antique*, l. II. c. 4, *De l'esprit municipal*), and which united the whole of Western Europe in antagonism to the Mohammedan world.

interconnection so close, that changes which occurred in one have necessarily reacted upon all the others[1].

72. The ruins of the Roman Empire were drawn on, in many ways, for the reconstruction of civilised society in the West. The very tradition of Imperial power exercised an immense influence as a unifying idea[2], which survived to give definite shape to the ambitions of Charles, and facilitated the general recognition of a central authority at Rome. These political influences are the most obvious, but others, which are more difficult to trace, are hardly less important; we find the signs of a new social order, especially when we are looking at its material side, not only in the one great centre of administration[3], but in many separate localities, where circumstances afforded an opportunity for the beginnings of progress. There was no province from which the barbarians effaced all traces of Roman occupation. Even in Britain, the cherry trees and quickset hedges, the wheat and the cattle, suggest the tradition of Roman agriculture[4]; while the roads, canals, and buildings afforded models that were followed in subsequent times. In some parts of Northern France the imperial influence had been comparatively superficial[5], but it was not obliterated; when some degree of order was once more secured there were ample materials which could be utilised in the new social structure. The physical relics of Roman civilisation remained

The Economic debt to Ancient Rome.

[1] On the importance of intercourse as a characteristic of Western Civilisation, see Volume I. p. 3.

[2] Bryce, *Holy Roman Empire* (1875), pp. 24, 72.

[3] The beginnings of civilised life in northern Britain, round the Columban churches, lay outside the influence of the Bishop of Rome; nor was it from Rome that the impulse came for the work of S. Columbanus in Burgundy and Switzerland, and of S. Boniface in Germany.

[4] Pearson, *England during Early and Middle Ages*, I. 56; Coote, *A Neglected Fact of English History*, p. 53; Hughes, *Royal Agricultural Journal*, 3rd Ser., v. 561.

[5] Dareste de la Chavanne. *Histoire des Classes Agricoles*, p. 51.

throughout the greater part of the West; and in some cities
vestiges of Roman administration were maintained.   There
was a great heritage of manual skill and mechanical arts which
had been slowly built up in Egypt, Phoenicia, Greece, and
Carthage, and which was incorporated in the culture which
the Romans diffused; and it may be doubted if any of the
industrial arts as known and practised by the Romans was
wholly lost in the West.   There were, besides, forms of economic life which reappeared when circumstances admitted of
the revival; there was no need to invent them anew.   The
organisation of the mediaeval estate has its analogue in the
Roman villa; the mediaeval city, with its gilds, is the reproduction[1] of the Roman town and its *collegia*.   The fiscal and
the judicial systems of the different lands were affected by the
methods of Imperial Rome.   In some regions there was a
revivifying of institutions that had decayed but were not
extinct; in others there was the direct imitation or transplanting of methods that had survived elsewhere; but in all
parts of Christendom there is enough to remind us of the
fact that the new civilisation was raised on the ruins of the
Roman Empire.   Nor need it surprise us that the revival
followed a course that was somewhat parallel to the original
growth; the transference from natural to money economy, the
organisation first of passive and then of active commerce, the
establishment of fairs and the regulation of industry recurred
in mediaeval times, just as we have already traced them
in the ancient world; there has been a "natural progress of
opulence" which can be discerned both in ancient and in
mediaeval society.   So far as industrial arts and the great
types of social and economic organisation are concerned, the
new development followed closely on the lines of the old.

73.   It is true, then, that the debt of Christendom to
ancient Rome is very deep, and that centuries of gradual growth

[1] Even though continuity can only be proved in some few cities of
Italy; see below, p. 24 n.

were required before mediaeval could vie with ancient civilisation in the external signs of material prosperity ; The Chris-
but it would be a mistake to suppose that the tian compared
new society was a mere reproduction of the and Roman
old ; it differed in every single feature. It has attitude to-
been pointed out above¹ that though the Phoe- terial oppor-
nicians were so highly skilled in all industrial resources.
and commercial arts, the character of Greek The recon-
civilisation was different from that of their remodelling of
Semitic instructors ; there was a similar contrast society.
between the Roman Empire and mediaeval Christendom ;
a difference not in skill or in organisation merely, but in the
whole spirit of the civilisation. Though this element is very
important, it is so subtle that analysis does not readily detect
it, and there is some difficulty in describing it ; but the best
that the Greeks had attained may be taken as the starting-
point from which the new advance began. The Greek regarded material wealth as a means to an end, and as offering
opportunities for the cultured life of free men in a City-State.
A high respect for the dignity of man and the possibilities
of human nature as essentially political, dominated his attitude
towards the material world, and the pursuit of agriculture,
commerce and industry. Christian teaching carried this Greek
conception of the supreme worth of human life much farther
by presenting it in its supernatural aspects. The doctrine of
the Incarnation² asserted that the human body had afforded

¹ Volume I. pp. 71, 98.

² There is no side of human life which may not have a bearing on
economic changes (Cunningham, *Growth of English Industry and Commerce*, I. p. 7), and though it is rarely necessary to call attention to philosophical beliefs or religious convictions, we are forced back on them if
we attempt to describe the spirit of a people or of an age. Thus, as
Professor Bury points out (*Later Roman Empire*, I. p. 188), the victory of
Athanasianism over Arianism was of world-historical importance. "The
very essence of Christianity was at stake. For the special power of
Christianity depended on the idea of Christ, and the doctrine of Arius

an adequate medium for the manifestation of the divine nature; the doctrine of the Resurrection held out a sure and certain hope of personal immortality for the human soul. Christianity thus involved a higher view of all human life, as such, than the Greeks had asserted of the noblest members of a selected race. The supreme dignity of man as man was set forth by Christian teaching, and the conscious and habitual subordination of material things to human ideals and aspirations was carried farther than it had ever been before, since man came to be regarded not only as a rational, but as an immortal being, and as one who has a place in a supernatural order.

One of the gravest defects of the Roman Empire lay in the fact that its system left little scope for individual aims, and tended to check the energy of capitalists and labourers alike[1]. But Christian teaching opened up an unending prospect before the individual personally, and encouraged him to diligence and activity by an eternal hope. Nor did such concentration of thought on a life beyond the grave necessarily divert attention from secular duties[2]; Christianity did not disparage them, but set them in a new light, and brought out new motives for taking them earnestly. The Christian monk, like the Roman slave, was deprived of civil rights, and was absolutely at the beck and call of his superior.

tended to depress Christ, as less than God, a tendency which, if it had prevailed, would have ultimately banished Christ" from the world. The tendency of much Eastern speculation was to exalt the divine at the expense of the human, and thus to refuse to accord to what is merely human its true dignity and value. See also Gwatkin, *Studies in Arianism*, 264.

[1] Volume I. pp. 189, 192.

[2] The legend, which was popularised by Robertson (*State of Europe* in *Charles V.* I. p. 26) and Michelet (*Histoire de France*, II. p. 132), of the general disregard of mundane interests and consequent shock to society at the close of the tenth century from the prevalence of the belief in the approaching end of the world, has been recently shown to be entirely contrary to the truth. Pfister, *Études sur le règne de Robert le Pieux* in *Bibliothèque de l'École des hautes Études*, Fasc. 64me, p. 322.

But there was no degradation in monastic obedience, since it was voluntarily undertaken by a freeman as a discipline through which he might attain the noblest destiny.

The acceptance of this higher view of the dignity of human life as immortal, was followed by a fuller recognition of personal responsibility. Ancient philosophy had seen that Man is the master of material things; but Christianity introduced a new sense of duty in regard to the manner of using them. The new teaching could not approve the wasting of material wealth in the mere perpetuation of regal pride, in pandering to the gratification of effeminate luxury, or in pauperising an idle and brutal rabble by providing them with bread and diversion. The wealth of the old world had been wasted in this fashion; provinces had been despoiled and ruined and their resources exhausted rather than developed; and Christian teachers were forced to protest against any employment of wealth that disregarded the glory of God and the good of man[1].

This then was the characteristic difference between the ancient civilisation and the new order which was beginning to flourish in the twelfth and thirteenth centuries. It is of course true that these principles were very imperfectly realised, but in so far as they had any influence at all on actual life, they help us to understand the nature and scope of the political contrasts between the Pagan Empire and Latin Christendom. A capricious and arbitrary human ruler had been hailed with divine honours in ancient times; in the Middle Ages the supremacy of Eternal and Supernatural Authority over all human beings who might exercise magisterial power was maintained; the contrast is exemplified in the controversy between the Popes and Emperors regarding Investitures. The Christian doctrine of price, and Christian condemnation of gain at the expense of another man, affected all the mediaeval organisation of municipal life and regulation of inter-municipal commerce,

[1] S. Thomas Aquinas, *Summa*, ii[a] ii[ae], q. 66, art. 2, 7.

and introduced marked contrasts to the conditions of business in ancient cities. The Christian appreciation of the duty of work rendered the lot of the mediaeval villain a very different thing from that of the slave in the ancient empire. The responsibility of proprietors, like the responsibility of princes, was so far insisted on as to place substantial checks on tyranny of every kind. For these principles were not mere pious opinions but effective maxims in practical life. Owing to the circumstances in which the vestiges of Roman civilisation were locally maintained and the foundations of the new society were laid[1], there was ample opportunity for Christian teaching and example to have a marked influence on its development.

74.   When measured by strictly economic criteria, it may

The age of discovery and the study of economic policy. be doubted whether the civilisation of the thirteenth century had made any advance on that of the Roman Empire in its best days; in the fourteenth century, the Black Death caused a shock to society from which it only slowly recovered, and in the latter part of the fifteenth century Europe was still seeking for inspiration by looking to the past and making closer acquaintance with the masterpieces of ancient literature and art. It was only with the close of the fifteenth century that Western Christendom obviously reached a stage of material progress beyond that to which the Romans had attained[2]. The discovery of America and of the new route to the East Indies revolutionised men's ideas as to the surface of the globe, and

---

[1] The old order was not completely subverted at Constantinople, and ancient civilisation, with many of its inherent defects, survived in the East; society there had a veneer of Christian teaching applied to it, but it was not completely recast under Christian guidance. The church in the East was to a considerable extent a department of state under imperial control (Bury, *History of Later Roman Empire*, I. 105, 186; Finlay, *History of Greece*, I. 196), though there were indirect checks upon the Emperor (Finlay, *op. cit.* 188).

[2] For some qualifications see below on the beginnings of capital and credit, p. 169.

gave them an entirely fresh conception of the scale on which commercial intercourse and colonisation might be attempted.

This was a second great step in intellectual advance, and important economic results followed directly. The Christian revelation had given man a new sense of his personal responsibility, and brought about the remodelling of civilised society; the age of discovery opened up a new idea of the world we live in, and of the possibilities of wealth which might be secured by obtaining possession of, or trading with, distant parts of the globe. These new opportunities became available at the very time when the unity which had characterised mediaeval Christendom was being shattered. The absorption of the smaller powers, partly through conquest, had favoured the rise of considerable monarchies,—England, France, Portugal and Spain; and their statesmen were consciously setting themselves to consider how it was possible to utilise the resources of each separate country so as to promote its power effectively.

The most obvious method was adopted by Spain, and consisted in endeavouring to procure the largest possible amount of the precious metals; but before long it appeared that this was a short-sighted policy after all. It was necessary not only to gather and hoard 'treasure' or bullion[1], but to open up the sources, from which 'riches' of any and every kind might be procured. The particular advantages of each country came to be carefully considered; and every great statesman gave attention to the special economic scheme which should be pursued, in order to increase national wealth and provide the sinews of war for his own land[2]. The rise of nationalities,

[1] Seventeenth century writers have been somewhat unjustly blamed for carelessness in confusing elements in wealth which they endeavoured to distinguish. By *treasure*, they meant the precious metals; by *riches*, the comforts and the conveniences of life.

[2] On the relation of treasure and military power compare R. Ehrenberg, *Das Zeitalter der Fugger*, I. 9.

together with the opportunities for the amassing of treasure which the silver mines of America had rendered available, gave a sudden impulse, not only to commercial undertakings and colonisation, but to the study of economic policy and of the best methods for fostering the wealth of a nation. Both in practice and in economic doctrine the sixteenth and seventeenth centuries made rapid progress beyond the limits which had been reached in the ancient world. It had been the shame of ancient Rome that so little was done to develop the resources of Gaul and the various provinces[1], but in the sixteenth and seventeenth centuries there was far less of this neglect; for each country was regarded as an estate, which was carefully examined in every direction so that its capabilities might be taken advantage of to the utmost.

The rise of nationalities has been a gradual process and has extended to our own day, when the formation of a United Italy and a United Germany has first made it possible for each of them to formulate and endeavour to carry out a policy of economic regulation and expansion. England, from its limited area and insular position[2], was the first part of Europe to organise its political and economic life on a national basis. Signs of a deliberate economic policy for the country, as a whole, may be found before the important year when Edward I summoned the model parliament and passed a *Statute of Merchants*. But though there have been such marked differences in the dates at which different European countries have entered on this phase of development, it may still be

---

[1] There are of course some limitations to this statement; probably corn-growing was encouraged, as in Britain, for the sake of supplies; and various fruit trees and breeds of cattle were introduced into this country. It may also be remembered that Justinian established silk cultivation in Syria. In the first two centuries things were probably at their best, but the *coloni* were being ruined, and the spoliation of a province was not unknown. Cf. Juvenal, *Sat.* VIII. 87 seq.

[2] Cunningham and McArthur, *Outlines of English Industrial History*, p. 24.

regarded as a general movement by which each has been affected in turn. The precise form of policy that suited one was not adapted to another; but there was in all cases a similar attempt to pursue the same end, and to utilise the resources of the country in such a fashion as to increase its power. The movement was noticeable at the Reformation period, when the disruption of Christendom gave the different nations a keener sense of independence, and fresh motives for rivalry; the policy of governments became favourable to the race for wealth which is such a marked feature of modern society, as contrasted with that of the early Middle Ages, and distinguishes the western world to-day from the stationary peoples of the East. It is, however, in the seventeenth century that the working and effects of this phase of economic regulation come into clear light; they are plainly portrayed in the country which was at that time the undoubted leader in European politics. The French monarchy of Louis XIV was able to overawe surrounding nations by its splendour, and demonstrated the wisdom of the policy which had re-created agriculture and industry after the devastation caused by the wars of religion.

75. The intellectual progress of the eighteenth century was very remarkable, and it gave rise to the startling economic changes which have come about during the last hundred and fifty years. We may speak of this epoch as the age of invention; for though human ingenuity has not been confined to any one period, the eighteenth century made a great advance in the physical and chemical sciences, and also afforded economic and social conditions in which this new knowledge of physical forces could be practically applied. The blast furnace and the steam engine, the self-acting mule and the power loom have wrought revolutions in industrial life which are even more startling than the commercial changes that followed the age of geographical discovery.

[marginal note: The age of invention, and the general application of capital.]

It appears indeed that the age of discovery with its search for treasure was a necessary preliminary that rendered the age of invention possible. The maritime adventurers had opened up distant markets to European commerce, and rendered it practicable for business men to manufacture on a large scale and introduce costly machinery. These same discoveries, too, supplied the material means of saving wealth which could be utilised as capital[1]. Despite the strict regulations of the Spaniards, the precious metals which were brought from the New World could not be strictly guarded and retained as public treasure; bullion found its way into circulation and passed from royal treasuries to private hands, where it served a more useful purpose, as it was utilised in industrial and commercial enterprise. We have already seen that the waste of capital had been one of the causes of the fall of Rome; and constant complaints of a deficiency of capital and of the tardy development of English industry occur in the writings of English pamphleteers in the seventeenth century. These complaints seem to have been well-founded, and much human ingenuity was doubtless lost to the world for want of the material means of rendering some experiment a practical success. The formation of capital and the increased facilities for credit in the eighteenth century did much to remove these obstacles to progress. The cost and risk of introducing machinery into the textile trades could be undertaken as soon as there was abundance of capital in the hands of enterprising men, as well as access to many and distant markets where a vent for the products could be expected.

Capital accumulated in larger masses, and seeking for remunerative investment, has also been the principal agent in diffusing the triumphs of Western Civilisation throughout the globe. Railways have been laid down, and factories created in distant parts of the old world, by the enterprise of English-

[1] Cunningham, *Growth of English Industry*, II. p. 14.

men, Frenchmen and Germans; while in the new world our efforts are surpassed, not only by the ingenuity of American undertakings, but by the vast scale on which they are carried out. Japan has caught the fever, and is copying the achievements of European peoples. Private and associated capital, with its extraordinary fluidity and power of transporting skilled labour and the products of labour, is diffusing the last results of our material progress among savages and half-civilised races. We might have continued to trade with them as the seventeenth century companies did and left them little affected by the intercourse; but Western capitalists, by introducing modern inventions, have brought about startling changes, for good or for evil, in the social conditions of every country to which they have found their way.

It is thus that Western Civilisation has come to launch out in its ruthless career of conquest. Its two salient features,— the subjugation of natural forces and its extraordinary facility for procuring material wealth—have a fitness of their own; they are sure to survive, they are bound to force their entrance into every land and to compel society to adapt itself to them. And herein lies the danger; we may come, in our admiration of these marvels, to regard material progress as an end in itself, and to lose sight of the ideals for human society and for individual life which are the most precious of earthly possessions. It will be sad indeed, if while multiplying the opportunities that might be devoted to the cultivation of a truly noble life, we lose the power and desire to use these opportunities worthily.

76. The foregoing paragraphs may have served not only to point the contrast between ancient civilisation and that of mediaeval and modern times *Divisions of the subject.* but to elucidate the principle of division which has been adopted in the following pages. There have been three great stages of progress, in man's knowledge of *himself,* and of his *place* and *powers* in the world; and each of these

has had far-reaching effects on industrial and commercial life. Under the influence of Christian teaching man attained to a new consciousness of duty; and we can trace the workings of these ideas in the institutions of Christendom, as they are most noticeably seen in the age of S. Louis. Again, when the period of discovery came, man's conceptions of the earth and of the possibilities it contained were suddenly enlarged, and we find the influence of this new knowledge, not only in the expansion of commerce, but in the national economic policies, of which France under Louis XIV affords a typical example. Lastly, with the age of invention there was an increase in man's acquaintance with physical nature, combined with special opportunities for applying that knowledge practically; and Englishmen have taken the lead, not only as inventors, but as pioneers in the work of diffusing the new industrial practices and organisation throughout the world. During each of these three periods attention has been concentrated in turn on one of the requisites of production. In mediaeval Christendom we find institutions for the regulation of labour; the phase of nationalist economic policy has been chiefly concerned with the development of land; while in recent times we see the remarkable results effected by the utilisation of capital.

BOOK IV.

CHRISTENDOM.

CHAPTER I.

THE FOUNDATIONS OF SOCIETY.

77. WE are accustomed to describe different political organisms as being in a healthy or unhealthy state, according to their success in affording adequate protection to person and property. This test applies not only to high civilizations, but also to primitive peoples; for wherever chronic insecurity prevails it is hardly possible for society to continue to exist, and there can be no hope of any advance in material wealth. Diligence in labour and enterprise in business will both be checked, when men have little hope of receiving a reward for their work or of enjoying what they have stored[1]. It is essential to progress that society should be defended alike against attack from without and disorder within.

Security for the prosecution of labour and enterprise afforded by Moral Authority.

In striving for these ends men have not always adopted the same principles. In some cases it has been possible to take advantage of geographical conditions; these may prove serious obstacles against hostile invasion, though they cannot afford complete immunity; but they give no guarantee of internal welfare. Tyre maintained her independence for

[1] Cunningham, *Modern Civilisation*, 12.

centuries, but her prosperity was shaken by revolutionary outbreaks. It seems as if a great military organisation would
suffice for the double purpose, as it did for a time at Rome;
but the army itself may become a danger to civil institutions,
especially if the sense of public duty is lost or the bonds of
discipline are relaxed. The most effectual safeguard of society
is found in the influence of moral authority; and this may be
relied on, in so far as there is a belief that right and wrong in
political affairs are determined by something deeper than mere
expediency. This has been more or less felt in many polities,
and it comes out very clearly in mediaeval Christendom. The
claim to enforce the omnipotent God's Will as supreme over
all men[1] by the simple appeal to the human conscience to
submit to that Will, is the strongest position that human
authority can take. This conviction of a divine commission
may give to rulers the dignity and courage which impress
outsiders, and the strength of character which commands
respect.

Moral authority will rarely attempt to dispense with all
extraneous supports. S. Columba and his monks in their
island home were glad of the protection afforded them by the
sea. There may be many occasions for summoning an army
to do battle for the right, but the secret of success lies not
in these external agents, but in inspiring ideas. The claim
to enforce right is the best basis for civil authority, and the
recognition of that claim by the subjects is a sufficient reason
for loyal obedience. As Christianity was gradually accepted,
with its new view of man's nature and his responsibility, an
enormous influence was placed within the reach of those who
had authority to speak in God's name, and who warned the

[1] This principle, which holds good both among Mohammedan and
Christian peoples, is derived from Judaism. Paganism, with its local
cults, could not supply a common religious basis for moral principles as
binding on all men alike. On the economic importance of this belief,
compare the Duke of Argyle, *Unseen Foundations*, 192, 219.

disobedient of the danger of incurring divine punishment here and hereafter. This religious power was steadily brought to bear in favour of securing protection to person and property; it was used to limit the frequency and mitigate the horrors of war[1], which was then the chief source of social disorder: while the conditions of tenure and the protection claimed for ecclesiastical property favoured the growth of secular proprietary rights[2], and helped to supply the legal forms by which they are defined and transferred.

The claim of the Bishop of Rome to speak with authority in God's name, and to declare the right, absolutely, was generally recognised in mediaeval Christendom in the thirteenth century; religious ideas permeated all civil institutions; and the force of spiritual censures was shown in the humiliation of the emperor Henry IV at Canossa. The papal authority had grown from small beginnings; and we must look very closely in order to see exactly how this influence was actually brought to bear. The heathens who routed the imperial armies had little cause to respect ecclesiastical institutions; but even in the darkest days of all, we may notice how the personal influence of one or another of the Christian bishops intervened to stem the tide of invasion for a moment, or to intercede in behalf of subject populations, and thus facilitated the preservation of some elements of ancient civilisation. Besides this influence of personal character there was also corporate religious influence which we shall have to consider[3]; the power of individual men was displayed in saving some of the remains of the old order, but corporate religious life had much to do with creating the new civilisation. This religious enthusiasm enabled the monks of the West to be pioneers

---

[1] Bethune Baker, *Influence of Christianity on War*, 87, 118. Semichon, *La Paix et la Trêve de Dieu*. Lecky, *History of European Morals from Augustus to Charlemagne*, II. 274.

[2] Cunningham, *Growth of English Industry*, I. 68.

[3] See below, p. 35.

in the work of reclaiming the regions that seemed to have been totally lost. The isolated action of Christian men and Christian communities supplied the groundwork on which the widespread influence of the papacy was subsequently raised.

78. Many beautiful legends have been handed down of

Personal
influence
and official
position of
Bishops in
dealing with
Heathen
Barbarians.

the heroic conduct of bishops in intervening in behalf of their cities, especially during the invasion of the Huns. The city of Troyes was unfortified and surrounded by a swarm of disappointed and retreating soldiers who were clamouring for the spoil, but S. Lupus succeeded in persuading Attila to draw off his troops before the pillage began[1]. Later in his career, the same warrior yielded to the solicitations of another bishop at a moment of uncertainty. " Upon these doubts and ponderings of his supervened the stately presence of Leo[2], a man of holy life, firm will, and dauntless courage—that, to be sure, Attila perceived in the first moments of their interview—and besides holding an office high and venerated through all the civilised world. The Barbarian quailed to his spell, as he had quailed to that of Lupus of Troyes, and according to a tradition which is not very well authenticated, he jocularly excused his unaccustomed gentleness by saying that he knew how to conquer men but the lion and wolf (Leo and Lupus) had learned to conquer him." A similar example of episcopal heroism had been shown by S. Anianus at Orleans[3], while the sufferings of the provincials were also mitigated by the ascendancy which bishops[4], or private persons like S. Severinus of Noricum[5], obtained over the barbarian conquerors. The responsibility

---

[1] Hodgkin, *Italy and her Invaders*, II. 122, A.D. 451.

[2] Hodgkin, II. 161, A.D. 452.

[3] Hodgkin, II. 119, A.D. 451.

[4] Compare the influence of Avitus, Bishop of Vienne (A.D. 490–523), and Caesarius of Arles (A.D. 502–542) during the transition from Burgundian and Gothic to Frankish authority.

[5] Hodgkin, II. 514 (A.D. 453–482).

taken by the bishops in encouraging successful resistance may be noticed in the east[1] as well as in the west, while the miserable population that remained alive looked to the episcopate for protection against barbarian[2] and imperial oppression[3].

This view of the salutary influence exercised by the episcopal order is rendered more probable by the fact that so many of the towns in Germany, which have the best claims to continuous existence from Roman times, are ancient episcopal sees[4]. Cologne, Trêves, Metz, Mayence, Speyer, Worms, and Strasburg are ancient *civitates*[5] which appear to have a continuous ecclesiastical history[6], though this does not seem to extend to their civil government. Archaeological[7] remains in some of the French cities go to show that the Roman *civitates* in Gaul did not share the fate of those in Britain[8] which ceased to exist as populous places.

[1] Compare the influence of the bishop of Heraclea, in Macedonia, in making terms with Theodoric (Finlay, *Greece*, I. 170). At Thessalonica the populace insisted on the transference of the city keys from the praetorian prefect to the archbishop. (Bury, *Later Roman Empire*, I. 267.) There was one notable exception in the bishop who betrayed Margus to the Huns (Bury, I. 164).

[2] Kemble (*Saxons in England*, II. 375, 393) calls attention to similar activity on the part of bishops in England.

[3] Finlay, *Greece*, I. 202.

[4] In England, on the other hand, most of the towns grew up round abbeys or castles; even in the cases, like that of York, where a *civitas* was the site of an English town, there is no continuous ecclesiastical history: Winchester is not an exception in this respect.

[5] Hegel, *Entstehung des deutschen Städtewesens*, p. 3. Rietschel, *Die Civitas*, 33.

[6] Rietschel, *op. cit.* p. 51.

[7] In not a few French towns the space within the Roman walls remained as a well-defined and separately administered district, known as the city; this was the core, round which the later expansions were arranged as faubourgs. Du Cange, *Glossarium* s. v. Burgus. Pirenne, in *Revue historique*, LVII. 60. Flach, *Les origines de l'ancienne France*, II. 237, 239, 245.

[8] The mediaeval towns, which grew up among the ruins of Roman cities in England, generally occupied a somewhat different site, or show

It must be remembered, moreover, that successful intervention in behalf of the safety of a city did not merely
benefit the space within its walls, but applied also to the
territory round about[1]; and the boundaries of the dioceses of
mediaeval France, like Touraine and Perigord, seem to
perpetuate the ancient civil divisions[2] and to mark out the
territory which shared the favourable lot of the episcopal sees
of Tours and Perigueux.

While the bishops thus endeavoured to protect their
cities from pillage, they would also help to secure favourable
conditions for trading within the walls.   There is good
reason to believe that the bishops took an active part in
regulating commercial and industrial life in their dioceses.   We
know that this task was formally imposed upon them in the
East, and it is unlikely that analogous duties were entirely
neglected in the West[3].   The bishops were concerned in the
audit of moneys expended in public works[4], in supervising
the sale of necessaries[5], and in controlling the excessive gains
of Christian merchants[6].   It has been commonly alleged that
the bishops held the office of *Defensor civitatis*[7] and thus

a considerable shifting of the main lines of traffic. Chisholm, *Journal
of Royal Geographical Society* (1897), X. p. 512. Winchester appears to
be an exception. Kitchin, *Winchester* (Historic Towns), p. 5.

[1] Hegel, *Geschichte der Städteverfassung von Italien*, II. 347. The
term *civitas* may apply to the diocese of a bishop. Rietschel, *Die Civitas*,
21, 59. Many of the Roman cities had lands from which they drew their
food supply. Pardessus, *Lex Salica*, App. VIII. p. 544.

[2] There is another striking contrast with England in this matter. The
ecclesiastical divisions of England have no obvious relationship with the
civil division of Roman Britain. In Merovingian France the *gau* followed
the lines of the diocese, even when there had been no Roman *civitas*, as at
Châlons and Macon. Rietschel, *Die Civitas*, 26.

[3] Compare the trading facilities which were brought into play by
Bishop Patiens of Lyons in feeding the population of Auvergne in A.D. 474.
Hodgkin, II. 488.

[4] *Codex Justin.* I. 4, 26, sec. 2.

[5] *Digest*, L. 4, 18, 7.   [6] *Codex Justin.* I. 4. I.

[7] Houdoy, *Droit Municipal* (1876), 650.

occupied one of the principal civic positions in the town and were responsible for keeping the city records (*gesta*); and though there is no evidence that any diocesan ever filled this post[1], it is highly probable that he exercised dominant influence over every side of life in these struggling towns[2]. It is quite unlikely that the towns in France preserved an unbroken tradition in the system of civil government[3], but there is on the other hand a high probability that many of them continued to be populous places through the period of barbarian conquest, and that the economic life of some has been steadily maintained. In so far as any elements of the old administration survived the Frankish invasion, their preservation appears to have been due in no small degree to the personal character and effective intervention of the bishops[4].

79. To assess the precise results of Christian Faith as it inspired the action of particular men in re- Restraining
sisting heathen barbarians is not easy, but there influence on
is still greater difficulty in estimating the in- Christianised
Barbarians—
fluence religion exerted as a restraining principle Theodoric the
in modifying the conduct of Christianised bar- Ostrogoth.
barians. We may certainly feel that Theodoric the Great deliberately desired to preserve the Roman institutions and administration. Living as a Christian within the limits of the Empire, he had the keenest admiration for its great traditions,

---

[1] Chénon, *Étude historique sur le Defensor Civitatis* in *Nouvelle Revue historique de Droit*, XIII. (1889), p. 555.

[2] Fustel de Coulanges, *Institutions politiques, L'invasion germanique* (1891), 70. Hegel, *Städte und Gilden* (1895), p. 14.

[3] The influence of Christianity had done much to undermine the system of government by the *curiales* [Fustel de Coulanges, *Institutions politiques, L'invasion germanique* (1891), 35]; and Hegel's careful investigation shows that, in Italy at all events, the municipal constitutions were completely transformed between imperial and mediaeval times (*Städteverfassung von Italien*, I. 199); see also Flach, *op. cit.* II. 236.

[4] In so far as the evidence of contemporary panegyric is of value, it is interesting to compare Fortunatus, *Opera Poetica* in *Mon. Germ. Hist. Auctorum Antiquissimorum*, IV. part 1.

and he tried to use the swords of his Ostrogoths to preserve
it from external and internal decay.   The magnificent monuments which remain at Ravenna testify to the greatness of his
nation while it lasted, and give it a wonderful interest; but
the Gothic kingdoms disappeared so suddenly and so completely, that it may seem doubtful whether they played any
part at all in the course of Western civilisation.   Nevertheless, though we cannot specify any one element for which
we are indebted to Theodoric, there are two grounds on which
it is well worth while to pay some attention to his kingdom,
as at least a transitional form.   By establishing good government in Italy, he gave an opportunity for the tradition of
Roman administration to linger on[1], so as possibly to facilitate
the revival of similar institutions among the Franks and elsewhere.   There is, however, a better reason for dwelling on
this reign; in the letters of Cassiodorus, his secretary, we have
a most valuable collection of state papers, which put on record

[1] The security which was then enforced afforded an opportunity for
the survival in Italy of many imperial and civic institutions of which all
traces might otherwise have disappeared.   The letters of Cassiodorus are
full of reference to the fiscal system (Cassiodorus, *Variae*, XI. 7), and show
that the survey of lands (*Ib.* III. 52) and collection of a *census* was in
regular operation.   The postal service was also maintained (*Ib.* I. 29), and
there were commercial facilities which rendered it possible to supply Rome
with food drawn from distant districts (*Ib.* I. 35).   Within the cities too,
attention was given to the repair and maintenance of the aqueducts (*Ib.*
III. 31, V. 38), fortifications and other public works (*Ib.* I. 25, III. 29, 30,
44, 48, 49); while there is evidence that the organisation of labourers in
collegia survived in some of the cities of Italy till a much later date.
There appears to be documentary evidence of the existence of associations of fishermen, and of merchants in Ravenna in A.D. 943 and 953
(Fantuzzi, *Monumenta Ravennitia*, t. IV. 174, and t. I. pp. 133 and 227,
as quoted by Levasseur, *Histoire des Classes ouvrières*, I. 124).   Hegel,
who argues that there was an entire breach in civic government, admits
the probability of continuity among the trading societies of parts of Italy
(*Städteverfassung*, I. 196) as e.g. at Rome (*Ib.* I. 255, II. 298); but see
also Rodocanachi (*Corporations ouvrières à Rome*, preface, viii.), who
regards the survival as doubtful.

the maxims of state craft which characterised his beneficent rule. These may well have produced more than a contemporary effect; Cassiodorus by his example and influence gave a new direction to the monastic life, and laid the seeds of the devotion to learning for which so many Benedictines have been conspicuous. It is not improbable that his political ideals helped to shape the principles which the monks of the West brought to bear on the distant kingdoms in which they settled; at least it is remarkable that we find in the correspondence of Cassiodorus clear anticipations of the politico-economic principles that prevailed throughout the Middle Ages. These far-reaching effects are somewhat problematical; but the influence of Christianity on the work of Theodoric is perfectly clear. We can see on the one hand that the political aims he cherished were completely consonant with Christian teaching, and that his Christian education had rendered it possible for him to adopt them : on the other hand, if we compare his administration with that of the Imperial system, we may notice differences of detail which Christian influence would tend to produce.

In the earlier letters of Cassiodorus we may find the ideals of Theodoric as expressed by his secretary. The fundamental aim of his whole system was the maintenance of law and order (*civilitas*). This ideal is depicted in philosophical rather than religious terms, as something that appealed to right reason[1] and to the welfare of the subjects; but for practical purposes it was the same social condition as the bishops of Gaul were trying to secure in their struggle with the heathen Franks. In the kingdom of Italy a serious effort was made to give the blessings of good government to two separate races, each with its distinct history and proper pride, each with its own ecclesiastical system and habitual sentiments. That such a problem could be steadily faced and that there should be considerable success in dealing with it

---

[1] Cassiodorus, *Variae*, IV. 33.

for a time, is the highest proof of the statesmanship of
Theodoric and his ministers; even though their measures
failed to provide a permanent solution of the difficulties of
the situation.

Theodoric's birth and up-bringing fitted him for making
this attempt; he was too proud of his race and royal descent
to stoop willingly to take a subordinate position, however
high, in the Empire; but he had been so deeply impressed
by its magnificence, during the ten years of his boyhood at
Constantinople, that he did not wish to overthrow it; he
respected and retained the Roman law and administration.
Like Ataulfus he appears to have consciously aimed at preserving the ancient commonwealth with its laws, and restoring
the Roman power by the force of Gothic arms, but not
in any sense at subverting or even Gothicising imperial and
municipal institutions[1]. To make such an attempt could never
have occurred to a heathen conqueror[2]; and but for the conversion of the Goths, it could not have had even a temporary
success. After all, the conquerors and conquered alike professed Christianity, and though they differed theologically[3], they
had a common standard of political right and wrong. This
state of affairs rendered it possible for Theodoric to found a
kingdom in which Gothic warriors and Roman subjects lived
side by side, each preserving their own customs and living by
their own laws. The establishment of law and order was a
fundamental need for the prosperity of both races[4].

[1] Orosius, VII. 43. Hodgkin, *Italy*, I. 822, III. 249.

[2] Dr Hodgkin remarks that much of Theodoric's scheme must have
jarred on Gothic sentiment. *Italy*, III. 245.

[3] The theological difference was not insignificant even economically,
so far as future developments were concerned. Arianism tended to be a
mere Theism, and could offer no effective resistance to Mohammedanism.
On the contrast between Christianity and Mohammedanism in their bearing
on economic life, see below, p. 118.

[4] To preserve peace appeared, under existing circumstances in Italy,
even a higher duty for the civil ruler than that of maintaining true religion;
in the kingdom of Theodoric, for a time, the Catholic and the Aryan lived

With the view of maintaining these favourable conditions Theodoric's first care was for the protection of property. He could not make himself responsible for the righting of wrongs that had been perpetrated before he obtained control in Italy at the battle of Isonzo, but he did his best to secure those who came under his rule at that date in the enjoyment of their possessions[1]. He was careful also to respect vested interests, even when the right in question was an abuse; certain persons had been tapping the Roman aqueducts and diverting the water of the city to work mills or to water gardens. Theodoric insisted on behalf of the public that these practices should cease, but at the same time enjoined that compensation should be given to those who could plead thirty years' prescription[2].

If we contrast the institutions and administration of this well-ordered realm with those of the Roman Empire, we find considerable differences, which may be fairly ascribed to Christian influence.

The ruthless manner in which taxation was exacted had been a matter of frequent complaint in the ancient Empire[3], and there seems to have been little improvement in this respect in the ordinary practice of the imperial administration in the sixth century[4]. But the frequency of the letters

side by side, enjoying what might be called concurrent establishment. As we find it discussed in the letters of Cassiodorus, this toleration rested on the sound reason of the power of truth to hold its own, and on the impossibility of compelling belief. As Dr Hodgkin writes, "This tolerant temper of mind is the more to be commended because it did not proceed from any indifference on his part to the subjects of religious controversy." *The letters of Cassiodorus*, p. 22. This attitude of mind is most obvious in the letters granting privileges to the Jews, and at the same time protesting against their rejection of the Christian faith. *Variae*, II. 27, V. 37.

[1] Hodgkin, *Italy*, III. 191.
[2] Cassiodorus, *Variae*, III. 31.   [3] Vol. I. 184.
[4] The success of the imperial arms in Africa appears to have been followed by increased rapacity in the collection of the taxes. Hodgkin, II. 264.

remitting taxation, on the ground of the poverty of the taxpayers, is a very noticeable feature in the correspondence of
Cassiodorus. Such a remission was made to the inhabitants of
Apulia[1], to the citizens of Arles[2], and later to the people of
Venetia[3], in consequence of the damage sustained through
hostile invasions; and in Liguria on account of imminent
famine[4]. The principle was laid down that the willingness
of the people should be to some extent a limit to the demands of the prince[5]; and the rates were revised from time
to time and lowered when they pressed too heavily[6]. It was
clearly the intention of the government to adjust the taxation
so that the cultivator should be able to live and thrive, and
should not be forced to deprive himself of the means of pursuing his calling[7]. This is a sound principle of finance, but
the imperial advisers were slow to recognise it as such; and
it was a benevolent practice that was at any rate consonant
with the dictates of Christian charity.

There appears also to have been a good deal of difference
in the manner in which another important civic duty was
performed. In the time of Diocletian an attempt had been
made to limit the opportunities and gains of middlemen by
fixing a maximum price for corn and other articles of ordinary
consumption, but this edict expressly disclaims any desire to
fix the precise rates at which commodities might be sold, so
long as the price did not exceed the maximum laid down
by law. But from the instructions given to the *defensores*, as
well as from incidental references, we gather that Cassiodorus
had a different conception of a magistrate's duty in this matter.
The phrases which he uses seem to involve the Christian

---

[1] *Variae*, I. 16.   [2] *Ib.* III. 39.

[3] *Ib.* XII. 7.   [4] *Ib.* XII. 28.

[5] *Ib.* III. 40, XI. 7. In practice the complaints of inability to pay were
of course scrutinised. *Ib.* VII. 45.

[6] *Ib.* IX. 10.

[7] Compare the exemptions in the English assessment of the 15th in
A.D. 1225. Cunningham, *Growth of English Industry*, I. 152, 296.

conception of price as expounded some centuries later.   The *curator* was enjoined to fix "moderate rates¹" and not to allow the seller to get the best of the bargain, and the *defensor* was called on to fix the prices for the citizens "according to the goodness or badness of the seasons²."   There was also, in a time of scarcity, a special effort to prevent forestalling and regrating³; the whole of the phraseology suggests mediaeval analogies and presents points of contrast with the practice of the ancient world.   It seems not unlikely, however, that Cassiodorus only gave expression to the principles which had more or less consciously influenced the bishops in supervising bargains about bread and other articles of common consumption⁴.

Such links with things ancient and such affinities with the mediaeval world give a special interest to the story of the Gothic kingdom; it was a judicious compromise, but it had the inherent weakness of all compromises.   There was no fusion between the two races on Italian soil; the Goths could not be adapted to the imperial system, and they did not become the patrons and protectors of Latin Christianity.

80.   Though Theodoric did so much to introduce law and order within his realm, he had little success *The conversion of the Franks and the recognition of a common ecclesiastical authority in Western Europe.* in establishing peaceful relations with neighbouring states.   Chronic warfare was a crying evil in the sixth century, and he sought to limit it by creating a system of alliances between the ruling families.   His wife was the daughter of the king of the Salian Franks.   His sister was married to the Vandal king, and his daughters to Burgundian and

¹ Cassiodorus, *Variae*, VII. 12.

² *Ib.* VII. 11.

³ *Ib.* IX. 5.   There had also been legislation under Zeno against monopoly prices for wares and combination by artisans.   *Codex Justin.* IV. *tit.* 59, c. 2, sections 1, 2, 3.

⁴ *Corpus Juris Civilis, Digest* L. tit. 4, sec. 18. 7.

Visigothic monarchs[1]. But the family ties thus formed were not effective in securing European peace. Nor was there any real hope, even in the days of Belisarius and Narses, that the Emperor would recover his ancient sway and wield authority over the Western world. The attempt to restore imperial power served to increase the miseries of Italy, and the temporary success of Justinian only made the burdens of life heavier than before. The *pax Romana* could not be re-established in the provinces of the Empire; but the gradual recognition of ecclesiastical authority, as wielded all over the West, and as centralised and strengthened by the influence of the Bishop of Rome, helped to supply the defects of civil rule. The Catholic bishops, with their political and social influence in their dioceses, did much to secure internal peace; they were drawn into a practical federation by their common hostility to the Arian monarchs of the Goths, Burgundians, and Vandals; and this widely extended power was supported and consolidated by the action of the Roman See. When the baptism of Clovis and the conversion of the Franks changed the balance of theological opinion in the West, the triumph of Catholic doctrine gave a decided impetus to the growing power of the leading bishop in the Latin church. From that time onward the eventual recognition of one common ecclesiastic authority[2] in Western Christendom was ensured. Civil government, when acting independently, had failed to restore law and order; there was better hope that they would be successfully fostered when spiritual power was also brought to bear.

It was of the first importance that the new authority was

[1] Hodgkin, *Italy*, III. 321.

[2] We are not concerned either with subsequent efforts to justify this claim in the Forged Decretals, or with the question whether ecclesiastically the papacy was a legitimate development of the Christian hierarchy, but only with the fact that the authority was recognised, and that the recognition of common authority of any sort made for law and order in Christendom.

spiritual, and demanded obedience not as a natural right but as due to God. It sought to assert an absolutely just Will[1] as binding upon all men, and thus endeavoured to restrain the self-will of Emperors and potentates, and the arbitrary government which they might choose to exercise. The claim was formulated most plainly in the conflict about Investitures, but there had been practical assertions of it long before. When S. Ambrose insisted that Theodosius should make public acknowledgment of guilt in connection with the massacre at Thessalonica, he was maintaining the principle that an earthly ruler was responsible to God for his actions, and that in dealing with him[2] God's ministers were bound to have no respect of persons; Agapetus showed himself equally firm in refusing to comply with the commands of Justinian[3]. The clergy of the East were not so successful in taking their stand on this principle, and partly on this account they have played a less important part in the history of Europe. As the spiritual head of Christendom, the Bishop of Rome claimed to exercise a universal supremacy in God's name; and obedience could be rendered to such an authority without any sense of servility or personal degradation.

81. The power of the head of Latin Christianity gradually increased, and it accomplished the work of unification which Theodoric had attempted by means of family alliances, and in *The fusion of the Franks and the Gallo-Romans.*

[1] Cassiodorus had viewed the matter from a philosophical standpoint and advocated obedience on grounds of Right Reason. From a religious point of view, the duty of obedience depends on the conception of a perfectly good Will. Christianity lays the foundation of all civil liberty by insisting that it is only as a man speaks for God, or holds office in God's name that he has any right to demand obedience. To barter a portion of personal liberty for the sake of retaining property is a mean method of establishing law and order; but this was the best basis which Locke could suggest as the foundation of civil government. *Civil Government*, § 123.

[2] In A.D. 390. See Hodgkin, *Italy*, I. 533.

[3] In A.D. 530. Hodgkin, *Italy*, IV. 91.

which he had failed. Ecclesiastical authority had served the double purpose of preserving elements of Roman life and of moralising the barbarian, and thus it helped to bring about the fusion of the Frankish rulers with the Gallo-Roman subjects[1]— a result at which the Ostrogoth had not even aimed. We can trace in the barbarian codes how the modification of ancient custom tended to remove the principal barrier between the two races which were living on the same soil and accepted the same faith. In the Salic Law—the earliest Latin code of Frankish custom—the racial distinctions are preserved, and a severer penalty is imposed for the murder of a barbarian than for that of a Roman[2]; but still, this code, by the mere fact of definition, made the way easier for gradually bringing both races under one legal system[3].

A more striking proof of the amalgamation of the two races is seen in the common action of the leaders of the two parties in political affairs. So early as the seventh century we find the Frankish aristocracy making common cause with the clergy in opposition to the Crown. At the council of Paris in 614[4], each of these parties obtained the redress it was seeking; the Franks resisted the encroachments of the Crown, and the clergy secured the right of free election to bishoprics, as well as other important privileges. The whole incident shows that the clergy and the Frankish aristocracy were coming to a closer understanding.

The Franks were able, too, to utilise some parts of the

[1] The Franks were willing to accept some of the civilisation of their subjects, along with their religion. But the Greeks in the Eastern Empire were less able to meet the barbarians half-way. There was less opportunity for the fusion of the new and old in the East, and this seems to have been one reason for the stagnation of Eastern Christendom.

[2] *Lex Salica*, XLI. 1, 6, XLII. 4. Pardessus, p. 23.

[3] Fusion had already begun, since the term *ingenuus* appears to include Romans as well as Franks (Pardessus, *Lex Salica*, p. 540). The longer preface shows that the code was compiled under Christian influence. Pardessus, p. 344.

[4] Lavisse et Rambaud, *Histoire Générale*, I. 154.

Roman system which survived, and these remains were not so scanty as is sometimes supposed. There is indeed no reason to believe that the administrative organisation remained unaltered; or that under the Merovingians the same officers, with the same authority, went on discharging the same duties as their predecessors had performed in Imperial times. We can never assume from the use of similar names at two different periods that there has been no change in the things designated[1]; when these early times are viewed from a constitutional standpoint, we may certainly doubt whether there was continuity in any part of the governmental machinery. But for all that, there seems to have been an unbroken economic life, not only in many of the cities, but in large areas; the Frankish kings endeavoured to collect taxation in much the same way as the Romans had done, and maintained the old fiscal system; they inherited something more than a mere tradition and endeavoured to work it to their own advantage.

It is clear, for one thing, that the official valuation of estates was not allowed to fall into abeyance, and that the land tax continued to be levied as it had been under the Empire[2]. Augustus[3] had instituted a cadastral survey of the Roman Empire; and the census, renewed each fifteen years at the *indiction*, was maintained in the East, though not, as it would appear, in the Frankish realms. Much of the revenue of the Frankish kings was drawn from the same sources[4] as of old, and the fiscal obligation of Roman landholders remained as a heritage from the Imperial system.

Again, this revenue system rendered it necessary to maintain or to organise a system of registration of title. Transferences of land from Romans to barbarians might often take

---

[1] Dareste de Chavanne, *Histoire des classes agricoles*, 136.

[2] Dahn, *Zum merowingischen Finanzrecht* in *Germ. Abhand. zum LXX. Geburtstag K. von Maurers*, 1893, p. 356. Pardessus, *Lex Salica*, VIII^mo App. pp. 559—562.

[3] Vol. I. p. 174.

[4] Fustel de Coulanges, *Institutions; La monarchie franque* (1888), 266.

place[1], and such transactions gave rise to the disputed question whether the new proprietor should pay the old tax or whether his new possession should become as free as the *alleu* he enjoyed as a Frank. There was in consequence a systematic registration[2] of such instruments as deeds of gift or deeds for the re-establishment of lost titles. A country is not wholly given over to barbarism where such a practice survives.

Nor was commercial intercourse entirely at an end[3]; the customs continued to afford a revenue, and dues similar in kind to those levied by the Romans[4] were exacted on waterways and in harbours, and as tolls on bridges. That commerce had suffered greatly we may believe, but it seems unlikely that it ever became wholly extinct, or that it had to start afresh from such trivial beginnings as are indicated[5] in the early English laws. Under these circumstances there is no improbability in the survival of mercantile associations which are said to have had a continuous existence since Roman times. The instances are very few; but there is an inherent probability in the allegation that the society of *Nautae Parisiani*, which existed in the time of Tiberius, continued their organised trading on the Seine through the early middle ages[6].

When we contrast the cases of England and France, we may feel how much of the heritage of Roman life remained in the continental country. In England the work of civilisation consisted in modifying barbarian custom under Christian influence and in fostering a rudimentary administration, by the conscious imitation of foreign models. There was no need for the fusion of two elements, for there was

[1] For one case see Rocafort, *Paulin de Pella*, p. 83.

[2] Chénon *op. cit.* in *Nouvelle Revue Historique de Droit* (1889), XIII. 527.

[3] The relays for the postal service were maintained in the sixth century. Pigeonneau, *Histoire du commerce de la France*, I. 59.

[4] For many examples compare Pigeonneau, *op. cit.* I. 63 n.; Fustel de Coulanges, *op. cit.* 247.

[5] Cunningham, *Growth of English Industry*, I. 128.

[6] Fagniez, *Études sur l'industrie*, 4. The Paris butchers also claim a continuous history.

only one social stock to be considered. But the Gallo-Roman population survived in Gaul, and their customs and usages were retained and made to fit in with the system of their Frankish conquerors.

82. In the four preceding sections an attempt has been made to show how Christian teaching and eccle- The economic siastical authority were brought to bear in favour influence of of securing law and order throughout Western monasteries— agriculture, Europe, and thereby helped to provide the industry, conditions essential for material progress. When trade. we turn to another side of religious life, and consider the results of the founding of monasteries, we find influences at work that were plainly economic. These communities can be best understood when we think of them as Christian industrial colonies, and remember that they moulded society by example rather than by precept.

We are so familiar with the attacks and satires on monastic life that were current at the Reformation period, that it may seem almost a paradox to say that the chief claim of the monks to our gratitude lies in this, that they helped to diffuse a better appreciation of the duty and dignity of labour. By the 'religious,' manual labour was accepted as a discipline which helped them to walk in the way of eternal salvation; it was not undertaken for the sake of reward, since the proceeds were to go to the use of the community or the service of the poor; it was not viewed as drudgery that had to be gone through from dread of punishment. There was neither greed of gain, nor the reluctant service of the slave, but simply a sense of a duty to be done diligently unto the Lord. It may be said that this side of the monastic life was specially accentuated as early as the fifth century, because of excesses and irregularities that had even then brought scandal on the religious profession[1]. S. Augustine insisted on the duty of honest labour; and this element of disciplined life found a prominent

[1] S. Augustine, *De op. monach.* c. 36.

place in the rule which S. Benedict drew up for the guidance of his monks[1]. The practice which crept in later, of regarding writing or illuminating as manual industry, tended to the preservation of ancient learning, but it introduced a disastrous division of employment within the community; and the example set by monastic institutions, as Christian colonies, became much less telling after the tenth century[2]. Till that time it may be said that they were living testimonies to the duty of labour, and set forth the true character and dignity of honest work[3].

The wickedness of the Merovingian rulers was so gross and palpable, that we can scarcely help feeling that their nominal Christianity was an added offence. Nevertheless, the fact that they made a profession of Christianity had real importance. There was at least this difference between the Frankish monarchs and their Saxon or Danish neighbours, that the former encouraged the planting of these Christian colonies[4], while the latter continued to destroy them. Whenever and from whatever motive a Benedictine monastery was founded in France, a little territory was reclaimed, and a new centre of civilisation was established. Much good work was accomplished by the monks in the keeping a love of learning[5] alive through the dark ages; and it is easy to show that their manual activity had great influence as an element in material progress, and that they did not a little to disseminate the industrial arts, to improve agriculture, and to develop more regular commercial intercourse.

---

[1] *Reg. S. Benedict*, cap. XLVIII. *De opere manuum quotidiano.*

[2] Levasseur, *Histoire des classes ouvrières en France*, I. 144.

[3] Cunningham, *Modern Civilisation*, 201. This conviction about labour, together with the inculcation of respect for life and property, are the fundamental principles in Christian economic teaching.

[4] By endowments of land, and by immunities which gave freedom from toll, rights to the profits of jurisdiction and rights to take toll. Berthelot in Lavisse et Rambaud, *Histoire générale*, I. 339.

[5] S. R. Maitland, *Dark Ages*, 172.

Considerable tracts of Gaul had reverted to mere forest[1] under the combined pressure of Roman misgovernment and barbarian invasion; there was hard work to be done in re-claiming land for tillage, and frequent danger from the brigands and even the wild animals that had come to haunt the secluded neighbourhoods where monasteries were planted. Each of the Benedictine houses was primarily a model farm, preserving the external aspects of a Roman villa[2], and prose-cuting agriculture according to the recognised methods. It may be impossible to distinguish the improvements in cereals or breeds which were due to the monks, from those that were introduced by the Romans into Gaul and Britain, but at least we may say that the religious colonists maintained the practice of tillage in places where it was in danger of being forgotten altogether.

The monastery perpetuated the traditions of the Roman villa, not merely in regard to the cultivation of the soil, but in its industrial activity as well[3]. It was essential for the prosperity of these establishments that they should be, so far as possible, self-sufficing, and that the monks should be able to provide necessary clothing and to repair the imple-ments of husbandry without relying on outside help. The abbot was therefore bound to organise the available labour so as to obtain the best results for the community; he might set an artisan to work at his own trade; but the conception of personal reward was rigidly excluded, and the skilled la-bourer was discouraged from taking a pride in his work[4]; all was to be done as part of the service of God and for the

[1] Montalembert, *Monks of the West*, II. p. 316.
[2] Paillard de St Aignan, *Changements de l'État social en Belgique* in *Mémoires de l'Académie royale de Bruxelles* (1844), XVI. p. 68. For a description of the Roman Villa see Meitzen, *Siedelung und Agrarwesen*, I. 352.
[3] Levasseur, I. 136, to which I am indebted for many of the subjoined references.
[4] *Reg. S. Benedict*, cap. LVII.

advantage of the community, in strict subordination to the directions of the abbot[1]. The Celtic tradition, as we find it in S. Columbanus, is equally strict in enjoining the duty of assiduous manual labour[2], and the founders of the reformed orders—the Cistercians and Carthusians—reverted strenuously to this ideal, from which the Benedictines had fallen away[3].

The most striking picture of this side of monastic life is to be found in the description of the monastery at Solignac, which was founded in A.D. 631 by S. Eligius, the celebrated gold-smith, with the aid of his royal master, Dagobert. It contained at one time as many as five hundred brethren; it was so well organised that the Archbishop of Rouen held it up as a model for all other establishments. Among the residents were great numbers of artisans who were skilled in different trades, and trained as Christians to render prompt obedience[4]. When we remember how easily the secret of a manual art may be lost, we cannot but feel how much the industry of mediaeval Europe owed to the scattered centres where an unbroken tradition of skilled labour was maintained, in the seclusion of the monastery and under vows of obedience[5].

In so far as the monasteries developed special industrial activity, they would have surplus commodities which it was advantageous to sell; in some cases they might require to

[1] J. Cassianus, *De coenobiorum institutis*, IV. cap. XII.

[2] See authorities in Levasseur, I. 138.

[3] As the Benedictine monks confined themselves to artistic or literary labour, they were dependent on outside help for the necessaries of life, and their houses came to be the nuclei round which towns grew up. Levasseur, I. 141.

[4] *Vita S. Eligii*, c. XVI.

[5] See below, Appendix. Household arts would also be perpetuated by the nuns, who devoted themselves to ordinary domestic duties in the kitchen and laundry, and also to the textile arts, including spinning and dyeing, and to such fine arts as embroidery. Levasseur, I. 139. Eckenstein, *Woman under Monasticism*, p. 222 and fol. There would be much economic convenience in the double monasteries like that of Hilda at Whitby or the houses of Gilbert of Sempringham.

purchase materials for their industry ; at any rate it was only natural that they should develop a commercial side, and thus be brought as communities into constant economic relation with the outside world.   This important business was assigned to an official specially selected for the purpose—the *nego-ciator ecclesiae*[1]; and the principles of fair dealing, by which he should be guided, were carefully laid down.   The "immunities" granted to abbeys by the Merovingian kings enabled the inmates to purchase the goods they required and to transmit them free of toll ; the religious houses gradually increased their commercial connections, and not only bought for themselves but traded on a considerable scale.   The wine of Burgundy was transported in large quantities down the Seine by the negotiators of S. Wandrille, Jumièges and Fécamp ; and Rouen[2] served as a port from which it could be shipped across the sea.   Our best evidence of the early development of the clothing trades in Flanders comes from the fact that in the eighth century the agents of the monks of S. Wandrille went thither to purchase woollen stuffs ; while the merchants of Prüm are mentioned as travelling to Aix, Cologne, Coblenz and other towns along the Rhine[3].   After the establishment of the Carolingian Empire there was an extension of this monastic trading, and Louis the Debonnaire granted to the monks of Tours freedom from toll in Provence and Italy, and throughout his dominions[4].

The existence of this large trade gave the monasteries a commercial as well as a religious interest in the improvement of internal communications.   The repair of bridges and maintenance of roads was, it is true, an obligation on land-

[1] Negociator ergo Ecclesiae talis sit, ut nunquam, vel raro decipi valeat et studiose neminem ipse decipiat : qui nec, ut charius vendat, nec ut vilius emat, ore suo fallaciam proferat, vel juramentum ab his exigat aut ipse exhibeat.   *Reg. B. Petri de Honestis*, III. c. XXIX.

[2] De Freville, *Commerce maritime de Rouen*, p. 50.

[3] Imbart de la Tour, *Des immunités commerciales* in *Études du Moyen Age*, dédiées à G. Monod, p. 74.

[4] Levasseur, I. 141.

owners generally[1], but it was also regarded as a pious labour, and is treated as such in the beautiful legend[2] of S. Christopher. This useful work was undertaken by many of the abbeys, and in the twelfth century some religious houses were specially founded to perform the duty[3]. We can also trace the beginnings of a regular system of transport. The great abbeys on the Loire and the Seine had large numbers of vessels for carrying on their trade; and the peasants on their estates were required either to provide oxen and carriages for land transport or to pay a commutation which enabled the monks to organise an independent service[4]. The foundations of this traffic were laid before the time of Charles the Great: but under his protecting care it was greatly expanded, so that religious houses became the chief centres of mercantile activity. When we realise the extent to which this commercial side of monastic life was developed, we can the better understand why Danish raids were so frequently directed against these establishments[5]. Perhaps they paid an even heavier penalty for their commercial success; for devout men seem to have felt, as early as the ninth century, that there was a danger that the business enterprise of the monasteries would divert the brethren from sacred occupations[6].

83. The effective rule throughout the West, which was revived by Charles the Great, was dependent on his own personal ascendancy, and the partition of his Empire was inevitable at his death; it was not possible to perpetuate Charles's system of government in the separate kingdoms inherited by his successors, and Europe was left to pass

The Empire of Charles, its importance, and its character as compared with the realm of Theodoric.

---

[1] *Capitulare*, A.D. 803; Migne, I. col. 254, c. 18.

[2] A. Jameson, *Sacred and Legendary Art*, II. 433.

[3] Levasseur, I. 143.

[4] Imbart de la Tour, *op. cit.* 75, 76.

[5] Keary, *The Vikings in Western Christendom*, 127.

[6] Levasseur, I. 143. Also *Capit.* Migne, I. col. 227, c. 17.

CHAP. I.]   *The Foundations of Society.*   41

through centuries of disorder and degradation. But though his rule was so short-lived, Charles has left a very deep mark on all subsequent history: he made a magnificent effort to organise society through the influence of one civil but conse-crated authority; and he so far succeeded that his reign is a turning point in the history of Western Europe. When we compare the centuries before his time with the succeeding age we see that in his reign the various elements which had been contributed by Romans and barbarians were at last amalga-mated under Christian influence into one great polity. The government which he created, though so personal to himself, was not a mere transitional form, like the kingdom of Theodoric; the *Capitularies* continued to have direct effects on the subsequent history of France and Germany; while Charles was taken as a model, consciously or unconsciously, by kings in Scandinavia[1] and England[2]. All the vague reverence for the name of the Roman Empire which survived in the West attached itself to his personality. From his time onwards it is to the Empire as revived by Charles that men looked for the type of what a well-ordered polity should be; and the administrative tradition[3] of classical antiquity only exercised a living influence, in so far as it had been per-petuated in the institutions which he established[4].

It is also true that the epoch of Charles is the beginning of the modern world, because the political problems with which we are still struggling are very similar to those which

[1] Compare the story of the baptism of S. Magnus. Laing, *Heimskringla of Snorro Sturleson*, II. 181.

[2] The activities of Alfred so closely resemble those of Charlemagne as to suggest conscious imitation.

[3] The reintroduction from Constantinople of commercial habits and industrial arts as practised in ancient Rome, or the rediscovery of any of them from literary references, is not in question here, but only the *tradi-tional* survival.

[4] Court etiquette he seems to have consciously copied from Byzantium. Gibbon, *Decline and Fall*, c. 58.

he tried to solve. We still aim, as he did, at bringing Christian influence to bear on political and economic life. We are still confronted by the problems presented by racial differences, and the difficulty of bringing all the subjects of a realm under one system of morality and justice[1]. Rulers still feel the public duty not merely of obtaining revenue but of developing the resources of the country to the best advantage. These are the recognised ideals of the great world-empires of the present day; and when we notice that Charles was dealing with modern problems, with which the ancient world hardly attempted to grapple, we shall feel that there is much to be said for the opinion of those who fix on the year 800 A.D. as the beginning of modern history.

It is hardly necessary to call attention to the contrasts between the realm of Charles and such precursors as the empire of Alexander or that of Rome. The Hellenistic world was so imperfectly organised that few elements of common law or administration have survived; it was only in city communities that the tradition of civilised life was maintained and handed down; but city life was the least noticeable feature of the empire of Charles. Some of the contrasts between the Roman Empire and Christendom have been already pointed out[2], and it is needless to dwell on them at greater length or to try to accentuate the differences in detail. It is, however, particularly instructive to compare the realm of Charles with that of Theodoric, and to notice that Charles, owing to the fusion of races and the wide extent of his rule, was able to aim at so much that had lain quite outside the field of practical politics at the time when the Ostrogothic kingdom

[1] There is, of course, a parallelism with the Roman Empire here, but the attempt to introduce similar morality differentiates the modern from the ancient world. The abolition of Suttee in India and the objection to Polygamy in the United States would hardly have occupied the attention of the civil government in the ancient empire.

[2] See above, p. 7, fol.

was founded in Italy. The most important difference for our immediate purpose lies in this, that Theodoric seems to have been contented if he could secure *civilitas*, while Charles set himself consciously to promote *utilitas*. Charles was not merely concerned to maintain law and order, though he knew how necessary they were, and could champion them ruthlessly in his dealings with the Saxons[1]: it was also his conscious effort after beating back the barbarians to make the best use of the peace he had secured and to develop the resources of his empire for the benefit of the people under his charge[2]. He endeavoured, not merely to obtain a revenue, but to foster the prosperity on which sound finance must necessarily depend, and set himself to reorganise the agriculture and industry of the royal estates, and to promote commercial intercourse[3]. The care that was bestowed on the sources of wealth also distinguishes the policy of Charles from that of his Frankish predecessors, who were chiefly concerned in amassing the precious metals[4]; while there is also a wide difference between his scheme[5] for

[1] The war against the Saxons was forced on by the difficulty of living with such neighbours (Eginhardus, *Vita*, c. 7), and was followed by systematic efforts to civilise the country (Giesebrecht, *Kaiserzeit*, I. 118).

[2] De communi omnium nostrorum utilitate. *Capit. Duplex Aquisgranense*, A.D. 811, title to second part. *Caroli Magni Opera Omnia.* Migne, I. 330. Nos considerantes utilitatem nostram et populi a Deo nobis concessi. *Capit. Ticinense*, A.D. 801. *Ib.* 212. In communem sanctae Dei ecclesiae et omnium nostrorum utilitatem. *Ludovici et Lotharii Capit. Aquisgran.* A.D. 817. *Ib.* 396.

[3] The development of these resources was necessary for the maintenance of military equipment. With this compare Oman, *Art of War in Middle Ages*, 78—83.

[4] Levasseur, I. 151 and notes. The contrast between the aims of the Frankish kings as amassing bullion and those of Charles, is analogous to the distinction between the bullionists and mercantilists in the seventeenth century, or between the colonial systems of Spain and England.

[5] In the Eastern Empire very little effort was made to organise active commerce, and a good deal of attention was given to planting exotic rather than to developing native industries.

the material prosperity of his realm and the economic system that had been in vogue in the Eastern Empire.

Some of the great difficulties with which Theodoric as an Arian Goth had to contend, were due to the fact that the Catholic clergy were always out of sympathy with his rule, while throughout Charles's dominions the Latin Church was established by his legislation. The Frankish kings had already given a great deal of encouragement to religious institutions, and much wealth had been devoted to the endowment of monasteries; but Charles[1] set himself to carry through the complete *establishment* of Christianity; that is to say, he used the civil power to support spiritual authority, partly by insistence on the performance of certain Christian duties, and partly by strengthening the position of the clerical administration. We find in his legislation or that of his sons, canons against holding markets or courts on Sundays[2]; and the observance of this day was imposed as a duty not only on the Franks but upon the Saxons[3]; both peoples were also required to devote a tenth of their substance to religious objects[4]. Attempts were begun to combat the evils of beggary by providing local maintenance for the poor[5]; in the case of religious foundations[6] this duty was specially insisted on, and it had a prominent part in schemes of monastic reform[7]. An endeavour was made

---

[1] Charles endowed new monasteries at Corbie and Fulda; the Fulda charters with his signatures are still preserved at Marburg.

[2] *Capit.* A.D. 813; Migne, I. 363, c. 15 (also I. 318, c. 9 .

[3] *Capit.* A.D. 782; Migne, I. 146, c. 18.

[4] *Capit.* A.D. 782; Migne, I. 146, c. 17. The State in imposing an obligation to pay tithe enforced a Christian duty on the subjects, and did not endow religion from royal property. Charles set an example by paying a tithe on royal revenue. *Ib.* c. 16.

[5] *Capit.* A.D. 806; Migne, I. 303, c. 9.

[6] See Ludovic and Lothaire; Migne, I. 389, c. 49.

[7] The Capitulare of Ludovic and Lothaire (A.D. 817; Migne, I. 383) is very interesting from the manner in which it goes into details, advising that the work on fast-days should be light (c. 18), and referring to the practice

to bring the monasteries under better rule[1], and the total mass of legislation on such subjects as these shows clearly how much Charles felt it his duty to follow the example of Josiah, and on the one hand to reform ecclesiastical abuses[2], and on the other to recall the kingdom committed to his charge to the worship of the true God[3]. It had been impossible for Theodoric to attempt such a decided course; and, as we find a closer connection between Church and State under Charles, so too we may feel that the influence of Christian teaching on civil duty is more strongly marked in the Frankish Empire than in the Ostrogothic kingdom. The responsibility of Christian princes to God for the manner in which they exercise their powers is very explicitly stated in the Capitularies of Ludovic and Lothaire[4]; while there is an attempt to impose a higher standard of fair dealing in commercial transactions[5] than that aimed at by Theodoric, and there are signs of an increasing disposition to put limits on the traffic in slaves[6].

---

of lending books from the library during Lent for private study by the brethren (c. 19).

[1] *Capit.* A.D. 802; Migne, I. 248, c. 19.

[2] There was need to guard against the malversation of ecclesiastical property (*Capit.* A.D. 806; Migne, I. 303, c. 4), extravagance in building and disregard of the duties of devotion (A.D. 811; *Ib.* I. 332, c. 11), and to warn against the evils which arose in connection with the development of monastic commerce. (A.D. 789—794; *Ib.* I. 185, c. 6, and 195, cc. 11, 14.)

[3] *Capit.* A.D. 782; Migne, I. 152.

[4] *Capit.* A.D. 817; Migne, I. 393.

[5] The principles are laid down clearly, and an attempt is made to define usurious and sordid gains (A.D. 806; Migne, I. 304, cc. 1, 8); we may note the condemnation of some special forms of bargain (A.D. 809; *Ib.* I. 318, c. 12). There is also famine legislation (A.D. 805; *Ib.* I. 284, c. 4), and in some cases the setting of a maximum price (A.D. 794; *Ib.* I. 193, c. 4; also A.D. 808; *Ib.* I. 313, c. 5).

[6] Pigeonneau, *Histoire du commerce de la France*, I. 75. See below, p. 133.

84. When we turn from ecclesiastical to economic affairs

we may see that Charles took a new and very important departure; he seems to have made some attempts to open up commercial relations beyond the area of the Empire, as well as to provide improved conditions for internal trade. Even though his endeavours had little immediate result, they are interesting anticipations of lines of progress that were subsequently pursued.

The Mediterranean had come to be practically a Mohammedan lake; and though Charles was not very successful in his attempt to drive the Moslems back beyond the Ebro and free the north of Spain from their control, he was able to obtain some important concessions for Marseilles and Narbonne[1], which began to be staples for trade with the Levant. His friendly relations with Haroun-al-Raschid[2] not only enabled Charles to establish these trading connections but also to secure privileges for pilgrims to the Holy Land.

The long campaigns which he and his son Pepin waged against the Avars gave greater security along an important route, but even before the practical extermination of that tribe, we find some occasional references to trading communications through the valley of the Danube[3]. Charles attempted to construct a canal which should join the Danube[4] and the Main; though this seems to have been primarily intended for military transport, it would also have served to bring the commercial traffic of the Danube and the Rhine into direct connection at Mayence.

This city was the starting point of a great commercial route in another direction. The conquest of the Saxons had added

[1] Pigeonneau, I. 73; Abel and Simson, *Jahrbücher des fränkischen Reichs unter Karl dem Grossen*, I. 257.

[2] Eginhardus, *Vita Caroli*, c. 16.

[3] Kurz, *Oesterreichs Handel in älteren Zeiten* (1822), p. 4.

[4] Eginhardus, *Annals*, 793. Heyd (*Commerce du Levant*, I. 80), shows that it had military rather than mercantile importance.

an enormous area to the Frankish Empire, and had given the opportunity for extending commercial enterprise among the wilder tribes in Pomerania and the Baltic lands ; access had also been obtained to Bohemia and Moravia. Caravans ot merchants traversed these dangerous regions at no little risk[1], and made large profits by their importations of furs and amber. There were depots for trade with the Saxons at Erfurt and Magdeburg[2] ; and Jumna[3] at the mouth of the Oder rose into prominence as a centre for Northern products.

We also find that attention was given to maritime commerce as well. The Channel ports, Rouen and Boulogne, were of considerable importance. Nantes, at the mouth of the Loire, had doubtless prospered through the activity of Bishop Felix[4], and Bordeaux had mercantile intercourse with the Iberian peninsula, and also with Ireland[5]. The trading relations with England were interrupted in 790 A.D.[6], to the loss of the men of Boulogne; and the treaty with Offa of Mercia in 796 A.D., by which they were re-established, gave security to English merchants and pilgrims who travelled in the Frankish Empire.

Commerce must have benefited by the provision that was made for protecting the coast from pillage ; Charles had a fleet on the Mediterranean which guarded the waters of Septimania and Italy against the Moors ; while he also kept ships in the northern rivers to provide against the attacks of the Norsemen[7]. Boulogne appears to have been the principal port on the Channel, and it was improved by the erection of a lighthouse[8].

---

[1] Pigeonneau, I. 61.   The story of Samo, a Frankish trader, shows that merchants visited this region in the seventh century.

[2] *Capit.* A.D. 805 ; Migne, I. 285.

[3] Heyd, *Commerce du Levant*, I. 77.

[4] Fortunatus, liv. III. c. 10.

[5] Pigeonneau, I. 60.   [6] Pigeonneau, I. 74.

[7] Eginhard, *Vita*, c. 17.

[8] Carlier, *Commerce en France sous les rois de la première et de la deuxième race* (1752), in Leber, *Collection*, XVI. p. 113.

The extension of foreign commerce must of course have reacted on internal trade. The towns along the Rhine valley,—Cologne, Coblenz, Mayence, and Strassburg—entered on more prosperous times than they had enjoyed for centuries ; and a great impulse must have been given to the trade of the old established fairs of Troyes[1] and Paris[2]. The increased number of similar fairs[3] made it necessary to attempt to improve the facilities for internal communication. The Capitularies insist on the duty of keeping the roads in good repair, and Charles expended much time and money on the construction of a bridge at Mayence[4].

But great as were the physical obstacles with which the trader had to contend, he must have suffered even more from frequent and arbitrary exactions to which he was subject. Charles was of course careful to collect the ancient revenue from merchandise, and he organised a customs department at different points along the frontier of his enlarged realm[5]; but he was also at pains to put down novel and extortionate demands[6]. Doubtless there were many local magnates who took tolls from the merchants on the flimsiest of excuses, and Charles had to legislate against those who compelled travellers to use an inconvenient route in order to force them to pay the toll at some particular bridge[7]. Such instances are instructive, not only as indicating the arbitrary extortion

[1] Sidonius Apollinaris, *Epist.* lib. VI. 4.

[2] The fair lasted for four weeks in October, commencing on S. Denys. Pigeonneau, I. 63. On other fairs see Huvelin, *Droit des marchés et des foires*, p. 146.

[3] Inama Sternegg, *Deutsche Wirthschaftsgeschichte*, I. 433 and refs.

[4] Eginhardus, *Vita*, c. 17.

[5] Pigeonneau, I. 75; Abel and Simson, II. 332, and *Capitulare*, A.D. 805, c. 7; Migne, I. 285.

[6] *Capitulare*, A.D. 805, c. 13. The practice of stretching a rope across a river and demanding a fee from travellers passing it was regarded as specially reprehensible. See also A.D. 806; Migne, I. 304, c. 10.

[7] A.D. 809; Migne, I. 317, c. 8: also A.D. 817; Migne, I. 408, c. 17.

from which merchants suffered, but as showing the value of the immunities which had been conferred on so many monasteries.

It would be interesting if we had fuller information about the men who had enterprise enough to face these difficulties and to devote themselves to commerce. It is probable that a very large part of the active trade was still in the hands of aliens. At an earlier date the Syrians—a term which included all merchants from Egypt and Asia Minor—had been the chief agents in the traffic between East and West; they had had a considerable settlement at Paris and had been able to exercise much influence there[1]; but we do not hear explicitly of them in the time of Charles, though they may of course have been commercial intermediaries in communicating with Constantinople. It seems more probable, however, that they had been superseded by the Jews, who had begun to come to the front during the reign of Justinian[2], and who enjoyed great privileges in the Frankish Empire[3]. They were better able than Mohammedans to trade in Christian lands, and better able than Christians to carry on business among the Mohammedans, so that the expansion of Islam gave them great opportunities. They had an ancient colony at Cologne[4] which may possibly have survived, and considerable numbers were settled at Aix, Magdeburg, Paris, Orleans, Clermont, and Narbonne; they were well established at the principal centres of trade. But though they may have been the most wealthy merchants in the time of Charles, they had no exclusive possession of the field. His biographer shows that there were Christian merchants, as well as Jews, even in

---

[1] Gregory of Tours, X. 26; Boichorst, *Zur Geschichte der Syrer in Abendland* in *Mittheilungen für oesterreich. Geschichte*, VI. 535.

[2] Vol. I. p. 203.

[3] Pigeonneau, I. 70; also Depping, *Les Juifs au Moyen Age*; Huvelin, *Droit des marchés et des foires*, p. 151.

[4] Hegel, *Entstehung des deutschen Städtewesens*, 112.

the Levantine trade[1]: monastic commerce must have assumed considerable proportions, and important immunities were granted to the Archbishop of Strassburg[2], for the advantage of the men of that city.

Charles exerted himself in another economic matter, and his legislation would have been of decided advantage to trade if it could have been carried out practically. He attempted to reform the standard of weights and measures[3], and also to deal with the problem of currency[4]. There was great risk of confusion in all calculations, as Roman and barbarian methods of reckoning existed side by side, and so many distinct authorities exercised the right of coining. The monetary system had been farther complicated by such general conditions as a scarcity of the precious metals[5], and a partial return to natural economy. But the precise motives which induced Charles to take this matter in hand are not clear. He may have desired to issue a standard rate at which revenue should be assessed when it was collected in kind[6], or he may have been anxious to establish a scale of reasonable prices, and to put an end to the sordid gains of middlemen[7] who traded in the necessaries of life. Accurate definition of weights and measures and values was a necessary preliminary for either object, and it would have also been a general advantage to the trading class to give precision to the terms they used in bargaining. He had little success in imposing the uniformity he desired; but his attempt has had a lasting influence on the metric system of a country which lay beyond the limits of his empire. The pound of silver, consisting of twenty solidi of twelve *denarii* each, was adopted by Charles[8] as his unit of currency, and this practice was introduced by the Normans into England, where it eventually displaced the

[1] Eginhard, *Vita*, c. 27.
[2] A.D. 775; Migne, I. 938.
[3] Inama Sternegg, I. 456.
[4] Inama Sternegg, I. 458.
[5] Pigeonneau, I. 83.
[6] *Ib.*, I. 469.
[7] Inama Sternegg, I. 480.
[8] *Ib.*, I. 456.

old method of reckoning by marks consisting of eight ounces of twenty pennies each. The English monetary system is a symbol of the long-abiding influence which Charles exercised, even in matters where his efforts seemed to fail utterly.

85. Even greater interest attaches to the famous *capitulare de villis* in which Charles dealt with the economic activities of the household. We are fortunate in possessing so much information about his efforts to foster civilisation in a territory where city life was so little developed; the normal economic unit, alike on royal lands, in monastic institutions, and in the possessions of lay proprietors, was the household. This may be a very large social group, but the mutual offices of the members are rendered as a matter of obligation, not as the result of agreements between men who are personally independent and drive their own bargains. It was already the military unit responsible for the defence of the realm[1], and was the territorial basis for the administration of justice and provision for the poor. In addition to this Charles aimed at so organising household life that agriculture and industry might be stimulated and improved.

The household as the unit of society for economic purposes.

The *capitulare de villis* was not propounded as a mere fiscal measure with the view of increasing the royal revenue; it aimed at increasing the efficiency of the economic organisation[2] of society as a whole. Charles was of course chiefly concerned with the administration of the royal domain; the *judices*[3] were to overhaul the administrative work of the *majores*[4], and to see that the king's estates were properly cultivated and the local products well utilised. But the royal example would find imitators, and pressure was brought to bear on the monasteries and lay possessors of *beneficia*[5], who

---

[1] A.D. 807; *Capit. Aquense* in Migne, I. 307, cc. 1, 2.
[2] Inama Sternegg, I. 349.
[3] *Capit. de Villis*, 3, 8, 9, 24, 29.
[4] *Ib.*, 10, 26.   [5] Inama Sternegg, I. 351.

held portions of the ancient Crown lands. The necessity of
being provided with the men and military equipment they
were required to furnish would tend to induce other magnates
to adopt improved methods of estate management. As it
appears that these large households were steadily increasing
and attracting the possessors of small holdings to become
members of larger organisations[1], the rules which were laid
down for the royal *villae* would serve, so far as their form
was concerned, for the economic regulation of the whole
territory.

The *de villis* recapitulates the matters into which the
judices ought to enquire, so that the estate management might
be carried on properly and efficiently both on its agricultural
and industrial sides[2]. To enable them to perform this duty
it was desirable that the condition of the estates should be
exhibited in writing, so that everything might be easily
checked, and the general state of the property readily gauged.
There were *surveys*, which gave a complete inventory of
the villa, including a statement of the labour available and
the personal obligations of each man, as well as an enumeration of the live stock, horses, cattle, and hens, and also
information about the condition of the buildings and the
supply of implements[3]. It was part of the duty of the *judices*
to keep regular accounts, with separate books for revenue
and for outlay, and to inform the king of the state of the
balance[4]. The surveys are closely analogous to the *extenta* of a
mediaeval manor, while the accounts, of which no specimen

---

[1] Inama Sternegg, I. 295; Lamprecht, *Deutsche Geschichte*, II. 89.

[2] On the industrial organisation of the villa compare Gareis, *Bemer-
kungen zu K. Karl's Capitulare de Villis* in *Germanistische Abhandlungen
zum LXX. Geburtstag K. von Maurers*, p. 246; Bücher, art. *Gewerbe* in
Handwörterbuch der Staatswissenschaft, III. 926; Guérard, Introduction to
the *Polyptyque de l'Abbé Irminon*, I. 617; *Explication du Capit. de Villis*
in *Bibliothèque de l'École des Chartes*, ser. iiime. t. iv. (1852), pp. 324—7.

[3] A.D. 812; Migne, I. 341. Compare Ulpian, in *Digest* L. tit. 15, c. 4.

[4] *Capit. de Villis*, c. 55.

seems to have survived, may well have set the type of the mediaeval reckonings which are commonly known as ministers' rolls.

The institution which is thus depicted for us, and the system which Charles introduced with the view of regulating it, give us a link with the distant past and help us to look back to the Roman villa, with its *ergastula* and its tillage, its vineyards, and its cattle breeding. This *capitulare* is also of great interest on its own account, since it shows us an almost unique effort to organise a highly civilised life on a basis of natural economy. Military obligations, justice, and poor relief are inseparably linked with the household, within which there is no money circulation. Money and commerce were not excluded; but the prosperity and strength of the realm were dependent primarily on the management of natural resources, and not on the accumulation of treasure. The amassing of bullion had been the Merovingian expedient[1] for equipping armies, and it gave the means for bribing barbarians to abstain from plundering.

Necessity was doubtless the mother of invention; and we need not suppose that Charles had consciously formulated any principles of political economy; but it is worth while to notice that the wisdom of his methods has been endorsed in later times. It was his policy to make the most of native resources, as the secret of strength; to promote agriculture, but without disparaging industry; and especially to encourage the manufacture of native products. This was practically an anticipation of the economic policy which was successfully applied to England in the days of Burleigh,—the development of industry generally, but in conscious subordination to the needs of agriculture, while the special advantages of particular districts for mining[2] or for the manufacture of salt were not neglected either in the empire of Charles or in the realm of Elizabeth.

---

[1] Dahn, *op. cit.* p. 343.
[2] Inama Sternegg, I. 426.

There is even greater interest in following out the subsequent history of the economic organ which Charles utilised—
the household. The system which he formulated was adopted
by the Normans, and was introduced into a country well
prepared for receiving it, when William conquered England.
The great household, as the centre of rural life, has had an
extraordinary influence on English development; it has shaped
the ambitions of the English plutocracy from the days of
William-de-la-Pole, and has led them to set their faces from
the towns where they made their money to the country, where
they exercised great power: it survived to stimulate the
energies of the great landowners of the last century, when
money economy had become completely prevalent, and induced them to give their energy to the improvement of English
tillage.   In the ancient world, and in much of the modern
world, the city has had exclusive attractions as the centre
of social life; but English civilisation has proceeded on the
basis that is implied in Charles's maxims of social regulation[1].

86.   The political history of the three centuries that
followed the partition of the Carlovingian Empire
seems to be a mere record of social disintegration and internecine warfare, and to have
been incompatible with material progress.   There

Town life—
its meaning,
elements, and
conditions.

---

[1] In the expansion of English influence beyond the seas, this household
type has sometimes been retained, but sometimes we have the land settled
in small homesteads.   The resultant civilisation in each case has varied
immensely.   In the tropical climates of India and Ceylon, of the West
Indies and the Southern States, with the exception of some parts of
Georgia and West Virginia, there are planters with labourers in practical
dependence, even where slavery is extinct and cash relations exist; and in
the pasture farms of Australia there are rich squatters.   In these lands
we get a diffusion of wealth and culture beyond the limits of cities.   In
the Northern States, in Canada and in South Africa, the rural districts
were occupied by little homesteads.   There are great drawbacks in this
latter system, since it concentrates all social advantages in urban groups
and leaves the rural population to a sordid struggle for independence, or
monotonous drudgery under giant capitalists.

is reason to believe, however, that there was more opportunity for cultivating the arts of peace than might at first
sight appear; there seems to have been such an increase
and diffusion of Teutonic population[1] that large areas, first
in the south and then in the north of Germany, were occupied
by agriculturists[2]. But more than this, the eleventh and twelfth
centuries supply ample evidence of the existence of vigorous
urban life in France, Flanders and the Rhineland: while
the founding of new towns in these districts and other parts of
Germany went on in the twelfth and thirteenth centuries[3].
Such commercial and industrial centres could not have come
into prominence unless there had been a real improvement in
the economic conditions of Western Europe.

There is no more complicated problem in mediaeval history
than that which is raised by this revival of town life. An
immense amount of research has been recently devoted to
the legal and constitutional aspects of the enquiry; for us this
is a subordinate consideration. The full solution of the
economic question can only be found by an investigation
of the special history of particular communities; but it is
perhaps possible to state the problem in general terms, and
thus to indicate the directions in which detailed research may
be pursued with profit.

One of the principal difficulties to be faced lies in the
uncertainty, or rather the want of agreement among historians,
as to the characteristic feature of town life; we want so far
as possible to be clear what we are looking for. If all that
we mean by a town is an unusually populous village[4] or

[1] On the motives for this colonisation see Lamprecht, *Deutsche Geschichte*, III. 351.

[2] Lamprecht (*Deutsche Geschichte*, III. 299) points out that the oscilla-
tion in migration began at least as early as the time of Charles. The
Germans ceased to move westward, and commenced to colonise towards the
east. Inama Sternegg, III. p. 1.

[3] Hegel, *Die Entstehung*, p. 37—42.

[4] Green, *Short History of the English People*, I. 369.

even a place which contained merchants among its inhabitants[1], we can hardly hope to distinguish it from other social groups. There were monasteries that had hundreds of inmates and dependents[2], and that were deeply interested in trading concerns. There is, however, some possibility of discriminating, when we look at the matter in its economic aspects. In the household there is only one proprietor, who has a power of controlling the resources of the establishment; the town is a social group in which there are several proprietors[3], and therefore several households. If these households were each self-sufficing, they could exist side by side, without entering into any relations with one another; but the group of households in a town supplement one another's industry and are mutually dependent for the necessaries of life. The town consists of an aggregate of households; each householder is free to manage the internal economy of his establishment—so long as he does no injury to the commonweal—and therefore each is economically distinct. In the religious houses and other large establishments there might be much division of labour, and the community might engage in constant trade with the outside world; but however numerously a monastery was inhabited it would only be a household in the economic sense, and not a town, so long as there were no separate proprietors, with exclusive rights in their possessions, and consequent independence within the group.

For the continued existence and growth of such a group of households, facilities of interchange are requisite; it may be impossible to say whether trade called forth a town, or

[1] Pirenne in *Revue historique* (1895), LVII. p. 70.

[2] See above, p. 38.

[3] "Proprietors" is here used in the widest possible sense, for all those who have exclusive rights to use land, or other requisites of production, whatever might be the precise terms of their tenure, or their legal status as persons.

CHAP. I.]   *The Foundations of Society.*   57

whether the presence of a town gave the opportunity of trade[1];
as a question of priority it is as insoluble as the problem
about the first hen or the first egg; logically, and as observed
fact, the existence of a town and the existence of internal trade
are inseparable; the progress of one would stimulate the
increase of the other. Something of the nature of a market,
in fact if not in law, is involved in the economic idea of a
town; such a market would be possible wherever the households, large or small, of distinct proprietors were closely
associated together, and were in any way inter-dependent so
far as their economic requirements or abilities were concerned.
But within the monasteries or large villas there was no similar
need or opportunity for the development of habitual interchanges and bargaining. Hence it seems to follow that
though towns were found under the shadow and protection
of monasteries and palaces, they consisted of the establishments
of several distinct proprietors, and therefore were outside the
organised life of any one household.

The formation of such groups and their increase in size
and importance could hardly have proceeded unless they had
been reinforced by the inhabitants of surrounding districts.
Herein is our difficulty. When society was organised in
households, and men were bound to the soil either by
proprietary rights or personal obligations, there could be little
freedom of movement; it is not easy to see from what sources
the population that was aggregated in the towns could be
drawn. It may be that there really was more fluidity than
is commonly supposed[2]; but in any case it is possible to call
attention to some social elements which were capable of
taking a part in facilitating the growth of towns, as populous
places with internal trade among the inhabitants.

We must remember, moreover, that there is no difficulty about
the origin of some of the most important towns of Christendom;

[1] Arnold, *Verfassungsgeschichte*, II. 126.
[2] Inama Sternegg, II. 31, and III. 29.

Cologne, Mayence, Strassburg, Paris, Bordeaux, and many others had probably survived as populous centres from Roman times; the inhabitants seem never to have lost their habits of economic independence even though their powers of municipal self-government were swept away. In many places in France the *cité* remained as a monument of the old days, to be the nucleus of a new growth[1]; and in all such cities there would be several proprietors, and facilities for the purchase of food and opportunities of hiring labour, or being hired as a labourer, would be perpetuated. The Roman cities of northern France and of the Rhine valley may have been reduced to the greatest poverty, but it appears that they continued to exist as towns, in the economic sense of the term.

The growth of a town at a wholly new centre presents greater difficulty; but where several distinct proprietors were residing in close proximity to any point which was favourable for trade, there would be at least the nucleus of a true town[2]. There were other social elements, however, which were ready to group themselves round this nucleus, and as they prospered they secured possessions and a footing in the towns. So far as the towns which grew up round monasteries are concerned, we see that the increased trade of religious communities during the eighth and ninth centuries involved the employment of a considerable number of outside agents. Whatever the precise status of the *negociatores* may have been, they are definitely distinguished from the *coloni* and *serfs*; if they were not so far dependent on the monastery as to be able to claim allowances from it, they would have to procure supplies by purchase and would find a market a convenience.

[1] Flach, *Les origines de l'ancienne France*, II. 244.

[2] The possessors of land on the site where trade was springing up were the ancestors of the urban aristocracies of which we hear in the eleventh and twelfth centuries. This was the principal period of the struggle between the landed aristocracy and the trading interests, for power to control the government of the towns.

Other elements would help to swell the lower grades of society in the nascent towns. Places which enjoyed the right of asylum and sanctuary[1] would attract fugitives from justice. Charles the Great insisted on the return of robbers and fugitive slaves[2], but other refugees were apparently retained; and as there was no obligation to maintain them in idleness they would probably be set to work for wages. There were other elements of roving population; pilgrims were passing to and fro, and alien merchants were constantly on the move. They were definitely recognised in the Carolingian legislation, for the *missi* were to report to Charles on the *advenae*[3] that came into their districts; some of them might be attracted to settle permanently and contribute to the growth of a town. Some of the artisans appear to have been free; but even those who were not their own masters might occasionally migrate; Bishop Gebhart was able to secure that a large number of his people should settle in the neighbourhood of the monastery he had founded at Petershausen[4].

One great reason which would induce men to draw together and reside in contiguity with their neighbours was the need of protection. This was especially felt in districts which were exposed to the ravages of the Norsemen and the Huns[5]; and the humbler classes would find it to their advantage to live under the shadow of a royal palace, an episcopal residence, or a great monastic household, where defence could be regularly organised. In its external aspects the tenth century town was before everything else a *burg* or fortified place, and many continental towns long preserved the character of military strongholds. The neighbourhood of a monastery might be less secure than that of a fort, but the trading immunities

---

[1] Imbart de la Tour, *op. cit.* p. 80.

[2] *Capitular.*, A.D. 806; Migne, I. 303, c. 5.

[3] *Capitular.*, A.D. 806; Migne, I. 303, c. 5, 306, c. 5.

[4] Hegel, *Entstehung des deutschen Städtewesens*, 117.

[5] W. Arnold, *Verfassungsgeschichte*, II. 130.

possessed by many of the religious houses must have been an attraction to settlers who hoped to share in these commercial privileges.

The towns of the thirteenth century were not, however, a mere congeries of atoms attracted by the opportunity of protection and maintained by the facilities for trade; there were connecting ties in each town, consisting of the rights and obligations which were common to the inhabitants, or to some portions of the inhabitants, and which helped to give these groups some semblance of unity.

There was, for one thing, in many of the Roman towns, common ownership of land. Besides the arable fields, which belonged to particular proprietors, there were common lands which supplied pasturage for the cattle[1]. The history of Nîmes supplies a case in point[2]; and in many other instances when an agricultural unit developed into an industrial or commercial town, the existence of the common fields must have been an important bond of union among the inhabitants[3], while it served as the basis for the usual food supply[4].

The common enjoyment of market rights was another bond of union among the townsmen. Practical facilities for the exchange of goods are, as we have seen, involved in the very idea of a town; but it seems to have been only gradually that the privileges, fiscal and legal, connected with the holding of a market were clearly defined; the grant of such privileges by charter may in some cases have instituted a market and in others have transformed an irregularly held market into a

[1] Lamprecht, *Deutsche Geschichte*, IV. 214.

[2] Dareste de la Chavanne, *Classes Agricoles*, 117. Rietschel, *Die Civitas*, 61, 87.

[3] Maitland, *Township and Burgh*, 50.

[4] On the agricultural organisation at Rome in 1030 A.D., see Rodocanachi, *Corporations ouvrières à Rome*, I. x. When new towns were planted in the twelfth century the agricultural conditions were carefully considered. S. Thomas Aquinas, *De reg. princ.* II. 4.

mercatum legitimum[1]. Markets are frequently mentioned in the *Capitularies*, and Charles endeavoured to keep the right of making these grants entirely in his own hands. It is by no means clear in many documents whether the market referred to was an annual fair which served as the resort of strangers and a centre for foreign trade, or merely the weekly market which furnished supplies to the townsmen. In either case transactions were carried on under regal (or seignorial) authority; this was symbolised by the market cross, bearing the glove and sword, as tokens of the impersonal presence of the king and the duty of preserving his peace[2]. Where a market was thus legally established it became the interest of neighbouring proprietors to obtain a house in the town[3], so as to share in these privileges, and bring their estates within the range of the increasing opportunities of trade.

The common obligations, which drew the townsmen together, were in part connected with the rights already specified; there were fiscal burdens connected with the ownership of land, and compositions to be paid in order to free the trade of the townsmen from the usual tolls. There were also military duties to be discharged; and the maintenance of the walls of mediaeval towns, together with the duty of manning them, must have been a very heavy burden on the property and the time of the burgesses. Much of the interest of the constitutional history of the towns lies in the story of the efforts of the inhabitants to free themselves from the discharge of these obligations, and to extort rights of self-government from the royal, noble, or ecclesiastical authority under whose patronage and by whose favour the town had grown up.

[1] Huvelin, *Droit des marchés*, 145, 175.

[2] R. Sohm, *Entstehung des deutschen Städtewesens*, 18. Of course successful attempts were made to encroach on this royal right, as on others, Huvelin, *op. cit.*, 183.

[3] In *Domesday Book* such houses were rated along with the estates, and did not form part of the town for fiscal purposes, *e.g.* Brightwell, *D. B.* I. 58; Maitland, *Domesday Book and Beyond*, 179.

Such were the chief elements which went to constitute twelfth century cities, and which were differently combined in the history of particular places. We certainly cannot account for the revival of city life in general by reference to any single element alone [1]; the increase of trade could not by itself [2] bring about the growth of towns as distinguished from the expansion of households. In the twelfth and thirteenth centuries the constitution of a town and the importance of fostering town life were generally recognised and understood; and conscious efforts were made by kings and nobles to plant such centres, and thus to develop the trade of their territories. Many towns [3] were established in Saxony in the thirteenth century in connection with the mining industry, and free towns were founded in the English possessions in France at favourable points for trade [4].

We may now turn from the consideration of the conditions under which towns originated and came to be organised communities, to look at their internal life before the thirteenth century. The scattered hints furnished by contemporary historians throw but little light on the subject; there is good reason to believe, however, that those who had proprietary rights in the land of the town formed a local aristocracy [5], and that their descendants long continued to enjoy a superior status; but they were not able to maintain their position as an exclusive caste permanently. The trading interests came more and more to be the leading factor in the prosperity of the towns; and the institutions which were organised for commercial purposes and which did not exclude either the

[1] Flach, II. 326; also see Pirenne (*Revue historique*, 1895, vol. LVII. p. 65), who shows by specific instances that the origin of towns cannot be attributed either to monasteries, fortresses, or markets alone.

[2] Pirenne (*Revue historique*, 1895, vol. LVII. p. 68), "Les villes sont nées spontanément sous l'action des causes économiques qu'a suscitées en Europe la renaissance du commerce et de l'industrie."

[3] Inama Sternegg, III. i. 2, 22 *n*.   [4] See below, p. 92.

[5] W. Arnold, *Zur Geschichte des Eigenthums in den deutschen Städten* 10.

landed or the landless man, gradually attained to considerable power. Some of these gilds and associations can be traced back to very early times, and we may also detect rudimentary forms of commercial regulation. The history of these bodies is exceedingly obscure, but it becomes less confusing if we fix our attention on the different functions they subserved.

The *active*[1] trade of the Carolingian period was carried on by caravans of merchants who travelled together for mutual protection, since solitary travelling was practically impossible. The caravan might swell to an extraordinary size as the merchants might be accompanied by a crowd of pilgrims who were glad of the convoy through perilous places; and some sort of rule and governance was necessary among this moving throng[2]. The organised caravan is the most primitive type of association among enterprising merchants; and would easily lead to the institution of depots at the points which these travellers habitually visited, and where they desired to find warehouses for their goods and accommodations for man and beast. The commercial *factories* of foreign merchants, like the Steelyard in London, where the men of the Emperor resorted[3], seems to follow naturally on the localisation of organised bodies of travelling merchants[4]. Such depots, which furnished permanent links between a town and distant lands, seem to have arisen with the growth of mediaeval commerce, but it is at all events possible that other forms of mercantile association survived from Roman times. In any case where the food supply of a city was drawn, not from its own fields,

---

[1] Active trade is done by merchants who buy goods and adventure with them, seeking for purchasers.

[2] Doren, *Untersuchungen zur Geschichte der Kaufmannsgilden* in Schmoller's *Staats u. socialwissenschaftliche Forschungen*, XV. ii. 162; Lamprecht, *Deutsche Geschichte*, III. 27.

[3] Lappenberg, *Geschichte des deutschen Stahlhofs zu London*, ii. 1.

[4] The hanse of which we read at S. Omer (Giry, *S. Omer*, 413) appears to be the local depot of Flemish merchants associated for active trade to England.

but by trading with outlying districts, the organisation of an active carrying trade was almost essential; the men who conducted the traffic on the Seine and the Loire were well-known associated bodies in the eleventh century; and it is at least possible that they were not a new creation, but maintained an unbroken tradition from the days of the Empire[1].

There is another commercial institution of which frequent mention is made, but the hints regarding its character and purpose are so meagre that it is impossible to speak of them with any confidence. The information that has come down to us is not, however, inconsistent with the hypothesis that the *gild merchant* was an organisation which was formed in many towns with the view of enabling the inhabitants to engage in *passive* trade, on the most advantageous terms[2]. The gild merchant seems to have consisted of all the inhabitants of a town, rich or poor, who had occasion to buy and sell[3]; it would doubtless be an advantage to them all to have the means of making purchases from travelling merchants by a collective bargain, with the view of afterwards sharing the goods among themselves. There seems to have been some stage of municipal development when the gild merchant was a highly prized institution; though many important towns dispensed with it altogether, and others soon outgrew it and allowed it to fall into desuetude. There does not seem to be any analogue to this institution in the municipal life of the Roman Empire.

---

[1] Pigeonneau, I. 33, 114.

[2] Rodocanachi (*Corporations*, p. xiv.) regards the possession of commercial tribunals as the main element in the formation of the Mercanzia at Rome. It appears to have arisen out of the combination of earlier associations in the xiith, and to have lost its importance as particular crafts withdrew from it in the xivth century. *Ib.* pp. xii, xviii.

[3] See Gross, *Gild Merchant*, I. 107; M. Bateson, *Leicester*, p. xxix.; Mayer, *Zoll, Kaufmannschaft u. Markt* in *Germanistische Abhandlungen*, p. 450: *Gild Merchant of Shrewsbury* in *Royal Hist. Soc. Trans.* N. S. IX. 99; Giry, *S. Omer*, 281; also Pirenne, *Revue historique*, LVII. p. 77.

The organisation of industry in *craft gilds* comes into clear light in the twelfth century, when we have documentary evidence of the cordwainers at Rouen, and the weavers at London and elsewhere. It seems possible that they are a branch of household organisation[1], which came to have a public position when any occupation ceased to be a domestic employment and was organised on an independent basis. But the analogy between the mediaeval craft gilds and the Roman *collegia* is so close that it is difficult to suppose that the craft gilds or industrial organisations were never a survival which was maintained among the economically independent inhabitants of ancient cities, but always a new development transferred from the royal household to the population that gathered beside it. There seems to be no conclusive evidence of the continuous existence of the *collegia* even in Rome itself[2], and the hints which we get of their persistence at other centres are very scanty[3]; but they are sufficient to make the hypothesis of survival in Roman cities and diffusion from them more probable than the view which assigns to them an entirely independent origin.

Of institutions which were formed for other than trading or industrial purposes it is unnecessary to speak here, though they may doubtless have had much to do with the development of municipal constitutions. There were *gilds* which Charles attempted to suppress[4], they seem to have been analogous to the English frith gilds[5] which served as associa-

---

[1] On the anticipations of craft organisation in the time of Charles, see Gareis, *op. cit.* p. 247. Compare the Assize of Bread under Henry II. Cunningham, *Growth of English Industry*, I. 568. In cases like the moneyers, when public administrative functions and work were combined, the household is a probable source of derivation.

[2] Rodocanachi, *Corporations ouvrières à Rome*, pp. viii, xi.

[3] Martin Saint Léon, *Corporations de Métiers*, 28; E. Mayer, *Deutsche u. französiche Verfassungsgeschichte*, I. 330.

[4] Inama Sternegg, I. 263.

[5] Pirenne in *Revue historique*, LIII. 63.

tions for the prosecution of felons. They possibly helped to train the inhabitants of a town to mutual help, and gave them practice in self-government so that they may have served as a preparation for the growth of the *communes*, when civic life received its great impetus at the era of the Crusades[1]. But from the economic standpoint such associations were not of first-rate importance ; and the city life to the growth of which they contributed was after all not a new social type, but only the reviving of a form that had already played a notable part in the history of the world[2].

87. The resuscitation of town life was the last stone[3] in the foundations of mediaeval Christendom;

The Roman Obedience.

many flourishing towns had revived or grown up in Flanders, Germany, France, and Italy before the thirteenth century, and if we attempt to survey society in Western Europe at that date, we cannot but feel that despite the political and racial divisions, and the area over which it extended, Christendom was extraordinarily homogeneous and was bound together by very firm ties deeply imbedded in its structure. Just as in India at the present time the common institutions of Brahmanism give a unity to the social system of all Hindus, whatever may be their language or their polity, so the common religious life of Christendom affected every aspect of society. We should remember, too, that there was a body politic, or at least a social organism, in the twelfth century : the peoples of Western Europe were no longer a military Empire held together by the personal ascendancy of a single ruler, like Charles the Great, but formed a vigorous polity which had grown up everywhere under similar influences, and which was in all its parts connected with the centre at Rome.

[1] See below, p. 89.

[2] See vol. I. p. 92.

[3] It had been the first thing of which we have any knowledge in the growth of Phoenician, Greek, and Roman civilisation.

The monasteries, as Christian colonies, had been brought
to conform to the rule of S. Benedict, and thus came to have
a special allegiance to the Holy See[1]; to Rome the trains of
pilgrims wended their way along the commercial routes; while
it was from Rome that archbishops received the pallium which
marked the dignity of their office[2]; and the papal theory of
the relations of Pope and Emperor triumphed at last.   Each
of the elements in the reviving civilisation of the Dark Ages
had close connections with the Eternal City, from which the
known world had been ruled in imperial times.

There were three great threads that ran through the whole
social system of Christendom.   First of all there was a common
religious life, with the powerful weapons of spiritual censure
and excommunication which it placed in the hands of the
clergy, so that they were able to enforce the line of policy
which Rome approved.   Then there was the great judicial
system of canon law, a common code with similar tribunals
for the whole of Western Christendom, dealing not merely
with strictly ecclesiastical affairs but with many matters that
we should regard as economic, such as questions of commercial morality, and also with social welfare as affected by
the law of marriage and the disposition of property by will.
Lastly, there was the payment of heavy dues to Rome; these
were partly connected with the administration of canon law,
and partly consisted of papal taxation of various kinds.   The
collection of this revenue gave rise to an enormous fiscal
system: the agents who administered it were Italian bankers
and their partners, and these papal merchants were settled all
over Western Christendom.

It was thus that a clerical organisation held the whole
social system together.   Each of these sides of the united
life of Christendom, whether religious, legal or financial, came
to be the subject of attack at the Reformation.   We may say

[1] Montalembert, *Monks of the West*, II. 345—347.
[2] Collier, *Ecclesiastical History of Great Britain*, I. 161.

that in Germany there was a genuine revolt against abuses in connection with religious belief and practice ; in Bohemia, on the other hand, the pressure of papal taxation had given occasion to indignant feeling for generations before the outbreak came ; this was also true of England, though the final breach in our country occurred in regard to the administration of canon law, and the hearing of the king's cause. But the violence of the rupture in each case helps to show how firm the ligaments had been that bound the social system together.

The advantages of the new order, as compared with the ancient empire of the Caesars or with the chaos that followed on its fall, are so obvious to us, that we are apt to underrate the difficulty of accounting for the growth of the new society, as we find it in the twelfth century[1]. If we are content to draw on our imaginations and people the Dark Ages with men of modern type capable of cherishing our ideals and being influenced by our motives, we can then trace the course of the change in terms that are plausible throughout, and that lay stress on utilitarian aims and motives of political expediency as accounting sufficiently for the progress that occurred.

But the problem is not so easily solved ; we have to do not merely with the revival of ancient society in its old form, but with its transformation. To maintain law and order when once they are established is comparatively simple ; it is a very different thing to create respect for life and property anew. We can only understand the course of the reconstruction of society when we enter into the definite ideals which the men of the Dark Ages set before themselves as concrete things to be aimed at, and the motives which appealed to them personally, with their experience and their beliefs.

[1] After the twelfth century there was more direct influence from imperial institutions through the revived study of Civil Law, and also through the more frequent intercourse with Constantinople which was brought about by the Crusades.

We must not only consider the enormous difficulties to be faced, but the means that were available for dealing with them. When we thus understand the complexity and conditions of the problem, we may see that there is only one suggestion which offers a simple, and at the same time a sufficient, solution of all the difficulties of the case. Christianity furnished the new ideals, and furnished also new and powerful motives which appealed to individuals strongly, so that they set themselves to realise their aims. The Roman Empire had lingered on as the type of a decadent society, which offered no high views of life, and supplied few effective motives for individual self-discipline and energy[1]. Christianity brought about the resurrection of a new society, because it was not the mere sentiment of pious individuals, but a living force which permeated all the remnants of civilisation, and guided the energies of those by whom these various elements were built up into the great mediaeval polity.

[1] Vol. I. p. 192.

CHAPTER II.

NATURAL AND MONEY ECONOMY.

88. In the preceding paragraphs we have endeavoured
to point out the chief factors in the reconstruction of civilised society in Western Europe;
we must now describe the character of the
economic institutions of mediaeval Christendom,
and examine their working when they were at
their best. Nor need we have much doubt as to the period
during which Christendom reached the highest point of material well-being, according to the test we have habitually
used[1]. The thirteenth century was one of the great eras of
the world's history, an age of remarkable artistic and poetic
production, of unrivalled philosophical and legal acumen[2], of
military expeditions and commercial enterprise. It was an
age, too, that has left abundant evidence of its material prosperity in the magnificent buildings which remain; sometimes
they are in ruins, and sometimes they have been restored; but
however they may have suffered, they force us to feel what
large resources were at the command of those who were able
to carry out their designs on so grand a scale.

The churches of Christendom—cathedral, parochial, and
conventual—as they still remain, are among the most impressive monuments of the architectural activity of the twelfth

(margin note:) Material relics of mediaeval prosperity; civic, ecclesiastical, domestic.

---

[1] Vol. I. p. 8.
[2] On the study of Roman Law, see below, p. 151.

and thirteenth centuries ; but many of them have perished
utterly.   The changed taste of a later age has done much to
obliterate the evidence as to the number and grandeur of the
edifices which were erected by the Normans in the lands which
they conquered[1].   Not only was there a very general reconstruction of the older and more meagre ecclesiastical buildings,
but there were also many wholly new foundations.   The
reform of the monastic life which emanated from Cluny
and Citeaux, and gave rise to the new orders, was the sign
of a fresh enthusiasm for a stricter religious life, which
expressed itself most fittingly in the severely beautiful churches
of the Cistercians.   The witness of the ecclesiastical buildings
is writ large as one of the features of the landscape throughout Western Christendom, and tells of a lavish devotion of
wealth and vigour to the maintenance of Christian worship
and the furtherance of pious objects.

There had of course been numerous sacred temples in
the old world, and a great deal of art was lavished on the
service of the gods ; it is easy to trace analogies between the
practices of paganism and the superstitions of the middle
ages ; it is not hard to shew that rites and legends from
the old world had survived, and were sometimes revested
in a Christian dress, when they were not so plainly unchristian[2]
that it was obviously necessary to stamp them out.   But
it is of less importance to note these superficial and occasional resemblances than to mark the fundamental differences.
In the ancient world, religion, springing as it did from family
rites and civic duties, was intensely local ; the philosopher
could find resemblances between the gods of different lands
and give the cults a spiritualised significance ; but the religion
of the individual, or of the city, was imbued with material
elements, personal and local[3] ; the one common bond

[1] E. S. Prior, *History of Gothic Architecture*, 34.
[2] L. Eckenstein on S. Agatha in *Woman under Monasticism*, p. 15.
[3] Fustel de Coulanges, *La cité antique*, (1895), pp. 37, 167.

through the ancient empire was the worship of the Emperor
—of arbitrary human will. In Christendom there was one
religion which was common to all; it might be localised at
some particular spot, which had been the scene of a spiritual
triumph—like the sepulchre at Jerusalem, or in a far less
degree the cave at Subiaco—it might be hallowed by the
treasured relics of some victor for the faith; but this was a
spiritual faith and therefore without distinctions of person,
place, or time, even when it was localised here by special
associations and degraded there by admixture with pagan
survivals. The internal struggles of Christendom gave rise
to the scandal of conflicting appeals to one God to support
the cause of rival claimants, but we no longer see the struggle
of gods with gods[1]. There was a fundamental unity of Christian faith and sentiment underlying all the differences of race
and interest. Religious motives might be brought into play
so as to give more vehemence to human passions; religious
principles might be alleged to excuse the direst crimes; but
there was after all a common ground on which men could
meet, one centre to which they could look, and a definite cause
which they had at heart. The churches of Christendom are
the outward and visible signs of a common religious life such
as was entirely strange to the ancient world; they are monuments which serve to remind us of the fact that one religious
and legal organisation ran through the whole social structure.

Churches and ecclesiastical edifices are among the most
prominent vestiges of mediaeval culture; but there are, besides,
buildings which remain to testify to the high development of
other sides of life. The crusades were the outcome of religious enthusiasm, but they were also partly due to commercial motives, and they proved to be the means of
introducing a new era of mercantile enterprise, which greatly
affected the towns of Italy and Flanders, and to a certain
extent of Germany, France, and England. Costly Town Halls

[1] Fustel de Coulanges, *La cité antique*, p. 175.

survive to commemorate the greatness of some of these trading centres. Such civic buildings served the same purposes as the basilicas of the ancient world; and, though there were no edifices which attained the magnificence of the range of *fora* which were grouped near the Capitol of Rome[1], there was enough grandeur to excite the admiration of those who look back from a utilitarian age. The piazza S. Marco at Venice, the Loggia at Florence, the city buildings at Bruges and Ghent, are at least striking memorials of newly developed commercial intercourse and of a municipal prosperity which had been unknown for centuries.

Though the arts of peace were thus flourishing once more, the thirteenth century was an age of frequent warfare; houses of every kind were built in a fashion which rendered them susceptible of defence. The great castles which overshadow the towns of France and Germany have their counterpart in the fortresses which Edward I created around and throughout the principality of Wales. The art of military[2] fortification had been greatly developed by contact with the East, and the means of defence far excelled the forces of offensive warfare. The castles of great nobles were places from which defiance could be easily hurled at an emperor or king; the walls of the cities enabled the burgesses to struggle for the maintenance of liberty; while the towers of parish churches and the buildings of mediaeval manors were capable of offering protection from hurried raids. The military and domestic, no less than the ecclesiastical and civic buildings which survive, tell us something of the characteristic features of life in the halcyon days of mediaeval Christendom.

The enumeration of these architectural monuments may serve to remind us of the different types of institution which we must study in turn, if we hope to understand their economic working. On the one hand these edifices bring before

[1] Hodgkin, *Italy*, IV. 104.
[2] As *e.g.* at Château Gaillard, Oman, *A History of the Art of War*, p. 533.

us the far-reaching *ecclesiastical* system which had been consciously developed on similar lines throughout the whole of
Christendom.   Other buildings enable us to recall the *city*
institutions, with the facilities they afforded for intercommunication and trade between different points throughout Europe.
There are others still which help us to form a vivid image
of *household* administration of different sorts, as it existed in
the castles of kings and barons, the palaces of bishops, and
even in the monasteries or the manors.   The principal groups
of architectural remains correspond to the three different types
of social organisation which have left their mark on Modern
Europe.

89.   The thirteenth century was, as has been pointed out,

The transi-
tion from
natural to
money
economy—
Constitutional
progress.

a period of great material prosperity ; but it was
also an age of rapid transition, one might almost
say of economic revolution.   The revival of
commercial intercourse and development of
trading centres had brought about a wide
diffusion of money, which tended to the substitution of money bargains for payments rendered in service
and in kind.   The government, ecclesiastical as well as civil,
was keenly alive to the financial convenience of a money
revenue, in respect to collection, transmission, and methods
of account.   The system of natural economy as embodied in
Frankish institutions was passing away ; and the pressure of
the demands of fiscal officials forced proprietors generally to
reorganise their establishments with the view of obtaining a
money income from their estates.   The course of the transition
from natural to money economy—from barter and payment
in service to the use of coin—gave rise to many practical
problems, and called forth a great deal of learned discussion.
A mass of records and some literature survive, especially
from English sources, which enable us to study some typical
phases of society, as drawn by contemporary hands, and to
distinguish the factors which contributed to this important

change. We can best understand the working of the social institutions of the day when we view them in connection with this economic revolution.

In the preceding volume of this essay it has been necessary to call attention to other instances of the same revolution, and to note the substitution of money for natural economy, as we find it in the ancient world[1]. The difficulty of collecting a money revenue from the rural population was one that taxed the ingenuity of Babylonian and Ptolemaic financiers. We have also seen what dangerous power was exercised by the moneyed class in Rome, and how greedily they availed themselves of their opportunities for becoming rich at the expense of subject peoples. Money economy had also imposed a heavy burden on the poor cultivators of Attica in the time of Solon. On the other hand we may remember that the introduction of a money economy into the Greek cities was one of the conditions which rendered the diffusion of political interest and power possible. All these phenomena may be found once more, in different forms and on a different scale, but with results that are at least so far analogous that they prove very instructive.

Though there were many mitigating circumstances in mediaeval as compared with ancient times, the pressure of the change was doubtless very severe; and there was a bitter feeling against the Jews and other bankers who had a partial monopoly of the medium of exchange. The convenience of the monetary system was, however, so great, both for fiscal purposes and as a means of opening up the possibility of commercial and industrial development, that the revolution was inevitable; had it not occurred, all human progress would have been arrested at a primitive 'stationary state,' with society organised in household groups. The economic advantages which have accrued from the general introduction of money are clear, if we contrast Western civilisation to-day with the

[1] Vol. I. 73, 100, 114.

condition of Europe in the time of Charles the Great; and
we must remember that this economic step in advance rendered
political and constitutional progress possible, both in the
ancient and in the mediaeval world. It was not until public
burdens were reckoned and collected in terms of money,
that it was feasible for the subjects to aim at controlling
the power of the purse. So long as revenue was obtained
in different forms, it was very difficult to unite the various
sections of the community in common action, and it was impossible to criticise the financial administration intelligently and
effectively. The connection between the new economic conditions and political progress is most noticeable in the history
of the European country which first adopted representative
institutions. Constitutional progress followed very closely on
the administrative changes which took place in England between the time of the Confessor and the time of Edward I.
The system of collecting revenue in money, instead of relying
on payment in kind and on service personally rendered, made
for more effective government in every department, and it
was a necessary step for the attainment of the prized power
of the English citizen to control and to adjust taxation. When
the customs on imports consisted chiefly of tuns of wine, and
traditional dues were habitually levied, there could neither
be the control of taxation, nor the attempts to adjust its
incidence with which we are familiar. The introduction of
money economy had been a necessary step without which the
Greek citizen could not be his own master and have free
time for political duty; it was also a necessary step in English
political development; it brought into light what concerned
all, and made it possible that the common obligations should
be discussed by all.

In the thirteenth century the life of cities, the ecclesiastical
organisation of Christendom, and the administration of kingdoms, were all becoming permeated by money economy; but
there must have been many relations of life into which it

rarely entered, even in advanced communities. After all, the
towns of Western Christendom were comparatively small ; the
rural population was relatively far larger than it is to-day,
and among the rural population in the thirteenth century
natural economy was dominant[1], and recourse to money
payment was not habitual, even when it was frequent. The
serfs put in their work, and were generally remunerated by
rations and by the holdings which they cultivated on their own
account ; in other cases the produce of a holding might be
divided proportionately between the cultivators and the owner
of the soil. Occasional pecuniary demands pressed heavily on
rural proprietors, who habitually dispensed with money and
organised their establishments on a self-sufficing basis, and it
is in their case that we realise most plainly the difficulties
caused by the transition from natural to money economy.

90. Commercial and financial questions became so prominent in the thirteenth century that they attracted
a great deal of attention from men whose intellectual acuteness was very remarkable. A considerable body of economic literature of various
kinds has survived from that time. In so far
as it is merely descriptive it is of great interest to the historian ;
but it has an even higher importance when it contains principles and enunciates maxims for the practical conduct of
affairs. There were many evils in the business life of the time
which it was desirable to check ; and definite principles as to
what was right and wrong in monetary transactions were formulated by contemporary moralists with the view of establishing
the grounds and limits of wise interference in matters of
trade. Their economic analysis was very defective, and
the theory of price which they put forward is untenable ;
but the ethical standpoint which they took is well worth

*The me-
diaeval theory
of price ; its
fundamental
mistakes and
its practical
applications.*

[1] In the middle of the eighteenth century a large proportion of the rent
of many estates in Scotland was paid in kind. H. G. Graham, *Social
Life of Scotland*, I. 4.

examination, and the practical measures which they recommended appear to have been highly beneficial in the circumstances with which they had to deal.   Their action was
not unwise; their common-sense morality was sound; but
the economic theories, by which they tried to give an intellectual justification for their rules and their practice, were
quite erroneous.

In modern times the form of economic doctrine has been
affected by the fact that it has been so much discussed by men
who were accustomed to deal with physical and mathematical
problems, and who brought their habitual methods of reason-
ing to bear on the phenomena of supply and demand.   In a
similar fashion the economic doctrine of the thirteenth century
in Christendom was affected, as far as its form was concerned,
by the engrossing studies of the time; economic problems
were discussed by men who were habituated to the methods
of metaphysics.   In accordance with current modes of thought,
they tried to determine an ideal standard which should be
realised in particular transactions, and sought for a definite
conception of a "just price"; the practical enquiries then
resolved themselves into means for discovering the just price
of each particular thing.   From the modern point of view
this whole quest was quite chimerical: prices are always fluc-
tuating, and must from their very nature fluctuate.   According
to the "plenty or scarcity of the time" there will be great differences in the quantities available, and therefore in the
relative values, of wheat, cloth, coal and commodities of every
sort.   We know too, that the commodity used for money
must vary in value from time to time, and that therefore there
must be continual fluctuations not only in values but in prices
as well.   The attempt to determine an ideal price implies
that there can and ought to be stability in relative values and
stability in the measure of values,—which is absurd.

The mediaeval doctrine and its application rested upon
another assumption, which we have outlived.   Value is not a

quality which inheres in an object, so that it shall have the same worth for everybody ; it arises from the personal preferences and needs of different people, some of whom desire a given thing more and some less, some of whom want to use it in one way and some in another. Value is not objective, —intrinsic in the object,—but subjective, varying with the desires and intentions of the possessors or would-be possessors ; and because it is thus subjective, there cannot be a definite ideal value, which every article ought to possess, and still less a just price as the measure of that ideal value.

This is one of the cases where the minute analysis of a conception has had practical consequences of a very far-reaching character. So long as it was held that every object had a definite value of its own, it was plausible to say that gain could never arise by a fair exchange between two individuals. If I give an equivalent in exchange for what I get, there seems to be no room for me to gain ; if I have gained by an exchange, it must be because I have not really given an equivalent, but have enriched myself at the expense of the man with whom I bargained. That one country was the better for intercourse with other countries was plain enough, since God had given different gifts to each, and the exchange of superfluities was desirable ; but the calling of a merchant who got rich in the process of exchanging was always more or less under suspicion, as it was not possible to see, from the mediaeval standpoint, how his gains could be really justifiable. This was one reason why mediaeval writers so strongly deprecated the action of the man who bought things in order to sell them elsewhere at a profit, and raised the price against another man who wanted to buy the same article for use on the spot. This misunderstanding, with the consequent prejudice against all commercial gain, was an element of confusion in thirteenth century discussion of business morality.

While mediaeval economic theory seems to us to be non-sensical, and we find it impossible to sympathise with the sentiment it encouraged, we may take a much more favourable view of these writers when we turn from their doctrine of what was right, to consider the practices they condemned as wrong. This is a subject to which but little attention is given in modern days: our economic analysis shows that wherever an exchange takes place, both parties gain by it, and we are apt to jump to the conclusion that if both parties gain the transaction is fair—not perhaps according to any standard of poetical justice—but as fair as can be expected in practical life. But there may be very hard bargains when one man is able to take advantage of the temporary distress of another, or where, from superior knowledge, the merchant is able to get the better of the native from whom he buys valuable pro- ducts with some paltry truck. We feel that it is unfair for the economically strong to wring all he can out of the economi- cally weak, or to trade on terms in which "common esti- mation" is notoriously set aside. We have given up as impracticable many of the old attempts to put down hard bargains with a high hand; but modern moral feeling does not sensibly differ from that of mediaeval times in the desire, if it were possible, to interfere with the action of any dealers who are able to enrich themselves through the necessities or the ignorance of others, and to gain at their expense.

If we tried to find a test by which to discriminate hard bargains we could scarcely do better than adopt the medi- aeval phrase and say that hardship arises when a bargain is made without reference to "common estimation." "Common estimation," according to mediaeval minds, was patent and obvious in an open market, where buyers and sellers met to- gether, and bargained over local products; but the *forestaller*, who made purchases in a private way before the goods were properly exposed to sale, seemed to be a suspicious character and to be trying to enrich himself by obtaining special terms. So far as manufactured goods were concerned, "common estimation" expressed itself in the deliberate opinion of the good men of any craft, who understood the conditions of production, the expense of materials and the cost in labour, and who could thus calculate a reasonable price for one group of commodities. The principle comes out in early regulations for the price of bread, and gives some justification for the statement that the reasonable price of the Middle Ages was based on a calculation as to the cost of production[1].

The prohibition of trading methods which ignored the reasonable price seemed well adapted for guarding against hard bargains: in some cases, however, it was possible to go farther, and to lay down definite limits to the range of prices, or even to prescribe lists which were to be authoritatively enforced. A maximum limit was set for victuals in towns; for there was reason to fear that if the licensed victualler was too extortionate and tried to take advantage of the ignorance and necessity of the travelling merchant[2], he might drive away trade from that place. On the other hand the *assize of bread and beer* supplied a sliding scale, which would reassure the public that a rise in the price of bread was really warranted by the state of the market, and was not merely due to the cupidity of the bakers.

The fixing of a minimum limit below which goods might not be sold was probably less common, but it occurs in connection with the English export of wool[3] to the Continent. Local feeling was very strong, and each little community would insist that it should have a prior claim in regard to the enjoyment of its own products, and that they should not be purchased at wholesale rates for transport to distant markets. The whole scheme of household economy was conducted on the assumption that each estate should be, so far as possible,

[1] Ashley, *Economic History*, I. i. p. 138.
[2] On the fixing of reasonable prices in Rome, Rodocanachi, I. p. xxx. Also for wages, *ib.* p. 20. Compare, for similar policy, Cassiodorus, *Variae*, XI. 11, 12.
[3] Cunningham, *Growth of English Industry*, I. 625.

self-sufficing, and that the bailiff should only sell the surplus
that could not be used; and, as a national economic system
developed, it took similar lines, and limited export trade to the
sale of the surplus for which there was no demand at home.

In these cases the range of prices was limited by authoritative regulation, but there were also many fixed or customary
prices, which arose from attempts to express payments, regularly
made in kind or service, in terms of money. Charles the Great
had devised a scale to show the rate at which tribute in kind[1]
should be accepted from the conquered Saxons. Similarly the
firma unius noctis[2] appears to have had a definite monetary
equivalent in the Angevin fiscal system. In many manors too
the serfs paid *quit-rents*, or regular sums at which their services
were commuted, so that, instead of doing definite works as
an obligation incidental to the possession of a holding, they
enjoyed their land at a fixed money rent. In such cases the
customary money payment came into vogue when natural
economy was beginning to give way.

91. While so much thought was bestowed on a theory
of price, and its application to business practice,
Royal Pre-
rogative and
the Minting
of Money.
it was only natural that attention should be also
devoted to monetary theory. The best example
of mediaeval opinion on this subject is to be
found in the *Tractatus de mutatione monetarum* of Nicholas
Oresme; there is no reason to suppose that this author made
any considerable advance on the scientific opinion which was
current before his time[3]; though, both from its systematic
character and its popular form, this treatise has a very special
interest. The author, who rose to be Bishop of Lisieux, was
a scholar and a lawyer, but he was also a keen observer of
actual affairs; his pamphlet, which is entirely free from scho-

---

[1] *Capitulare*, A.D. 797, c. 11; Migne, I. 202.

[2] Vinogradoff, *Villainage in England*, 303.

[3] Endemann, *Die nationaloekonomischen Grundsätze der canonistischen
Lehre*, p. 75 n. Brants, *L'Économie politique au moyen âge*, 187.

lastic pedantry of every kind, was written with special reference to the reckless debasement of the French coinage which had taken place under John the Good of France. Much of the interest in the treatise arises from the decided view which the author expresses as to kingly responsibility, and the limits of royal prerogative. The money of the realm belonged to the community, and the king could have no right to treat it as his own, or to alter it arbitrarily at his pleasure; if he stooped to do so for the sake of gain, he was worse than an usurer, for he was not driving a hard bargain, but extorting money from those who never bargained with him at all.

His political philosophy defines the standpoint from which Nicholas Oresme treated the questions of currency. He discusses the importance of the stamp on the coins, and shows that the ratio of gold to silver coin depends on the relative value of gold and silver as commodities. He deals with the expedient of altering the denominations of current coins in order to raise their nominal value, and with the mischiefs that result from reducing the weight or debasing the fineness of the money issued from the mint. He recognises that it may be convenient to coin token money of some inferior metal, but insists that the purity of the standard coin should always be maintained. His exposition of economic doctrine is so thorough and clear, that centuries were to elapse before his treatment of monetary problems was superseded.

The treatise of the French bishop is an admirable exposition of the principles of a sound monetary system, but it gave little guidance on the practical difficulty which was felt in commercial circles of exchanging the money of one country for the current coin of another. This was a very complicated business, as there were real differences of size and fineness with which travellers could not be fully acquainted; but account had to be taken of even more obscure phenomena; the same coin might have a different purchasing power in one country that was well supplied with the precious metals, from that which it had in a land where bullion was very scarce, and the range of prices low. This simple fact of commercial experience was entirely at variance with the theory of a "just price," intrinsic in the thing itself; and the selling of coins and making a price for coins, as was done at fairs and other places of resort, appeared to be in itself a disreputable occupation, by which the exchanger succeeded in obtaining a sordid gain. The real justification for varying rates of foreign exchanges was unintelligible to the ordinary man of probity at the time; and the merchant had little means of checking the cambist's calculations. In the interests of commerce it was advantageous, when it was possible, to commit money-changing to responsible officials[1], who were under the direct control of the highest political authority.

(i) *Ecclesiastical and Royal Finance.*

92. Such was the condition of opinion on prices and

Ecclesiastical and administrative system. Papal Revenue; its collection and transmission.

currency at the time when the system of money payment was being rapidly introduced in connection with transactions of every kind. The pressure of papal taxation, the necessity of collecting it, and the convenience of transmitting it were widely diffused influences which were steadily exerted in favour of the change. The popes had created an immense fiscal system all through Christendom; part of their income consisted of the rents drawn from the patrimony of the Church of Rome in Italy and Sicily[2]; but large annual payments were also received regularly from the lands of the numerous monasteries that had commended

[1] The banker's business at Rome was regulated by the Holy See. Rodocanachi, *op. cit.* ii. 6. Exchange tables were organised at Dover by Edward I. in 1299.

[2] Fabre, *Étude sur le Liber Censuum* in *Écoles françaises d'Athènes et de Rome*, p. 8.

themselves to the Apostolic See[1]. Very large sums were also levied as fees in connection with legal proceedings in the ecclesiastical courts, or as taxation insisted on under various forms. It would have been impossible to administer this revenue if it had been taken in kind, but when it was rendered in money it could be conveniently collected and transmitted to Rome by authorised agents, who had established themselves throughout the whole of Western Europe.

The Papacy was not uniformly successful in obtaining a full recognition of its claims to raise revenue in all lands alike; some sources of income were available, however, to a greater or less degree in all Christian countries. England was pre-vailed on to bear the burden of ecclesiastical taxation in its heaviest forms[2]; the sums collected there were exceptionally large, when estimated in relation to the total wealth of that outlying and little developed land. Peter's pence had been raised since the ninth century, and the success of the Norman invasion, which had been in some sort a crusade, tended to strengthen the papal influence over ecclesiastical affairs in England[3]. The re-organisation of the ecclesiastical courts opened the way for more frequent appeals to Rome; while the administration of canon law within the realm by papal officials appears to have been much more general than is commonly supposed[4]. These charges were a large item in the papal revenue; the income drawn, under various pretexts, from the endowments of different parishes, cathedrals or abbeys was also large. In addition to these habitual contributions there

[1] Fabre, *op. cit.* pp. 37, 116.

[2] Milman, *Latin Christianity* (3rd Ed.), VI. pp. 83, 290. For France see Glasson, *Histoire du droit et des Institutions de France*, V. ch. V. p. 263; also Gasquet, *Précis des Institutions politiques en l'ancienne France*, II. 19, 24.

[3] The monastery of Battle was placed under direct papal control, and a great deal of English preferment came to be in the hands of papal nominees.

[4] F. W. Maitland, *Roman Canon Law in the Church of England*, 113 fol.

were also extraordinary dues, such as the tithe of all ecclesiastical property which was levied in connection with the
second crusade. The claim to tax the people and the clergy
was submitted to with a bad grace; but the ecclesiastical
contention that the temporalities of the Church should be free
from the payment of taxes to the Crown roused a prompt and
effective resistance. The demands of the papal court became
more and more exorbitant throughout Christendom generally
in the fourteenth and fifteenth centuries[1]; the increased revenues of the Church in Bohemia[2], which had suddenly become
a wealthy country, excited widespread jealousy and gave rise
to premonitory symptoms of the Reformation.

The *camera*, as the papal treasury at Rome was called, had
an elaborate organisation[3]; and the money obtained in the
different countries of Christendom was collected by Italian
bankers who were generally known as the Pope's merchants;
the papal fiscal requirements were thus the principal cause which
led to the development of foreign banking[4]. The revenue from
England was transmitted by bills of exchange, which were
generally met by the exportation of English wool to Italian
markets; there must, however, have been a considerable drain
of bullion from the lands which were destitute of valuable
products for export trade[5]. The chief agents in forwarding the
money to Rome were known as *depositaries*, and they were

[1] Gottlob, *Aus der Camera Apostolica*, p. 183.

[2] Kautsky, *Communism in Central Europe*, p. 42.

[3] Compare Gottlob, *Aus der Camera*, p. 70 fol.

[4] Military requirements sometimes necessitated the transference of large
sums of money. Servois, *Emprunts de S. Louis* in *Bibliothèque de l'école
des Chartes*, 4me serie, IV. 113. Besides the facilities for such business
afforded by the Italian bankers [Bond, *Loans supplied by Italian Merchants*
in *Archæologia* XXVIII (1840)], an elaborate system for the transmission of
the precious metals had been built up by the Templars. Delisle, *Operations financières des Templiers* in *Acad. des Inscrip.* t. XXXIII. (1889).

[5] On the collection of the tithes in Greenland in 1282 see Heywood,
*Documenta selecta e tabulario secreto Vaticano quae Romanorum Pontificum
erga Americae populos curam testantur*, No. 8.

almost exclusively Italians; but the actual work of obtaining the papal dues was done by *collectors*. Much of this income was doubtless collected in coin; but some of it, such as tithes, appears to have been paid in kind in the thirteenth century, and it would then be the duty of the collectors to realise the money worth of the corn or other products which came into their hands. They had also occasional opportunities of advancing silver to persons who were temporarily unable to meet the papal demands, and of engaging in a great deal of profitable, but not very reputable business. In so far as the Pope's merchants gained by carrying on foreign exchanges, they were condemned by the public opinion of the day; and in so far as they took advantage of the necessitous, they gave rise to public scandal and brought religion into contempt.

93. The papal revenue system seems to have been entirely organised on a monetary basis. When we turn to the administration of royal income we get clearer light on the transition from natural to money economy, especially in the case of England, which is peculiarly rich in its financial records. The organisation of the English Exchequer as it existed in the twelfth century has been fully described by Bishop Richard in the *Dialogus de Scaccario*; and so many of the *Pipe Rolls* have been published that there is abundant opportunity for becoming acquainted with the whole system of account[1].

Collection of Royal Revenue in kind and in money.

There is an analogy between the sources of royal and papal income; in both cases there were certain landed possessions which yielded a revenue; there were profits of jurisdiction and an income arising from taxation; though the items included, and the proportions of revenue obtained under each title, would not correspond very closely. The regular income of the king was assessed in one payment as the *ferm* of the shire; and the sheriff of each county had also to collect the sums that had accrued from any occasional or

[1] Hubert Hall, *Introduction* in Publications of *Pipe Roll Society*.

additional source. In cases where he had expended money on
the king's behalf, he was called upon to show his authority for
making the payment; and the balance due to the Crown was
handed over in money. The coin was carefully scrutinised and
tested before it was accepted and the sheriff could be de-
clared quit of his responsibility as royal collector for that year.
The English evidence is especially interesting, not only because
it goes so fully into the system of account, the reckoning and
testing of money and the giving of receipts, but because we
find that so late as the early part of the twelfth century a
portion of the royal taxation had been collected in kind[1], and
the monetary fiscal system which is so fully described was,
at least in its completeness, of comparatively recent introduction.

In the time of Edward I special arrangements were made
for the collection of the customs revenue. This is a matter of
considerable interest, as we see that in one branch of the
import trade payment in kind still held its own; the ships
from Gascony were expected to contribute one tun of wine
from before and one from abaft the mast. During the reign
of Edward III we have other instances of collecting taxation
in kind, and the staple export trade of the country was seriously
affected by royal demands. Parliament voted supplies to the
king, to be taken up in the form of wool, and transmitted by
royal agents to Flanders, where the proceeds of the sale were
to be expended in military operations[2]. It thus appears that
the fiscal system of England in the fourteenth century was
not quite completely established on a monetary basis, since a
temporary reversion to the primitive methods of natural
economy was still possible.

This revolution in fiscal practice could only be accomplished
by the help of capitalists as intermediaries. It had been the
deliberate design of William the Conqueror to organise his

[1] *Dialogus de Scaccario,* I. c. 7.
[2] Cunningham, *Alien Immigrants,* 78.

revenues on a monetary basis, and he induced some Jews to accompany him to England, as his scheme could not be carried through without the presence and assistance of moneyed men. The Crown desired to have command of money, and the wealth of the subjects generally consisted of land and goods. The Jews could be called upon by the Crown to make advances in money, while the taxes were being collected in kind and realised; or in other cases the capitalists might be willing to lend money to a taxpayer, so that he could meet the royal demands with current coin; the English Jews seem to have been of little service either to industry or commerce, but they undoubtedly facilitated the important fiscal changes which were carried out in the period succeeding the Norman Conquest. They attained their greatest prosperity and highest importance in the Jewish world[1] in the latter part of the twelfth and beginning of the thirteenth centuries. After that date, the more general diffusion of money economy may have limited the field for their operations, while their practical monopoly was broken down by the Italian bankers. It is at all events instructive to note that whereas William the Conqueror found it necessary to introduce the Jews into England, circumstances had so far changed that Edward I was able to dispense with their services and to expel them from the country.

(ii) *Civic Life.*

94. When we turn from ecclesiastical and royal to civic economy, we find ourselves in a sphere where the use of money had probably been in vogue from time immemorial, since facilities for trade Civic Life. Rise of the Communes. were implied in the very idea of town life[2]; urban society and the institutions it evolved necessarily rested on this basis[3].

---

[1] Jacobs, *Jews in Angevin England*, Introd. p. v.
[2] See above, p. 57.
[3] The full social effects of money-economy cannot be seen, however, in

Commerce had been an essential condition without which the
towns of Western Christendom would not have come into
being, and the development of trading intercourse in the
eleventh and twelfth centuries afforded opportunities for the
growth of civic wealth and power.   We can trace how the tide
of commercial prosperity flowed farther and farther north, first
affecting the Italian Peninsula and the towns of Septimania
and Provence, then showing itself in the Rhine lands and
Flanders and the north of France, and penetrating at last
across the Channel to England[1].   As the towns profited by
increasing trade, they were able to secure a larger measure of
political freedom.   Sometimes, as in Languedoc, they fought
for it; in other instances, and particularly in England, they
purchased it; but by different stages and on different occasions, the towns of Christendom were able to secure municipal liberties.   Thus the growth of commercial prosperity
was the chief condition which rendered possible the great
movement known as the rise of the *communes.*

As we have seen above, many towns had had their beginnings under ecclesiastical tutelage and protection; but in
the twelfth century they had so far outgrown it as to aim at
enjoying powers of self-government.   They may have been
inspired to make this attempt by some tradition of popular
rights embodied in ancient customs[2].   They would find encouraging examples as they came to understand the practical
independence which was enjoyed by Venice and Amalfi in
their relations with the Emperor at Constantinople; the free
cities of the Holy Roman Empire eventually attained to similar
political independence[3].   The townsmen in France came to
adopt one regular method of procedure in their opposition
to the arbitrary exercise of seigniorial authority; they usually

those urban communities where elements of an old order survived and
police duty was done personally, and office undertaken gratuitously.

   [1] Giry, in *Histoire Générale,* edited by Lavisse and Rambaud, II. 420.
   [2] *Ibid. op. cit.* II. 423, 424.   [3] *Ibid. op. cit.* II. 439.

formed *communes* which were sworn associations for mutual support in their struggle for independence, and the wealthier merchants appear to have taken a prominent part in organising the movement. The formation of these *communes* could be represented as the action of "usurers[1]," and it led to the transference of power from the landed authority of Bishops and Counts to a moneyed aristocracy in each town. This revolution doubtless had its analogue in the history of ancient cities[2], and it is also an interesting anticipation of the contest between the landed and the moneyed interests over the power of directing the national policy of England in the eighteenth century.

There were two points in regard to which the townsmen were particularly inclined to resent the interference of the lord—on the one hand they desired to evade his rights in connection with tolls, since these might prove very oppressive[3], and on the other they preferred not to have their legal business decided by tribunals which ignored *law merchant.* There was ample justification for the desire of the townsmen to have privileges of self-government; while the great landed pro-prietors, under whose patronage and protection the town had grown up, would feel a not unnatural resentment at the de-mand of the townsmen to set aside immemorial obligations and to withdraw themselves from long-established jurisdiction. The clergy and the seigneurs were on the whole decidedly jealous of the rising power of the *communes.*

But it would be a mistake to suppose that the townsmen had to encounter uniform hostility. It was at least the occa-sional policy of the French kings to play off the rising towns against the great feudatories, and to show a friendly spirit

---

[1] See the Synod of Paris in 1213. Giry, *op. cit.* II. 428.

[2] Fustel de Coulanges, *La Cité Antique*, p. 381.

[3] On tolls in the Frankish Realm see E. Mayer, *Zoll, Kaufmannschaft und Markt* in *Abhandlungen zum LXX. Geburtstage K. v. Maurers*, p. 380 foll.

towards *communes* outside their own domains.   There were seigneurs too who realised that the commerce which centred in towns might be a source of wealth; they allowed the *villes-de-bourgeoisie*[1] to obtain limited privileges[2], which were granted by charter to townsmen, who yet had neither the common seal nor the belfry, which were the outward marks of the corporate life of a true *commune*.   After the crusades had opened the eyes of the western rulers to the value of commerce, there was an additional incentive to the founding of city colonies which has been noticed above[3].   New towns and large suburbs were laid out on a definite plan, both by French kings and by Edward I in his French dominions. Montpazier[4] and Carcassonne are among the most beautiful examples of the types that were preferred, when a town had to be laid out afresh[5], or when any considerable additions were required beyond its existing limits[6].

Among the cities of mediaeval Europe there were great varieties of political status and prestige; their constitutions were very different, though most of the continental towns were ruled by an oligarchy, and the commons had but little voice in the management of affairs.   The history of each town was distinct; but in their economic conditions and in their economic institutions they were much alike.   Together they formed a system of similarly organised but distinct communities, which served as depots for commerce, and provided facilities for inter-municipal trade.

[1] Giry, *op. cit.* II. 470.

[2] These have no analogue in England, but seem to correspond to the Scotch Burghs of Barony as distinguished from Royal Burghs.

[3] See above, p. 62.

[4] Turner and Parker, *Domestic Architecture in England*, II. 154.

[5] Compare the migration from Old Sarum and the founding of Salisbury; see also below, Appendix.

[6] Such as Bury, Norwich, and Peterborough.   Compare my paper on *The Corrupt Following of Hippodamus of Miletus at Cambridge, Camb. Ant. Soc. Communications,* 1899, IX. 421.

Each of these towns was an independent centre of civic life, and responsible for its own internal affairs; and each was forced to raise considerable sums of money for the expenses of its government and police, and the payment of the composition by which its privileges were secured. This revenue was raised by taxation, which seems sometimes to have been assessed on the various mercantile and industrial companies according to their standing, and sometimes to have been levied on the inhabitants by a house rate. The burgesses who paid their contributions and who had the freedom of a town were always careful to guard themselves against any intrusion on their privileges by outsiders; as citizens the former had a recognised status wherever they travelled, and hence there came to be a marked distinction between them and those who were mere upland men and had no footing in the commercial society of Christendom.

The importance of city life, as a factor in civilised society, has been discussed in connection with the ancient world. In mediaeval times cities such as Venice and Genoa rivalled or excelled the commercial centres of classical times; they attained to immense wealth, and their industrial development gave them a measure of stability which Athens never enjoyed. Their commercial colonies, unlike those of the Greeks, continued to be a strength to the mother cities; but for our purpose it is unnecessary to dwell on the greatness of their military and naval power, since it was destined to pass away as national government became more effective. Civic organisation for commercial and industrial purposes has a more lasting interest; for towns remain as great economic centres, though their political importance as independent communities and the power which many possessed of pursuing separate economic aims have vanished. The very full information which survives in regard to the mercantile and industrial associations of mediaeval cities, renders it clear that their gilds and companies were more highly organised and enjoyed a better political status than corresponding societies in the ancient world.

95. The merchants engaged in active trade appear to
have been the leaders in forming the *communes*,
and they obtained a dominating influence in
the government of each town[1]. They were the
moneyed men and they naturally came to the front in an urban
community, though the particular commercial calling that had a
leading position in one city might not be specially prominent in
another. The bankers, who acted as agents for the collection
of papal revenue, were important people at many centres; at
Florence the merchants, who imported cloth[2], had a leading
position; in London, the grocers, who dealt in bulky goods
which were weighed by the large beam, seemed to monopolise
all city dignities for a time, though the mercers, who dealt in
silk and other valuable goods weighed in a small balance,
had the older organisation there. These groups of merchants,
associated in companies for the wise regulation of their own
trades, had a practical control of the government of their city.

Merchants
and Fairs.

The whole mechanism of the commerce of the day
becomes more intelligible when we study the regulations
of the fairs, which were the principal trading resorts of
Christendom. The most celebrated marts of the early
middle ages were held in Champagne and Brie[3]; but
there were similar gatherings in every land. The streams
of commerce were too feeble to provide a constant market
all the year round, at any one centre, for valuable goods
brought from a distance; trade was only occasional; and each

[1] In England, where there were few resident merchants engaged in
active trade, the wealthy oligarchies did not show themselves until the
fourteenth and fifteenth centuries.

[2] The *Arte di Calimala* was engaged in the dressing and dyeing of
imported cloth; the *Arte di Lana*, a manufacture of cloth in Florence, was
a distinct trade which arose in the thirteenth century. Doren, *Entwickelung
und Organisation der Florentiner Zünfte* (in *Staats- und socialwissenschaftliche Forschungen* edited by Schmoller, xv. p. 7).

[3] Bourquelot, *Études sur les foires de Champagne* in *Mém. Acad. Inscrip.*
2me Serie, v. p. 75.

fair in its turn gave the transitory merchant an opportunity of attending and disposing of his goods. The rules for the construction of the booths and the conduct of business were very elaborate, and when disputes arose, the courts of pie-powder exercised summary jurisdiction according to Law Merchant. But there were differences that could not be so easily settled, and that gave rise to long correspondence between the authorities of different cities. A creditor would attempt to obtain payment by getting the mayor of his city to correspond with the mayor of the place where his debtor resided. We come to see that it was not as an Englishman or a Frenchman that a merchant claimed commercial status, but as a citizen of some one city ; his position in his own community gave him his status in any place where merchants congregated, and assured him that any wrongs he suffered in his transactions would be dealt with, not by a local custom of which he was ignorant, but according to the Law Merchant which prevailed in similar form throughout Christendom.

96. In addition to these associations of moneyed men engaged in active trade, there was also a great deal of industrial organisation in mediaeval towns. Manufacturing of various kinds was *Industrial Organisation. Craft Gilds.* doubtless stimulated by commerce ; it had to be carried on with a view to other than the local markets, or had at least to meet an increased demand as the town grew in size and population. It is difficult to believe that there could be much local organisation in any industry until there was need for the work of ten or twelve men engaged in the same craft ; and it is consequently surprising that societies of craftsmen should be found so widely diffused in the twelfth century. There were weavers' gilds in Marlborough, Beverley and Oxford, as well as in London in the time of Henry I, and there was a similar institution[1] among the cordwainers of

[1] Martin-Saint-Léon, *Histoire des Corporations de Métiers*, p. 57. Inama Sternegg II. 323—325.

Rouen, the tanners of Ghent and the drapers of Valenciennes. Though these are the earliest recorded instances, it is highly probable that some similar bodies were of very long standing in certain continental cities; we have an account of the crafts of Paris in the thirteenth century, and when we see how largely manufacturing was developed in that city and at that date, and also how completely it was organised, we can hardly suppose that the industrial associations were all of very recent growth[1]. Étienne Boileau[2] set himself to give a complete account of the *corps de métier* as existing in his time, and in his book we get a very clear picture of the habits and usages of the aristocracy of labour[3]. There were no fewer than a hundred such craft-gilds in Paris, and though they differed in many matters of detail, their general character was similar.

The boy who desired to enter any of these crafts was apprenticed to a master, who was responsible for supplying the youth with food and shelter, and who was not only expected to train his charge in the knowledge of his business but also to exercise such supervision over his apprentices that they might form the habits of good citizens. After serving his time as an apprentice, the workman became a valet or journeyman, who was hired by the master for longer or shorter

[1] The early rise of craft organisations in the mediaeval world, as contrasted with their late development in Greek cities, is very remarkable. In so far as the gilds were utilised for grouping the inhabitants and assessing taxation, it is possible to find a clear motive for the formation of such bodies. But, when once formed, they supplied a recognised want in civic life and they continued to exist in many places till the industrial revolution changed all the conditions of work. The gild merchant was a passing phase, the craft gild came to stay.

[2] *Le Livre des Métiers.* Edited by Lespinasse and Bonnardot. The royal attention to the organisation of industry in France dates back to the thirteenth century; in England the organisation and control of craft gilds was attended to by the municipal authorities, who were inclined to resent outside interference in this matter.

[3] The unskilled labourer seems to have been very little considered in the labour organisation of the day.

periods to work for wages. If the journeyman saved or borrowed enough money to start on his own account he would try to qualify as master in the trade ; and for that purpose he was, at least in later days, required to produce an *essay* or masterpiece as proof of his qualifications. We are able to gather that industry was generally conducted by small capitalists ; they were not mere employers, but worked themselves at the trade in which they instructed the apprentices ; they might however hire additional hands, and thus be employers on a small scale as well as workmen. The masters associated in the *corps de métier*, or craft-gild, made regulations for the good conduct of the trade,—not merely for the technical training of workmen, but for the quality of the material and the conditions of work. Within each city, the *corps de métier* was empowered to enforce its rules on those who were working at the craft ; no unauthorised men who did not conform to its usages were allowed to work at the calling ; and great pains were taken to prevent outsiders from acquiring any knowledge of technical processes, or other trade-secrets. In order to make and enforce these rules, a good deal of government was required, and it was necessary to provide for the administration of common funds, which were obtained partly by the entry money of apprentices and the gifts of members, and partly by fines imposed for infractions of the rules. The funds were occasionally used for charitable purposes among the members, such as gratuitous loans to a needy brother ; and they were sometimes increased by trading speculation. In some towns, the members of a gild had the option of sharing in an advantageous purchase made by one of their number ; and they were drawn more closely together by the enjoyment of common festivities and participation in the same religious rites.

Such was the general type of the craft-gild[1], but there were

[1] The care of the mediaeval craft-gilds for the welfare of the skilled labourer distinguishes them from their analogues—the *collegia* of ancient Rome. Levasseur, *Classes ouvrières*, I. 195.

minor differences in different countries[1]. On the Continent, generally, the artisan classes were separated by a hard and fast line from the moneyed men, as far back as we can trace the history of town life; in London, the differentiation of the industrial and the moneyed classes can hardly be observed before the fourteenth century. In Germany, the valet or *Geselle* was encouraged to travel and acquire a more complete knowledge of his trade; in England, there seems to have been no such provision for industrial intercourse between different towns. The distinctions are so marked that it is important to study the craft-system of each city and to be careful about the danger of pressing analogies too closely.

The mutual supervision by respectable tradesmen which was a prominent feature in the gild system operated in the interests of the public and of the workmen alike; it remained in force till the organisation of business by large capitalists superseded the older system by securing thorough-going supervision under a more flexible system. This latter method could be successfully carried on with workmen scattered in rural districts; whereas gild supervision almost necessarily involved the residence of the workers within easy reach of one another. The highly skilled industry of mediaeval times was concentrated in cities, where it was regulated by gild officials in the exercise of powers conferred on them by civic authority[2]; but as

[1] On the position of women in English and French craft-gilds respectively, see E. Dixon, *Economic Journal*, v. 225.

[2] One important craft, that of the masons, necessarily had an extra-municipal character. A great deal of castle and church building was carried on on sites which lay beyond the range of any municipal powers; and we may think of this craft in the thirteenth century as forming a part of great royal or ecclesiastical establishments. We read of royal masons, and of a school of masons at Saintonge. Isenbert, their master, was recommended by King John to the city of London as a suitable person to undertake the rebuilding of the bridge. (3 John, *Rot. Lit. Pat.* memb. 2, no. 7.) We get much light from Cathedral fabric rolls on the organisation of the building trades in the fourteenth and fifteenth centuries, when it still retained something of its exceptional character; like other crafts, it was

it prospered and established distant connections there was need for the intervention of capitalists. Many trades were dependent on commercial facilities which could only be obtained at such resorts of wealthy merchants as Venice and Genoa, Florence, Augsburg or Bruges. The materials for the manufacture of silk and the finishing of cloth were imported; and much of the wealth of these cities was due to their success in catering for distant markets, but their progress was incompatible with the maintenance of a purely civic policy. The necessity of procuring materials or of controlling a food supply forced some of the cities to take account of considerable stretches of territory. The city was the all-important unit for economic purposes in the later Middle Ages as the households had been in the Carlovingian times; but economic necessities, no less than political ambitions, rendered a change inevitable, and brought about a reconstruction of the economic system, not on the narrow lines of a city community, but in accordance with the resources and requirements of extended territories[1].

(iii)   *Household Economy.*

97. Long after money economy had been taken for granted in the industrial organisation of the urban population, it was hardly known in rural districts, where natural economy still played an important part. There is, in English sources, much literary evidence as to the administration of a well-managed estate in the thirteenth century. Economically considered, the best type known at that time was practically identical with the ideal of proprietors a thousand years earlier.

[marginal notes:] Household Economy. Household Management. Commutation.

conducted on a money basis, but as it had not grown up under municipal authority, it does not seem to have conferred on its members municipal status till a comparatively late date.

[1] See below, p. 148.

Land was owned in large areas, and cultivated by dependents who rendered service or payments in kind. Such an institution was fundamentally the same as the Roman *villa*, though there might be the greatest possible variety in the status and obligation of the dependents; and it bore the closest resemblance to the agricultural organisation in Carlovingian times[1]. We have ample evidence as to its working from the countless surveys of estates[2], which are in existence and record the precise local condition of particular places in detail; but the fullest description of the principles to be followed is to be found in treatises[3] on estate management which obtained a wide circulation in England during the thirteenth and following centuries. The best known of these is the *Husbandry* of Walter of Henley, which deals with practical problems of agriculture; the *Seneschaucie* gives an account of the various officials in a great household, and their respective duties; the *Rules* of Robert Grosseteste are also instructive as showing the general scheme of household economy in a well-managed establishment. When we remember that great households—whether monastic or noble—were not only the chief centres for regulating agricultural work, but served the purpose of places of education, either in learning or in manly exercises, we see the importance of the part they played, and the interest of examining their economic side.

In many parts of the Continent, and at the great English abbeys, there were large permanent establishments which could be supplied with food from adjoining territory; but the policy of the Conqueror had been to give scattered and separate grants to his followers, and the lands held by any one of the nobility were not contiguous, so that they found it con-

[1] Besides the Capitulary *De Villis*, we have the detailed *Polyptyque* of Abbot Irminon, edited by Guérard, and containing careful surveys of the Abbey Estates.

[2] Cunningham, *Growth of English Industry*, I. 576.

[3] *Walter of Henley*, edited by E. Lamond.

venient to pass from one estate to another in turn. The long
cavalcade of the travelling household must have been a familiar
sight in mediaeval England, and its approach would often
cause consternation to the Abbot or Prior to whom it appealed for hospitality during its progress. The period which
the noble owner could spend on each of his estates was
calculated with care; the bailiff was responsible for the corn
which was gathered at Michaelmas, and for keeping accurate
accounts of the stock, as well as of the service of the villeins,
or payments made in lieu of services, and of other receipts.
Each estate was meant to be self-sufficing, and to furnish
food for the owner's household; but there might be a surplus
of produce which it was wise to sell, or there might be occasion
to replenish the stores by purchase. With all his careful
efforts, it was not possible for even the most prudent landowner to keep entirely outside the circle of commerce and
monetary transaction; and the more he was drawn into it
by the demands for payments to royal or ecclesiastical officers
or by other forces, the more ready he would be to reorganise
the internal management of his estate on a monetary basis.

The mass of manorial documents which survive will doubtless afford some future student of economic history the means
of tracing the progress of this change in great detail, as it
occurred on one estate or another. At present, we can only
trace the main types of economic relationship. We hear of
free tenants, who may be regarded as appendages to a
manorial estate rather than a constituent part of it. The
payments they made to the lord seemed to consist chiefly of
their contributions to the royal taxation, for the collection
of which he was responsible. Within the *manerium* or *villa*,
as an economic unit, the serfs were responsible for tilling the
domain of the lord, and received their recompense in the
form of land, which they cultivated on their own account, in
their own time. The *extent* of the manor carefully noted for
each season the precise number of days' work to which the lord

was entitled, as well as the payments in kind which he had
an admitted right to exact; the records of the annual reckonings,—or *ministers' accounts*,—show what services were rendered and payments received. In the thirteenth century
this seems to have been the prevailing system; but there
is ample evidence that it often proved convenient for the
lord to accept money payment in lieu of service; grudged
labour was not always worth having, and he might find it
more prudent to supply seed himself than to rely on the
quality which his serfs provided for him. Each part of the
serf's obligations was assessed in terms of money; and we find
entries, even in the earliest rolls, of *opera vendita* when the lord
exercised his right of choosing to receive money-compositions
instead of exacting certain days or forms of work. In some
instances, this came to be a matter of formal and permanent
agreement; but in such cases the payment made by the serf
had no direct economic relation to the precise value of the
holding he continued to enjoy, but was based on the value
of his services, from which he was now *quit*. In the rapid
changes which followed the Black Death, the substitution of
payment in money for the practice of rendering service went
on apace[1]; but there was a more startling revolution im-
pending. On the one hand, the hired labourers, on whom
the landlords had come to depend for the tillage of their
domains, demanded that their wages should be settled by
competition, instead of being paid at the old customary rates
of assessment; on the other, the landowners sought to recoup
themselves for the loss of their power to exact labour by
adopting the principle of competition in the management of
their estates and letting the land to those who offered them
most money for the use of it[2]. It was not till the seven-

[1] Trevelyan, *Age of Wycliffe*, 191. T. W. Page, *Die Umwandlung der Frohndienste in Geldrente*, 37, 38.

[2] In the fifteenth and sixteenth centuries the largest bids were made by sheep farmers.

teenth century that the new method of estate administration, on a monetary basis, came to be accepted as creditable, and that the principle of competition was unhesitatingly applied to the letting of land for arable purposes. The change, so slow and so painful, and accompanied as it was by so much social disorganisation and misery in the rural districts, was inevitable when agricultural life was drawn into the range of monetary influence[1]. Permanent personal obligations were at first only expressed in terms of money, and from mutual convenience they came to be more and more frequently discharged in terms of money. These customary payments, whether of rent or for work done in the rural districts, did not rest on any clear economic basis, like that of the reasonable prices which were calculated by the authorities of craft-gilds; the sums demanded were only the expressions of servile obligations, not the result of free bargaining over the terms of voluntary exchange. The stability of customary rates had many advantages; but occasional and obvious variations in the value of service or the value of land gave rise to a sense of grievance under this system; and when once its advantage was questioned, there was no possibility that customary rates should be maintained. Competition was attractive, for it had the appearance of fairness at each particular moment; while rates fixed by custom only secured a fair average on the whole. The misery which would accrue from the loss of stability was not obvious; and despite the disadvantages in connection with competition we cannot regret this step in progress: it has given freedom to enterprising men to make the most of landed resources, as they could never have done while they relied on the household organisation of labour and were hampered by the restrictions of natural economy.

98. This cursory survey of the economic life of Christendom in the thirteenth century brings out some important contrasts

[1] More, *Utopia* (ed. Lumby), p. 32. *Discourse of Commonweal*, edited by E. Lamond, Introd. p. xlv.

with the ancient world, not only in aspirations but in actual

Mediaeval institutions. Social progress had on the whole
and Ancient followed the lines laid down in the *Capitularies.*
Institutions. It almost seems that the dream of a well-
organised empire of the West which Charles had had before
him was at length realised, though in other conditions, and
under the control of a spiritual head, not of a Frankish king.
The civilisation of Charles's realm had fired the imagination
of the northern peoples, and called forth their imitative efforts.
They inherited much from the old Rome, but they inherited
it in the form in which it had been recast by Charles the
Great, both as regards political and civic organisation and
in respect to commercial and industrial life, whether in town
or country.

This mediaeval society was in consequence permeated with
moral conceptions which had been entirely strange to the ancient
world ; the institutions of the Middle Ages had been gradually
formed under the influence of religious principles which the old
world would have explicitly denied. There was, first of all,
a keen sense of personal responsibility in the employment of
secular power of every kind ; the responsibility of rulers to
God for the exercise of their power over their subjects was
strongly insisted upon, as well as the fact that the rich man
must render account of the use he made of his wealth ; it
had been entrusted to him by God, and he ought to use it
for God. That the forms of using wealth, which piety and
beneficence dictated, were not always wise, is true enough.
The problem of applying wealth to the best purpose for the
good of man is not an easy one, even in the present day ;
but there was an extraordinary contrast between the spirit
of the Roman like Cato, whose only sense of duty was to
become richer, and that of the mediaeval proprietor who had
learned that he was merely a trustee, and responsible for the
manner in which he used his money. This lesson, so deeply
ingrained in mediaeval Christendom, was an immense gain, as

we see when we compare the tone of opinion in the ancient world ; it is a doctrine that can never be discarded without serious danger so long as society continues on the lines of personal possession. The truth that property has duties and responsibilities must be realised with greater and greater clearness.

The difference between the mediaeval and the ancient world comes out still more clearly in the new conception of labour. In the ancient world labour was drudgery ; and all possibilities of human advance were connected with the possession of leisure. This was fundamental in Greek life, and it was adopted in the old Rome ; but Christianity insisted that labour itself might be a discipline and might thus conduce to the ennobling of human character. When the beneficent influence of labour on character was once recognised, and a life of labour was voluntarily adopted by those who were in positions to escape it, it could no longer be regarded as in itself degrading. Serfdom existed so long as natural economy lasted, and the mediaeval conscience was only partially awakened to the evils of slavery[1] ; but the dignity of labour began to receive adequate recognition. Here again we see a permanent gain for which society is indebted to the Middle Ages ; that work is a duty to be done, and that a life spent in idleness and self-pleasing is wasted, is another belief which has entered deeply into the very structure of modern society in Western Europe and which had no corresponding influence in the ancient world.

The main contribution of mediaeval society to the economic progress of mankind lay in its success in moralising industrial and commercial conceptions and institutions. Just as the Greek made an advance on the Phoenician by treating material plenty as subservient to human well-being and regarding it as means to an end, so Christianity reconstituted the economic life of the old world in accordance with a fuller appreciation of personal responsibility in the use

[1] See below, p. 133.

of property, and a recognition of labour as a method of personal self-discipline. This moralisation was a very important change ; as we look back we are apt to say that there were the strangest contrasts in the Middle Ages between high ideals and gross outrages, and that though there was so much parade of religion and so much machinery for the maintenance of a better morality, they were merely superficial. It is easy to assert that underneath the high claims of the papacy to represent God's Will there was only priestly ambition, and that the great religious foundations of the Middle Ages were partly due to vanity and partly to base attempts to cajole an offended Deity with gifts. But it is an error to suppose that because the religion of the age came prominently before the eye, it was therefore merely external, with no real vitality ; or to imagine that because the moral conscience of the day exhausted itself over casuistical distinctions between honest and oppressive bargains, it had no real hold upon the minds of men. The piety and morality of the age were very apparent, but they were not empty and lifeless ; just because they had expressed themselves in external forms and institutions, they had a chance of influencing individual character and working deeply into the moral consciousness ; at all events they were powerful enough to stay the disasters under which the Roman Empire fell to pieces and to pass on a great and improved tradition of active economic life.

CHAPTER III.

CHRISTIAN RELATIONS WITH HEATHEN AND MOSLEMS.

99. In describing the civic life of Christendom, and the progress of commerce, it has been impossible to avoid all reference to the non-Christian world; in- **The Crusad-** tercourse with distant lands was one of the factors **ing Spirit.** which helped to develop trade and town life during the twelfth and thirteenth centuries, and there have been occasional allusions to it in the foregoing pages; but these scattered hints must now be gathered together, and we must try to take account of the trading activities of men who lived in regions where the papal power was not recognised as authoritative[1]. We may thus come to understand more clearly the causes which were at work in the movements that have been already discussed. Such a survey is also necessary if we would trace the tendencies which were leading up to the age of discovery and preparing for the commercial revolution of the sixteenth century.

[1] The trading relations with Constantinople are not treated separately; much of their importance was due to the fact that that city was a depôt for the commerce with more distant regions. In the period before the Crusades the intercourse between Rome and Constantinople was frequent (Heyd, *op. cit.* I. 94), while a great deal of commerce went on with Bari, Amalfi, and other towns of Southern Italy which still preserved a political connection with the Eastern Empire. Heinemann, *Geschichte der Normannen in Unter-Italien*, p. 22.

Unity of religious belief and similar ecclesiastical institutions were the ties which bound Christendom into one organic whole; the outside world consisted of the lands where these conditions did not obtain. There were heathen peoples who had never come under the influence of Christianity at all, and they had no scruple in plundering Christian shrines and in destroying consecrated buildings. There were also Mohammedans whose profession prepared them at any time to engage in active attacks on the Cross; at best they treated the Christian population with contemptuous tolerance. The relations of the people of Western Europe with outsiders were necessarily affected by these religious differences, and were more often hostile than friendly; indeed they were coloured by what we may call the crusading spirit. Devotion and commerce were closely interrelated in the Christian attempts to recover possession of the Holy Land[1]. Mercantile enterprise combined with religious zeal in subtle proportions from the outset of the struggle, but the only lasting gain went to the trading interest, as merchants obtained a permanent footing in lands where the dominion of Christian rulers had been destroyed. The initiative in the earliest interference with the Heathen and Moslem worlds had been chiefly taken in the cause of religion, though organised commerce soon seized upon the lines which were thus opened up. It is most convenient to describe in turn the relations of the men of Latin Christendom with the non-Christian peoples on the Northern Seas, in the Western Mediterranean, and in the Levant and to take the beginning of the ninth century as our starting point in each case.

100. There is no more pathetic incident in the history of Charles the Great than the account of his sorrow at seeing the sails of the Norsemen in the Mediterranean[2] and his premonition of the mischief

The Vikings and the Baltic commerce.

[1] Heyd, *Commerce du Levant*, I. 131.

[2] *Monach. Sangallensis* II. 14 in Pertz, *Mon. Germ. Script.* II. 757.

which they would work in his dominions. Their rude and vigorous energy proved the scourge of many parts of Christendom for generations; but when it was gradually absorbed and controlled, it furnished one of the most potent factors in the subsequent triumph and diffusion of the civilisation which Charles appreciated so highly. In the history of the lands over which Charles ruled, it has not been easy to distinguish the various racial elements, or to say how much of his system was due to Roman survivals, and how much to the Teutonic grafts which had been introduced in larger or smaller proportions by successive conquests. But at all events none of these peoples had betaken themselves to maritime enterprise; the piratical expeditions of the Norsemen were a new element, with which the nascent civilisation had to engage in a life and death struggle. It was the crucial test whether the new empire would succeed where the old empire had failed, and would be able to convert this strenuous barbarian life to be its defence and the means of extending its boundaries.

The sagas, and the relics which have been discovered in the north, reveal the existence of a vigorous commercial life in the Baltic lands during the ninth, tenth, and eleventh centuries. It offers points of comparison which take us back to the Homeric poems and the early days of Phoenician trading in the Mediterranean. The picture of the Viking—half merchant and half pirate—reminds us of old acquaintances in the *Odyssey* and in Herodotus[1]. The seafaring man made a raid on the banks of the Seine or the Trent, and then, as a merchant, disposed of his booty and captives at one of the great seaside fairs. The description which Adam of Bremen gives of Birca[2] supplies an instance of the commercial activity which was found at different points all through the Baltic lands, but which centred chiefly in the island of Gothland.

So far as we can gather, however, this commercial activity

[1] Vol. I. p. 66.
[2] Adam of Bremen, *Gesta Hammaburgensis Ecclesiae Pontificum*, I. 62.

was different from that of the Phoenicians and their Greek imitators in two important particulars. It was much less completely organised; the Phoenicians had settled factories at special points; and these were permanent off-shoots of the mother-city in distant lands, and had recognised rights and ob- ligations. But the Norse commerce does not appear to have arisen between towns and colonies; the Viking was rather the adventurer who went out to improve his fortunes as best he might, and who, if he found a favourable opportunity, established himself on an estate. The Norsemen may have had more aptitude for town life than some of the other Teutons[1]; but they were ready to become cultivators and colonists, and did not confine their energies to industry and trade.

From their sagas, too, we get an impression of the extraordinary individual enterprise in their voyages[2]. The most profitable commerce of the Norsemen was apparently conducted by the Elbe and the Oder and their tributaries, till they came within reach of areas from which they could find their way to the Black Sea and Constantinople. It was probably along the primeval amber routes that the vast quantities of Arabian coins were carried which have been found in Sweden[3]; but the Vikings ventured far beyond these limits and forced their way round the North Cape to Archangel; they even sailed to Iceland and colonised it after their fashion[4]. The story of the voyage of Eric the Red to Greenland gives a singular picture of their audacity; and though doubts have been cast on the alleged discovery of

[1] A Danish settlement was the nucleus of Cork, Waterford, and Dublin, and an important element in Derby, Leicester, London, and many English towns.

[2] Toulmin Smith, *Discovery of America by the Northmen*, 321.

[3] Montelius, *Civilisation of Sweden*, 191; Heyd, *op. cit.* I. 58.

[4] The contrast between the legal and social conditions in Iceland (Dasent, *Burnt Njal*, I. xi., xlv.) and at Carthage (Vol. I. 145) accentuates the differences between Norse and Phoenician colonisation.

America by the Norsemen, there is no inherent improbability in the accuracy of the legend[1]. The whole description of their ruthless activity and grim humour in the sagas is of the keenest interest, as it describes the new strain which was introduced into Christendom, and which has perpetuated itself in the maritime enterprise and individual energy which characterise the modern world.

101. Such were the men who were harrying Western Christendom from the north in the ninth, tenth, and eleventh centuries; but as they were gra- *The Hanse League.* dually converted to the profession of Christianity, the danger which threatened the rising civilisation was averted. We need not pause to consider how far this process implied a complete alteration of personal religious belief; however unintelligently and unwillingly they may have accepted the new faith, it brought them into line with the other peoples of the West. They ceased to plunder sacred places; and, as a consequence, the most important centres of agriculture, industry, and commerce were respected, and opportunities for the uninterrupted pursuit of peaceful avocations were greatly increased.

There were various agencies through which this change was brought about: it was accomplished partly by the individual heroism of missionaries like S. Boniface, and partly by the militant Christianity of the soldiers of Charles the Great or the Teutonic knights; and despite its defects and weaknesses, the civilisation of Christendom could not but command the respect of the peoples of the North. The tradition of the Imperial name was impressive; the arts and culture of the great monasteries would move the barbarians' admiration. When any considerable bodies of the Norsemen came to settle on the territories they had ravaged, they were soon brought under the influence of the Christian religion, and adapted them-

---

[1] The evidence has been discussed with great care by Dr O'Gorman in an article on the *American Mediaeval Church* in the *Catholic University Bulletin* (Washington D.C.), I. 416.

selves to the habits and usages current in Christendom.   The
transformation in the case of the Dukes of Normandy was
singularly rapid ; and the rule of Cnut must have done much
to leaven lands which were still half heathen, with influences
derived from his Christian dominions.

The progress of Christianity, by limiting the field for
Viking enterprise, appears to have exerted a repressive influence
on the vigorous life of the north.   Much of the Scandinavian
commerce passed into other hands, especially into those of
the Germans.   There was a remarkable power of combination
among the German townsmen in the thirteenth century ; the
cities on the Rhine[1] formed a political confederation for the
security of merchants engaged in trading along the river ; and
the towns of northern Germany worked in unison for the
object of promoting active commerce.   There had been plenty
of personal enterprise in the Baltic trade from time immemorial,
but the new movement, which emanated from Lübeck[2], led to
the founding of regular factories ; an element of organisation
was introduced, and Wisby became the centre of trade which
had been previously carried on at other points.   The German
influence had made itself paramount by means of colonies
established in Denmark and Prussia, and the associated towns[3]
were able in 1284 to force the Norwegians to accord to the
men of the Emperor commercial privileges of which they
availed themselves greedily.   These mercantile colonies of
the Germans really had a civilising influence ; among other
things, they helped to extinguish the traffic in slaves which
had been a regular and flourishing business in heathen times.
Towns which had grown out of factories established in connection with trade served as centres where new churches were
planted, so that there was a genuine expansion of Christendom

---

[1] Frignet, *Histoire de l'Association Commerciale*, 131.

[2] Lamprecht, *Deutsche Geschichte*, IV. 146.

[3] Lübeck, Riga, Wismar, Stralsund, Greifswald, Rostock and Wisby.
Beer, *Allgemeine Geschichte des Welthandels*, I. 249.

towards the North and East[1]. The work was carried still
farther by the Teutonic Order, in accordance with the militant
Christianity of the day, so that the whole of the southern
shores of the Baltic, as well as Scandinavia, were brought
within the circle of Western Christendom.

Under the influence of these German towns the occasional
commerce of the Norsemen was systematised and developed;
Lübeck, the leader, controlled the policy and directed the
energies of the associated cities which eventually came to be
known as the Hanse League. This body succeeded in putting
down the bands of pirates, who maintained something of
the old Viking tradition; they rendered the Baltic an inland
sea from which intruders were warned off; and they secured
a practical monopoly in the export of amber, of furs and tallow
from Russia, and of fish, iron and copper from Sweden[2], and
they imported cloth and other manufactures in return.   They
had important factories at Bergen, the staple town of the Iceland
trade, while they had access to Eastern routes through their
establishment at Novgorod[3]. They thus commanded lines of
trade which lay beyond the purview of Charles the Great, and
they had also important connections with the Danube valley,
with Italy[4], and with Bruges and London.   During their most
flourishing period they present a picture of intermunicipal
commerce at its very best; they formed a great mercantile
federation, the members of which were independent internally,
while they pursued a common policy in distant lands[5].   Their

---

[1] Lamprecht, *Deutsche Geschichte*, III. 395.

[2] Worms, *La ligue hanséatique*, 84, 90.

[3] Buck, W., *Der deutsche Handel in Novgorod bis zur Mitte des xiv. Jahrhunderts*, 37.

[4] W. Stieda, *Hansisch-Venetianische Handels-beziehungen im* 15 *Jahrhunderte*.

[5] There was considerable friction between the different groups of towns
in the League, but the union was none the less remarkable.   The Confederation of Rhodes is an interesting analogy in ancient times.   The

subsequent fall is often ascribed to the discoveries of the
fifteenth century, and to their inability to adapt their restrictive methods to the new fields of commercial activity that were
then opened up; but it seems to have begun before that era,
through a general antagonism to the League as a monopoly,
and in consequence of the rise of new nationalities which
resented the presence of alien merchants enriching themselves
out of native products. In the fourteenth century the English
forced their way into the Baltic[1] and deprived the League of its
exclusive trade in cloth. This attack from the West was almost
simultaneous with strenuous measures which were temporarily
taken against the merchants of the Hanse League in Russia[2];
and eventually they fell before the rising spirit of English and
Russian nationality; but yet it must not be forgotten that,
divided as Germany has been since the sixteenth century, the
Hanse towns by their combination and by the manner in which
they organised the commerce of the north, initiated a national
commercial policy[3] at a time when trading was ordinarily
regulated in the exclusive interest of particular cities.

102. Charles the Great had been called upon to take an
active part in rolling back the other great wave
which threatened western civilisation. The in-
coming tide of Arabian victory had already
been checked by Charles Martel; but Charles the Great
assisted in the first stages of the conflict which was to last
for so many centuries. During his reign the Crescent was
driven from the Pyrenees, and Christian kingdoms were
established on the north-east side of Spain. Septimania and
Provence, thus set free from the fear of subjugation, formed a
suitable area for the revival of Mediterranean commerce and
a basis for farther encroachments on the territory of the infidel.

The Cali-
phate.

Italian cities were much less able to lay aside their mutual jealousies and
combine together for common purposes.

[1] Daenel, *Geschichte der deutschen Hanse*, 44.
[2] *Ibid.* 47.   [3] *Ibid.* 191.

There are, however, many striking contrasts between the struggle in the north against the Norsemen and that in the south against the Arabs. The English, and the dwellers in Germany, the Low Countries, and France, were forced in self-defence to attempt to subdue the Danish plunderers; the warfare in the south was an act of Christian aggression. In the north militant Christianity had to deal with expeditions hastily set on foot by particular leaders; in the south it had to face well-equipped armies backed by the resources of a well-organised state. The results, too, were very different. In the north, the people of the Baltic lands were converted; there was a real expansion of Christendom, such as there had also been along the Danube valley through the conversion of the Hungarians. On the south, however, though new territory was added to Christendom, the people were not christianised; they withdrew before the advances of Spanish chivalry, and many of those who attempted to remain on the Peninsula were eventually expelled by Philip IV. The Moslems were not willing, like the Norsemen, to adopt the Christian faith, and to range themselves among the Christian nations. Bitter hostility between the two continued by sea and land, though their supremacy on the Mediterranean was gradually wrested from the Arabs and they were at length forced back to the African shore.

The success of the Christian arms in this struggle with an organised society is all the more remarkable, if we remember that the civilisation of the peoples under Arabian rule was, when tried by almost any test, and certainly by any economic test, incomparably higher than that of Christendom. The court of the Caliphs was the resort of men who were eminent in mathematical and astronomical science, and who had made considerable progress in chemistry and in medicine. They were acute and enthusiastic students of philosophy and cultivated an elegant taste in literature. They had carried the arts to a very high degree of perfection, both as regards metal-working and the textile trades; they were adepts in irrigation, and made the most of all opportunities for horticulture and agriculture. There was no art in which they could not have given much instruction to their Christian antagonists. Even though so much hostility severed the two polities, there was sufficient intercourse between the Arabs and their northern neighbours to exert a very great influence on the thought and art of Languedoc and Provence. The admiration which Arabian society excited and the infiltration of their ideas, came in the thirteenth century to be a serious danger to the Christian faith in academic centres like the University of Paris, and the Emperor Frederick II was practically a convert to their tenets[1].

It is no exaggeration to say that the Arabian conquerors had accomplished much that Alexander the Great seems to have aimed at. In their hands there was a curious fusion of the East and the West; the long heritage of both was combined in the learning and material prosperity of the Caliphate. Acceptance of the teaching of the prophet—a pure Theism— was an easy condition for religious consciences that were half-prepared for it by the prevalence of Arianism; and all forms of secular activity and learning ultimately found a home under this common conviction. The Arabian civilisation thus pre-sented a curious amalgam of elements that had little in common; Hellenism, as it had survived in the East, furnished its quota, and the remnants of ancient philosophy and Greek science, in so far as they were kept alive in Armenia and were not destroyed at Alexandria, continued to influence men's minds; while the luxury of oriental courts was reproduced in the palaces of the West, and the industry and commerce which ministered to it were prosecuted with success. The Caliphs had the wisdom to give full scope to the talents of the conquered, when once they accepted Islamism; and thus,

---

[1] Frederick II was much influenced by Arabian models in the adminis-tration of Sicily. Nys, *Researches in the History of Economics*, 36 foll.; Huillard-Bréholles, *Historia Diplomatici Frederici II*, Preface, ccccxxii.

while the Arabs originated so little themselves, they raised a great civilisation that was brilliant for a time, though it was barren in its after-results.

There was, however, a curious want of vitality in the Arab civilisation, when the period of conquest had come to an end; and though it is easy to represent the Latin Church as merely obscurantist in her constant hostility to such a highly cultivated society, we cannot but recognise that subsequent events have done much to justify this attitude. As we look back, we can see that the Arabian society was lacking in the physical and spiritual qualities which would have fitted it to take a great part in contributing to the progress of the race; it did collect and disseminate the elements of well-being that remained from the old world, but it did not carry them farther, or found anything that was really new. There was a strong probability for a time that the heritage of ancient civilisation would be taken up by the Moslem peoples, and diffused over the world under their guidance. The brunt of the struggle was borne by the Greeks of Constantinople[1]; and the Crusaders, all unconsciously, took action which helped to decide that this thing should not be, and that the progress of the world should be continued, not under the auspices of the Crescent, but of the Cross. When we see the decadence of society in lands where Mohammedanism has had a dominating influence, we may feel that the issue was of vital importance for the whole future of the race.

The fundamental weaknesses of the Arab civilisation can be noticed as we look back even to its greatest times. On the physical side we may contrast the Western Arabs with the northern races, who were then mere ruthless barbarians and who had little in common with the cultivated gentlemen of the south; but the northerners had a special aptitude for individual enterprise which rendered them ready to go out

---

[1] Lenormant, *La grande Grèce*, II. 376.

of the beaten tracks, not merely as soldiers obeying a divinely commissioned commander, but from the very love of adventure ; of this racial characteristic, however, enough has already been said.

There is a striking contrast too between the religion of the Prophet, inspiring as it was and is, and the Christianity to which Mohammedans were actively opposed. Their pure Theism, just because it is a pure Theism, could not give fruitful maxims for mundane affairs, or lay the basis for a doctrine that should ennoble secular life. The rule of the Caliphs was, in its ultimate basis, a theocracy ; it would submit to no limitations, and the objects which it set before itself, in the conquest of the world to the faith and the attainment of paradise by fighting for it, gave no scope for a doctrine of the responsibility of civil rulers, and of duty towards the governed. The popular imagination which filled the future life with dreams of sensuous enjoyment gave no check to reckless indulgence in luxury here ; and failed to lay down any clear and effective teaching on the obligations of those who were possessed of wealth ; nor was there any doctrine of the value of human personality as such, to tell in favour of the gradual extinction of slavery or the improvement in the position of women. Work was encouraged not as a wise discipline, but merely because of the remuneration of the work, and the independence it afforded. From every point of view we see that there was no advance beyond the doctrine of secular life which we find in the Old Testament. Christianity is not a pure Theism, but a worship of an Incarnate Deity, Who has established a kingdom among men ; it is, in its very essence, a religion of Humanity ; it has proved itself capable of inspiring an enthusiasm for the service of man which lies outside the sphere of any mere Theism. Christianity had the power, which Islam had not, of bringing the highest motives and the loftiest principles to bear on mundane affairs, and of remodelling political, civic and industrial life. Islam, with all its enthusiasm and all its faculty for adopting alien elements, failed to supply a firm basis for social life, or to give inspiration for human progress.

103. In the relations between Arabians and Christians on the Western Mediterranean, during the early Middle Ages, we have much that is analogous with the intercourse between Phoenicians and Greeks in earlier times. There is the same racial conflict of Semites and Aryans; there is the same apparent superiority of the Semitic race at the outset, and the same steady encroachments of the Aryans, who succeeded in wresting point after point from the power of their rivals. The precise course of the struggle is very obscure in each case; for though we have some mediaeval chronicles, and even important civic and ecclesiastical documents bearing on the later contest, they only throw occasional light on particular incidents, and hardly help us to understand the course of the struggle as a whole. There were, besides, so many conflicting interests at work that the tale is hopelessly tangled, and one which it would be impossible to attempt to unravel here. The Arab empire, like Western Christendom, was split into many separate groups, which neither supported each other's interests in war, nor followed a similar policy in their peaceful relations with Christian powers. Without dwelling on minor divisions, we have only to remember that Charles the Great had been in friendly communication with the Caliph of Bagdad, while he was raising armaments against the Arabs of Spain; and that the rulers of Morocco were developing commercial relations with the cities of Italy and the South of France at the very time when the crusading wars were being carried on most assiduously in Syria. In the East, as in Spain, there was constant hostility between the representatives of the Cross and the Crescent; but though a great struggle was waged by sea, as well as by land, it was less persistent. At the end of the eighth century the Arabian influence had been paramount in the Mediterranean; before the close of the

The Western Mediterranean.

reign of Charles, the maritime towns of Italy were beginning
to send out their fleets and to contest the Arab supremacy;
while two centuries later the Normans established themselves
in parts of Southern Italy, which had been the prey of Mohammedan invaders, and effected the conquest of Sicily. After
the loss of Sardinia and Majorca, the Arabs were thrown more
and more upon the defensive, so far as their African dominions
were concerned; but during this long and bitter struggle the
maritime relations between Christians and Moslems were by
no means uniformly hostile. It may suffice to indicate and
to illustrate the different occasions of intercourse by which
the Arab civilisation was brought to bear upon the relative
barbarism of Western Christendom.

In pursuing their career of conquest in Africa and Spain
the Arabs had been glad to preserve the Christian population,
and assure to them the enjoyment of rights and privileges, including the exercise of their religion, on the condition of their
paying a regular tribute; hence there was a considerable, though
diminishing, Christian population in Morocco and other parts
of the Arab dominions. When Cordova was recovered by the
Christians in 1085 A.D., they found that the churches had not
been desecrated during centuries of Arab domination; and in
similar fashion, there was a large Mohammedan population
which preferred to remain in Sicily under the protection of the
Norman Conquerors, rather than to seek new homes among
their co-religionists. As the wave of Christian conquest rolled
onwards, it swept over, rather than swept away, some elements
of Arabian civilisation. The habits and tendencies of thought,
which took such a firm hold in Languedoc and called forth
the Crusades against the Albigenses, were partly due to a
deeply rooted oriental influence in that area. The territory
which passed from one set of masters to another formed a
fringe where the two civilisations met, and to some extent
blended.

The existence of a Christian population under Moslem rule

also brought about a certain amount of ecclesiastical inter-communication. In the tenth or eleventh century there were still forty-seven bishops in the north of Africa; and in 1053 A.D. the Roman pontiff intervened to maintain the ancient supremacy of the Archbishopric of Carthage among the other remaining sees[1]. Though the settled Christian population was steadily decreasing, new elements were added; war and piracy were frequent, and many Christians were carried away to languish as captives in Moslem lands. The order of the Redemptionists was founded with the view of aiding in their release[2]; it was commended by Innocent III to the good offices of the Sultan Almanzar, while the Dominicans and Franciscans also took an active part in this charitable work, which continued to be a recognised duty of Christian philanthropy in the seventeenth and the early part of the eighteenth centuries. This intercourse, for religious objects, between Christendom and the Moham-medan rulers of Africa, is of interest; it at least indicates one kind of intercommunication, and it shows that the prohibition of commerce, from which Genoa suffered in the fourteenth century, is not to be regarded as the constant and permanent policy of the Holy See at earlier times.

Morocco had access by caravan routes to the products of the East, while it could also draw gold and ivory from the interior of the dark continent; but it required the oil and wine and wood, as well as furs and metals, which were produced or could be purchased in Italy, France and Spain. These mutual needs rendered commerce inevitable, even though religious differences, and inter-municipal jealousies, frequently inter-rupted it and enormously increased the risks of trading. In the twelfth and thirteenth centuries, when the crusades were being actively prosecuted in the East, there were ample and regular facilities for Christian merchants trading with Morocco.

---

[1] Mas Latrie, *Relations et Commerce de l'Afrique Septentrionale avec les nations chrétiennes*, p. 29.

[2] *Ibid.* p. 130.

These were secured by numerous treaties, which specified on one hand the privileges which Christian merchants were to possess, and on the other, described the conditions to which they were personally to conform[1]. It is curious to observe that there is little difference between the provisions laid down and those which were necessary for the prosecution of ordinary trade within Christendom, or even between the towns in any one realm at the same date.

According to the most important stipulation, the persons of Christian merchants were to be secure; it was agreed that they should not be held responsible for the debts of other men, and that they should have legal protection and remedy against wrongs done them. Each trading city had its own consul, who had the right of direct access to the Sultan; the consul had complete jurisdiction over the merchants of his own colony when alive, and administered their goods when dead; disputes between the merchants of two Christian cities came before their consuls, without any interference on the part of the Sultan and his officials. Each Christian city possessed its own factory in Africa, where the merchants could live, where their goods were stored and from which they might be re-exported; these were mercantile strongholds, as they were liable to attacks from many quarters and on many occasions. There was, moreover, a common understanding between Mohammedans and Christians as to the desirability of suppressing piracy, and the protection of those who had suffered shipwreck. It was also a recognised principle that Christians were not to run unnecessary risks by attempting to trade at any points on the coast, and that they were to show reasonable respect to the religious sentiments of the Arabs; though they were free to practise Christian rites in their own chapels, within their own factories, they were not permitted to have public worship in Mohammedan cities, or

[1] Mas Latrie, *Relations et Commerce de l'Afrique Septentrionale avec les nations chrétiennes*, p. 160.

even to sound a *sanctus* bell which might be heard outside their own establishments.

The trading cities of the south of Europe were much less inclined to combine for a common cause than those of the north; each town pursued its independent policy and had its separate factories. The men of Pisa had a specially favoured position at Tunis in 1157 A.D.[1] The Genoese had a large establishment at Ceuta in 1234 A.D.[2], and helped to protect that city from the attack of a crusading fleet; the men of Marseilles also had a factory even earlier[3]; and all these towns had establishments at Bougie. The factories appear moreover to have been used to some extent by the merchants of other cities. The Florentines trafficked for a time in conjunction with the Pisans[4], and the factory of the men of Marseilles was used by merchants from other towns in Provence. The Venetians also had a consul at Tunis in 1281 A.D.[5]; they had besides carried on a considerable commerce with Morocco and enjoyed special privileges for the purchase of lead[6].

Such was the nature of the arrangements that were made for the traffic of Christian merchants in Morocco itself; and enough information has survived to enable us to understand the plan on which their voyages were organised. Associations were formed by traders and other capitalists for the purpose of engaging in a voyage to Africa, deeds of partnership were drawn up, and on the return of the ship and sale of its cargo the profits were paid to the various partners in proportion to the sums they had contributed for the venture. This collectivist system is probably very ancient, and survived as the business form which was adopted in the sixteenth and seventeenth centuries for undertaking distant voyages.

---

[1] Mas Latrie, *Relations et Commerce de l'Afrique Septentrionale avec les nations chrétiennes*, p. 71, also pp. 90, 107.

[2] *Ibid.* p. 150.   [3] *Ibid.* p. 154.

[4] They used Pisan ships though they had trade privileges of their own.

[5] Mas Latrie, p. 170.   [6] *Ibid.* p. 162.

104.   The intercourse with Africa which had been established on these carefully restricted lines was
beneficial to particular cities, but so far as Western
Europe in general was concerned it had comparatively little importance.   The awakening of
a spirit of adventure in the northern parts of Christendom
was due to the preaching of the Crusades.   This movement
appealed to the two strongest sentiments of the age, and
found a ready response among all classes of the community ;
it came as a call to fulfil a sacred duty, and it opened up new
fields for the boldest military undertakings[1].   Its effects were
very deep and lasting ; it did not merely afford scope for the
mercantile classes to carry on commerce at new points and
along fresh routes ; it also diffused new conceptions of civilised
life and its possibilities among the Germans, French and
English, and introduced a taste for Eastern products in places
where they had been hardly obtainable hitherto.

The marginal note reads: The Crusades and the Opening of the East.

The reaction of this movement on society at large had
far-reaching consequences ; and it is almost impossible to
exaggerate the results on the mercantile class in particular.
There was much business to be done in assisting in the
equipment and transport of troops, as each new Crusade was
organised.   The commercial colonies which were soon established at Tripoli in Syria and elsewhere on the Mediterranean
were far more important than their analogues—the factories in
the cities of Tunis and Morocco ; for they gave access to more
important lines of trade with the East[2], and furnished many
valuable products, such as sugar, cotton and silk, from their
immediate neighbourhood[3].   The trading connections which
were then established continued to be maintained—though not
without interruption—till the discoveries of the fifteenth century

[1] The conquest of Sicily by the Normans was in part an anticipation of
the Crusades, and it gave a basis for conducting them on a larger scale.

[2] Heyd, *op. cit.* I. 163.

[3] *Ibid.* I. 178.

revolutionised the character of commerce with the East. The prosperity of the mercantile classes also tended to improve their political status; as the towns increased in wealth, they were able as communities to purchase larger and larger privileges, and even to assume the character of territorial powers; but at the same time the differences between the rich and poor within the cities became more noticeable. The rise of capitalist oligarchies, and the struggles against their pretensions, were really though remotely connected with the impulse which was given to commercial activity by the Crusades.

The Christian commerce of the Eastern Mediterranean was never so completely extinguished as that of the West had been; in the years when the Arabs ruled Septimania, Spain and Africa, as well as Sicily, Sardinia and other neighbouring islands, Constantinople still held her own; and under her prestige the commerce of Venice and of Amalfi began to flourish. The Norman invasion of the Mediterranean was fatal to this latter city, but Venice made rapid advances; the Greeks were content that active maritime trade should be undertaken by strangers, and the Venetians not only secured an important establishment in Constantinople, but founded depôts at Caffa and other points on the coasts of the Black Sea. They had little sympathy with the Crusaders at first, for, like the Greek Emperor, they were tempted to look askance on the crowd of military adventurers who flocked into the territories where their trading interests lay.

Owing to these circumstances the Venetians held aloof on the whole from the earlier expeditions[1], and the profitable undertakings connected with the transport of the Crusaders fell to a very large extent into the hands of their great rivals— the Genoese. When we consider on what a small scale shipping had hitherto been carried on, we see at once what an enormous impetus must have been given to business of every kind by

[1] W. Lenel, *Entstehung der Vorherrschaft Venedigs an der Adria*, p. 35.

the necessity of finding the means of conveying and of provisioning whole armies. The Genoese, who had taken an active part in the struggle with the Arabians in the West, threw themselves heartily into the new field of maritime employment which the Crusaders opened up. They were perhaps better prepared than their neighbours to take advantage of the great opportunity; but Marseilles and Montpellier were also engaged in catering for the demands of the Crusaders in the matter of equipment and transport. The successive expeditions, which followed one after another, served at all events to make money circulate among shipowners on the Mediterranean, as it had never done before.

During the brief *régime* of the Latin kingdom of Jerusalem, the merchants of Genoa and other cities of Italy and of Provence made the most of their opportunities and established considerable factories on the coast of Syria. The Italian merchants had access for a time to the caravan routes which had formerly contributed so much to the prosperity of Tyre and to that of Antioch in Roman times; with the reassertion of Mohammedan influence, the Christian traders failed to maintain their position. Experience had already shown, however, that crusading had its commercial aspect, and that it could be made to pay; and in the Fourth Crusade the religious interest fell entirely into the background. It was an expedition which was directed by the Venetians to forward their mercantile projects; they succeeded in upsetting the Greek Empire in Constantinople, and in reducing their Genoese rivals to a subordinate position in that emporium; for sixty years the Venetians appear to have enjoyed a complete monopoly of the trading stations in the Black Sea, and to have commanded the Northern caravan routes to Persia and the East. But they were not sufficiently careful to maintain the valuable monopoly they had won: the Genoese were willing to assist[1] in restoring the

[1] Michael Palaeologus succeeded in his expedition before the Genoese fleet arrived. Heyd, *op. cit.* I. 428.

Greek Imperial line in 1261 A.D., and in their turn attained a supremacy which, though less extensive, was similar to that which Venice had enjoyed[1]. They concentrated their attention on the Black Sea trade; while the Venetians developed their Levantine trade from Cyprus[2], and consolidated their position in Egypt. The trade with this latter country had suffered, but it had never been suppressed, either by the fortunes of war or by papal prohibition[3]. The Venetians endeavoured to monopolise it, but they were unable to prevent the intrusion of other merchants from the Adriatic[4], and a very large commerce was carried on by the Catalans[5] and Provençals. At the beginning of the fourteenth century there were several well-established lines of communication between Western Europe and the East through the Moslem world. The Hanse towns worked eastwards through Russia, and the Genoese from Constantinople; Venice, Barcelona, and Marseilles had factories in Egypt, and various Italian towns maintained prosperous establishments in Morocco. It was of course restricted intercourse, conducted at factories, but it was regularly organised and fairly constant.

There was occasional agreement for common commercial objects among the Provençals and Catalans[6], but between the Italian towns there was little sign of any confederacy such as grew up among the traders in the Baltic; and the rise or fall of one or another of these centres was for the most part due to political causes and had but little economic significance. Intercivic quarrels were often connected with the desire of each town to maintain its monopoly, and especially to secure exclusive access to the harbours on the more important

[1] Heyd, *op. cit.* I. 430, 441.
[2] Heyd, *op. cit.* II. 7.
[3] After the fall of Acre in 1291. Heyd, *op. cit.* II. 34.
[4] Heyd, *op. cit.* I. 418.
[5] Heyd, *op. cit.* I. 422.
[6] Mas Latrie, *op. cit.* 213.

commercial routes[1]. Genoa succeeded in establishing her supremacy on the Western coast of Italy, and closed the harbours of Messina and Syracuse to the Pisans[2] and Marseillese[3]; while Venice continued to gain at the expense of Ancona and Ferrara, and attained at length to the sovereignty of the Adriatic[4]. Apart from these rivalries, the policy pursued by these cities was economically sound; since their commercial prosperity and industrial activity were made to react on one another[5]. Each had to some extent its own character; the Venetians imitated the imperial policy in the endeavour to introduce the manufacture of articles of luxury which had hitherto been imported at great cost; they set themselves to encourage the silk industry[6], as well as the production of glass and mosaic, and the fine kinds of metal work. Genoa was perhaps more of a mere commercial depôt than her great rivals, but her people were specially skilled in the manufacture of arms and munitions of war. The Florentines had devoted themselves to the textile trades and the dressing and dyeing of fine woollen cloth[7]; it was only gradually that they forced their way to the sea, and superseded Pisa in a profitable trade with Morocco; but the prosperity of their town was built on the most secure foundations, and they suffered less than their neighbours from the changes which were brought about by the age of discovery.

The impulse which was given to the Italian towns was communicated with more or less rapidity to other centres in Europe[8]. The cities in the Danube valley must have profited

[1] Compare Vol. I. 64, 89.

[2] Heyd, *op. cit.* I. 183.

[3] *Ibid.* I. 188.

[4] Lenel, *op. cit.* 47—84.   [5] Vol. I. 67, 119.

[6] Broglio d'Ajano, *Die Venetianische Seidenindustrie*, 27.

[7] E. Dixon, *Florentine Wool Trade in the Middle Ages*, in the *Royal Historical Society's Transactions*, XII. 158. Doren, *Entwickelung und Organisation der Florentiner Zünfte* in Schmoller's *Forschungen*, XV. iii 60.

[8] The increase of commercial intercommunication undoubtedly affected

to some extent by catering for the armies which passed along that route; while Augsburg and Nuremberg, which were in direct communication with Venice, gained with the increase of her commercial activity. Nor was it only by mountain passes that communication with the North took place; from the early part of the fourteenth century regular commercial voyages were organised from Venice to the Low Countries. The Flanders galleys began to carry a portion of the trade which had gone in previous times by the French rivers, and after the middle of the fourteenth century, when the Hundred Years' War interfered with the peaceful avocations of merchants, this stream of traffic was almost entirely diverted to the Alpine and maritime routes. In the fourteenth century we can estimate the full extent of the impulse which had been given by the Crusades. We see the organised commercial communication between all parts of Western Christendom, and with the countries which lay outside, and we see too that a new development of industry followed in connection with the improvement of the facilities for trading intercourse.

105. It is rarely the case that the personal life of any individual embraces and illustrates the most momentous issues in the contemporary history of his country; and it would be difficult to find

Prince Henry the Navigator.

any single character that summed up the tendencies of his age so completely as did Prince Henry the Navigator. His work led to the discovery of the new world, and to the opening of direct maritime communication with the East; through his personal energy, and interest in founding a school of navigators,

the industrial arts in the North and West of Europe. This is particularly clear in regard to the art of fortification (Oman, *Art of War*, 526). It is noticeable that many of the terms in use in the building trades in England are of Greek origin—*laothomi, cheirotheca, schola*—and that the organisation of masons had little in common with that of other crafts in England, while it was closely analogous to that which existed in Byzantium in the ninth century. Jules Nicole, *Livre du Préfet*, p. 82.

the preliminary difficulties were overcome and complete success was brought within sight. The change which has revolutionised European trade and has drawn the whole world within the influence of Western Civilisation was indirectly the doing of this Portuguese Prince. Yet though his action rendered modern life possible, with its cosmopolitan commerce and giant industry which far outstrip the greatest efforts of the ancient world, he was not in any sense before his time; he was emphatically a man of his time. The various threads which we have followed in the preceding paragraphs appear to meet and to be united in him. Prince Henry came of a stock which had a strain of the old Norse blood; the kingdom of Portugal had been founded by Norman adventurers; and his mother was a Plantagenet and therefore a descendant of Norman William. Thus the first impulse in the age of discovery came from a scion of the race that had made their homes on all the lands of the Northern Seas, and had swept the Mediterranean with their ships. He lived at a time, too, when his native country had come to occupy a new place in the commerce of the day; the fleet of Flanders Galleys touched at its ports, and native enterprise was fired more and more with the ambition to obtain at least a share in the trade which the Venetians found so profitable. It is noticeable also that Prince Henry resided in the one corner of Christendom where the old crusading fervour burned most fiercely; the continued presence of the Mohammedans at Grenada was an offence to Christian sentiment and a challenge to Christian chivalry. Prince Henry had won his spurs in a brilliant attack on the infidel fortress of Tangier; and there was in him a combination of the scientific and missionary interest in discovery with the military and religious desire of conquest, which was characteristic of the mediaeval world in which he lived rather than of the modern life he was helping to introduce. Islam had hemmed Christendom in on every side; on the east as on the south, the Crescent raised a barrier against the advance of the

Cross. It was the ambition of Prince Henry to turn the flank of these ancient foes, and thus to obtain direct access to the great world, and to the Heathendom that lay beyond the wide belt of Mohammedan influence.

With this object in view he organised a school of maritime exploration, where all the geographical knowledge of the day and technical skill in seamanship might be combined for one definite object. Year after year his expeditions were sent out, and pushed their way farther and farther along the African coast; but few of his emissaries were inspired by his far-reaching ambitions; they preferred to reap the immediate profits of commerce on the African coast, rather than to push on to the continents that lay beyond. They obtained gold from the Guinea coast by barter with the natives, and made a new beginning of that trade which has been the immemorial curse of Africa, by bringing negroes to work in Portugal.

At the time of Prince Henry's death the Portuguese had already found their way to the Madeiras (1418 A.D.) and rounded Cape Bojador (1434 A.D.); and a few years later they pushed as far as Senegal and the Cape Verde Islands (1446 A.D.); the impulse which the prince had given was not allowed to die out, and the work of discovery became a settled part of Portuguese policy, though it was not pursued with the same assiduity in every reign. Explorers were sent by land to the East, and attempts were made to utilise the caravan routes across Northern Africa; but the crowning success was attained in 1498 A.D. when Vasco da Gama arrived after a nine months' voyage at Calicut. Six years previously Columbus, relying on the experience accumulated by Prince Henry's school and aided by the resources of Ferdinand and Isabella, had found his way to the West Indian Islands, and fired the ambition of a crowd of other explorers; so that in the course of a few years the coasts of enormous continents were sketched in the map of the world, and a field was opened for military and commercial expeditions, which was wide indeed compared with the narrow area which the Crusaders had striven to occupy.

It were invidious to compare the heroism and persistence displayed by the discoverers in one great area with the virtues of other men at other times. The Portuguese and Columbus accomplished a magnificent work that has changed the face of the globe; but it may be doubted if they showed more enterprise in penetrating the unknown or more skill in seamanship than the Phoenicians in their voyages or the Vikings of whom we read in the sagas. The times were ripe for the fifteenth century discoveries; facilities were at hand to take advantage of the new vista they opened up. The Norsemen had not had the means to transport armies which could conquer the lands they reached, or the skill to frame a government which could even enable them to explore the new territories systematically; but the world had advanced since their time. The business training which had been developed by merchants in the Mediterranean could be brought to bear in the Eastern hemisphere; the Portuguese did not fare forth half as pirates and half as merchants, but as men who meant to obtain a regular establishment from which they could organise a steady trade. The preceding centuries, with their limited commerce and futile expeditions, had been a long apprenticeship and had fitted the men of the sixteenth century for the career of conquest and commerce and colonisation which had become possible for them alike in the East and the West.

106. However highly we may rate the gain that has accrued, on the whole, from the age of discovery we should not overlook the mischiefs that accompanied it. The moral results in Europe of intercommunication between Christendom and the Moslem world had not always been wholesome; and the contact between Christendom and heathendom induced a terrible relapse from the improving standard in regard to the treatment of labourers, which had been the most striking economic

Mediaeval and Modern Slavery.

feature of mediaeval society, for it led to an immediate recrudescence of slavery. When the African slave-trade had once been started, it continued to develop and increase till the horrors of the revived traffic nearly equalled or possibly even exceeded the miseries endured by slaves in the ancient world.

The reintroduction of the slave-trade was a singular aberration, for which it is not at first sight easy to account; the influence of Christian sentiment and economic changes had alike tended to raise the status of the labourer in Europe; but, for different reasons, these forces did not serve to prevent or discourage the export of slaves to the new world. The attitude of the Church towards slavery had always been perfectly clear; from the time of S. Paul onwards there had been no condemnation of slavery as an institution, or attempt to interfere with it as a condition of life in ordinary society; there was no assertion of any inherent right of man as man to be free. While, then, there was no condemnation of slavery as such, there were frequent efforts made to lighten the lot of the slave, and to protect him from arbitrary and cruel treatment by his master[1]. Many signs of this influence are to be found in the legislative codes of the East[2], as well as in the *Capitularies*[3]; and the partial freedom which was afforded by limiting the master's rights gave the slave an opportunity for gradually bettering his position. Besides contributing in this way to the gradual improvement of the circumstances of the class, the Church treated freedom as an ideal, which ought to be kept in view. The liberating of slaves was encouraged as a form of charity, though it was not regarded

[1] Yanoski, *De l'abolition de l'esclavage ancien au moyen âge*, p. 37 fol.

[2] Brownlow, *Lectures on Slavery and Serfdom in Europe*, p. 30 fol. *Cod. Theod.* lib. IX. tit. 55. 1, 5; *Cod. Justinian.* lib. VII. tit. 15. 1. Wallon, *Histoire de l'Esclavage*, III. 389.

[3] Brownlow, *op. cit.* 69, *Capitula excerpta ex lege Longobardorum*, c. 14 in Baluze, *Capitularia* (1677), I. 351; Guérard, *Polyptyque de l'Abbé Irminon; prolégomènes*, 331.

as a duty of strict obligation[1]; to keep slaves was not wrong, but to free them was kindly and commendable. Hence we have the numerous wills, like that of King Alfred[2], where the manumission of slaves comes in as a generous benefaction, much as the endowing of a college might appear in the present day. There are other examples, such as that of S. Eligius, whose methods of effecting the redemption of slaves were so strangely unlike those of modern abolitionists[3].

There were, moreover, certain cases in which Christian sentiment was not content with improving their lot or making occasional efforts for setting individual slaves at liberty; a traffic which consisted in removing men from Christian homes and leaving them uncared for in pagan lands roused the strongest indignation. To be willing for the sake of mere money to sell a Christian man into a country where it was hardly possible for him to maintain Christian habits of life, and where he must die 'unhouseled, disappointed, unanealed,' was an outrage on religious sentiment. Hence, while there was little decided feeling against slavery as such, there was the deepest pity for those who were sold into captivity beyond the pale of Christendom[4]; a pity which was based, not merely on sympathy with their physical lot, but on fears for their loss of the means of grace and the hope of glory.

The Christian sentiment on the subject was not primarily humanitarian, but simply religious, and herein lies the secret of its limitations. When the sphere of Mohammedan influence in

---

[1] A precisely similar distinction was drawn in regard to the use of money; to lend money without interest was a commendable sort of charity and kindliness, but it was not a duty incumbent on every man who had wealth at his disposal.

[2] Thorpe, *Diplomatarium Anglicum Aevi Saxonici*, 492, also 513.

[3] S. R. Maitland, *The Dark Ages*, 88. For the Viking slave-trade compare Torfaeus, *Rerum Norvegicarum Historia* (1711), vol. II. p. 332.

[4] Great pains were taken by the Genoese to prevent the inclusion of any Christian among the slaves they exported from Caffa to Egypt. Heyd, *op. cit.* II. 557.

Africa had been rounded by Prince Henry's exertions, and Christendom had come into direct contact with heathendom, this strong religious feeling was not shocked by the action of those who imported heathen slaves into Christian lands; it would have been possible to regard such conduct as a pious work, since by its means the imported slaves were brought within the range of Christian instruction. It does not appear clear that any one ever advocated the traffic on this ground[1], and Cardinal Ximenes and the Spaniards generally regarded the trade with dislike, as at best a necessary evil, but a real evil; still the point remains that the Christian sentiment which had protested vigorously against the export of slaves from Europe was not roused by the importation of slaves to Europe, or to lands dominated by Europeans and in which Christian institutions existed.

Apart altogether from this religious influence, economic causes had been at work in improving the condition of the rural labourer in Western Europe. They had doubtless had something to do with the diminution of slavery; for its decline in the ancient world had been partly due to the fact that no sufficient source of supply continued to be available[2]. It had been necessary to introduce new methods of estate management, and to rely on the labour of serfs who were restricted to particular estates and remunerated by the assignment of holdings which they worked on their own account. The mediaeval villein was in a very different position from the slaves of classical times, for despite the disabilities to which he was subject, he had a definite legal status, and he frequently enjoyed proprietary rights which enabled him to improve his position as opportunity arose. The gradual substitution of money for natural economy in rural life told decidedly in his favour; this gave him an increased measure of economic

---

[1] Columbus appears to have taken this view in his treatment of the natives of the Caribbean Islands. Ingram, *History of Slavery*, p. 142.

[2] Vol. I. p. 179.

independence and much greater freedom for movement[1]. The change has not proceeded at a uniform rate in all European lands; the occasions which have brought it about have been different in each country, though the general result has been similar in all alike[2]. For the most part this revolution occurred at a date when there was little tendency to utilise capital in the cultivation of land[3]; there was no considerable demand for hired labour, and no need at all to import it into Europe. A large body of peasantry, engaged in work upon their small holdings, inhabited the areas that could be most profitably cultivated[4]. The circumstances in the New World were so different that the importation to it of slaves from Africa proved to be a remunerative business. There were many large capitalists in America who were eager to obtain numbers of labourers so that they might carry on mining operations and work their plantations, while a supply that was practically unlimited could be easily drawn from the dark continent. These exceptional circumstances, under which the traffic revived, bring into clearer light the reasons for its decline and practical disappearance from European lands[5], and help us to gauge more precisely the effect of religious ideals on the course of affairs. In the one case where Christian sentiment failed to make its protest, the horrors of slavery revived. The introduc-

[1] T. W. Page, *End of Villainage in England*, in the *Publications of the American Economic Association*, 3rd series, I. p. 382.

[2] Ingram, *History of Slavery and Serfdom*, 91 fol.; see also Brownlow, *op. cit.* p. 210, for the influence of the Crusades.

[3] The large Tuscan estates appear to have been exceptional. Pohlmann, *Die Wirthschaftspolitik der Florentiner Renaissance*, p. 5. In the *Preisschriften gekrönt von der fürstlich-jablonowskischen Gesellschaft*, 1878.

[4] The pressure of the moneyed and industrial interests tended to depress the condition of the peasantry both in France and Germany, but not to enslave them. Lamprecht, *Deutsche Geschichte*, V. 87 fol.

[5] Slavery was not extinct in Europe so early as is commonly supposed. Cibrario has collected numerous instances of sales of slaves in Italy in the xiiith, xivth and xvth centuries. *Della Schiavitù e del Servaggio*, I. pp. 227—235.

tion of money-economy gave the command of more capital to invest in slaves; the opening up of commercial intercourse afforded wider opportunities for engaging in the traffic; these elements in material progress were perfectly compatible with the maintenance of slavery and the oppression of the workman. It was so far, and only so far, as Christianity made itself felt as an effective force, by constant pressure exerted through many centuries, that the condition of labour was sensibly improved from what it had been in the ancient world.

BOOK V.

NATIONALITIES.

CHAPTER I.

SECULARISATION.

107. THE resemblances between the Roman Empire of the second or third century and the Latin Christendom of the thirteenth have been already pointed out. Both attained to a high state of civilisation, and a large part of the areas they occupied was common to both; they were ruled from the same centre and included a similar independent city life. These points of similarity lie so much on the surface as to tempt us to overlook and ignore the deep and real differences which were inherent in the very structure of these polities; but the marked contrast between them is forced on our attention when we compare these two great systems of society in their decline. The Roman Empire preserved its apparent grandeur, while it was tottering to its fall, and one after another of its provinces sank away into utter barbarism. In Christendom, however, there was disruption rather than decay. The central authority fell into disrepute and the cohesive influences gave way; but the distant provinces were by no means exhausted; they were, on the contrary, full of vigorous vitality, and were so far from

The Disruption of Christendom.

relying on the central power for defence, that they resented attempts to exercise any interference and control.

The radical distinction between the breaking up of the ancient and of the mediaeval system lies in the fact that the Empire succumbed and fell to pieces as the result of a long period of economic failure and decadence; the weakness was obvious enough, even though there may be some dispute as to the precise diagnosis of the disease with which the mischief began. In Christendom however there was no similar blight. The era of the Crusades had been a time of extraordinary material prosperity; even despite the devastation caused by the constant struggles in Italy, and the Hundred Years' War between England and France, in spite too of the destruction consequent on the Black Death and of the commercial readjustments necessitated by the fall of Constantinople, economic progress continued in many directions. Under the influence of developing trade, industry was stimulated; the towns of Flanders and of Germany are full of fourteenth and fifteenth century monuments which testify unmistakeably to the vigour of their industrial life, and the wealth of the merchant princes of the time. The outlying parts of the Empire had been the first to show the numbness which betokens a mortal malady; but there were no analogous symptoms in the distant parts of Christendom.

A strange glamour had attached to the very name of the Roman Emperor; the mere survival of the imperial dignity had overawed the barbarian invaders; while their admiration for the imperial authority persisted, in spite of their experience of its inability to resist them. In Christendom, on the other hand, the rivalry of Pope and Emperor was too intense, and their struggle too long continued, for either to command the un-questioning obedience of the world. The subsequent triumph of the Papacy over the Emperor was spoiled of its effect by the great schism and the Babylonian captivity, when the spiritual head of Christendom became a mere puppet of France.

When not one Pope but three demanded the obedience of mankind, and the new era of Councils opened, there was a patent confession that the Papacy had ceased to be an effective instrument for the government of Christendom. Nor had the Papacy been successful in organising effective resistance to the common foe; the greedy intrigue, which brought about the fall of the Templars, discredited its instigator, and opened up fresh opportunities for Mohammedan aggression. The Emperors had been forced to yield to the Popes, but the Papacy was unable to wield the power at which it had grasped, and failed to maintain its dignity as a spiritual head directing all the energies of a great and complex civilised society. The economic inanition, which proved fatal to the Roman Empire, had nothing to do with the disruption of Christendom; that was entirely due to the inability of the central power to maintain an effective authority.

108. This loss of prestige on the part of the ecclesiastical head of Christendom became a serious danger to the institutions of the mediaeval world, because it directed attention to the principles on which the whole social system rested and rendered them the subject of much hostile criticism. The claim that Christian influence should be supreme in all the relations of life had been admitted in the foundation, and had guided the construction of the fabric of mediaeval society; this principle seemed to imply that there was no sphere of human interest which did not come under the cognisance of spiritual authority, and with which the activity of ecclesiastics might not be rightly concerned. Practical reasons rendered it convenient to entrust the management of civil affairs to the clergy, as educated men; they were also regarded as especially trustworthy, since bishops and priests were particularly bound to discharge their duties with the fear of God before them[1]. Directly and indirectly an immense amount of secular business

Secular Functions of the Clergy and Criticism of the existing System.

[1] *Dialogus de Scaccario*, Pref.

came into the hands of clerical functionaries; ecclesiastical tribunals had control over all matters connected with wills and marriages; and much administrative work, both fiscal, judicial, and diplomatic, was carried on by ecclesiastical personages, who held high civil offices in the various states of Europe.

This attempt to control the life of man in all its aspects is of the very essence of the Christian religion. *Homo sum, nihil humani a me alienum puto*, is the Divine Word to the world. Still it is true that those who have aimed at giving effect to this principle have often discredited it by their failure to apply it. The effort to control and direct all the various interests of mankind may distract attention from the supreme end which ought to be in view. The Benedictines had devoted themselves to the study of letters, that they might consecrate learning, and to the pursuit of wealth that was devoted to the service of God; nevertheless they had so far lost their hold on the end and aim of the *Rule* under which they lived, that there was need in the twelfth century for the founding of the reformed orders at Cluny and Citeaux. In precisely the same manner the absorption of ecclesiastical officials in civil and political activity tended to distract them from the duties of devotion, and laid them open to the charge that their claim to spiritual authority and respect was a mere pretext, which was used to cloak an absorbing interest in worldly dignities and earthly gain. There was a consequent reaction of religious feeling, which carried many earnest men into the opposite extreme and led them to disparage secular life altogether. The rise of the mendicant orders was a protest against a secularised hierarchy; in their devotion to spiritual things and to acts of mercy, they deliberately refrained from secular duties, and alleged the example of our Lord and the Twelve Apostles as an excuse for neglecting the discipline of work, and living on the alms of the faithful. Mediaeval thinkers rightly insisted on the supreme value of that which is spiritual; but they erred in giving it exclusive importance; indeed, the hard and fast line which they drew is inadmissible. We cannot sever the merely secular from the purely spiritual and contrast them one against the other; the problem which confronts the Christian man in all ages is that of so using earthly things as to turn them to the highest uses. He is bound to endeavour to bring the common affairs of daily life into just subordination and to limit an absorbing interest in them; but any attempt to ignore them altogether as unworthy of attention must end in disaster. That which is secular has a place in the divine order and will reassert itself if neglected. Those who, as friars, were wholly true to their vows of poverty and were personally most self-sacrificing and devout, might yet be deeply concerned about the worldly welfare of their community and vehement sticklers for its privileges or wealth. Still, the view of Christian duty which they asserted, in all its exaggeration and crudity, came to be widely popular; in the time of the Emperor Lewis of Bavaria the enthusiasm for the purely spiritual was dexterously used by William of Occam as a weapon for attacking ecclesiastics for their readiness to attend to worldly matters and to control or exercise civil functions.

This teaching was formulated with such skill and acumen that it was diffused and perpetuated in academic circles; similar criticism on the existing system was uttered more forcibly, in the fourteenth century, by those who regarded the affairs of the times as plain men, exercising their common sense. There was a sharp contrast between the recognised duty of labour,—of accepting work as a personal discipline,— and the lives of the friars who lived in idleness as beggars. The management of the religious houses failed to show that ecclesiastics were actuated by a sense of responsibility in fulfilling the duty of administering their property carefully; the exactions of the monasteries from their serfs or from the townsmen, who were their neighbours, gave continual cause for complaint and were the excuse for occasional outbreaks. A more scandalous violation of another fundamental Christian principle—that of fairness in monetary transactions—was afforded by the practices of the papal merchants, whose sharp dealings rivalled those of the detested Jew. When tried by the standards, which the Church had introduced and disseminated, the existing ecclesiastical system was emphatically condemned. It must be noted, however, that this popular criticism was saner and wiser than that of Occam and the friars; it did not discard the old conceptions as mistaken, but, in the face of existing abuses, it challenged the papal claim to unquestioning obedience, as the unique authority in interpreting and enforcing Christian duty. The old ideals have survived the disruption of Christendom and are retained in Christian lands as setting the standards by which right and wrong are judged; there is still the recognition of an Absolute Will as the ground of all human authority and the guarantee against the encroachments of arbitrary human will on personal liberty; there is frequent insistence on the responsibilities of the wealthy, and a general admission that work is a duty to be done. All this remains in the modern world, though the Latin Church is no longer accepted as the sole illustration of every Christian virtue; the maxims of its jurisprudence have been set aside in many lands as no longer applicable, and its methods of enforcing them have lost much of their power. The mediaeval world, which owed everything to the work of the Christian Church, had gradually outgrown and ceased to rely on the forms through which that guidance had been habitually given.

109. These opinions, so hostile to the existing order, must have sooner or later had their effect in undermining clerical authority in Christendom; but their influence was greatly accelerated by the terrible pestilence which devastated Europe in the middle of the fourteenth century. The

The Black Death and Social Disintegration. The Renaissance.

Black Death, passing as it did from country to country and

sweeping off about half of the population in land after land[1], brought about many fundamental changes, both in urban and rural districts.   Some of these are matters of local and special history, but one result was common to the whole of Western Europe.   The Church as an organised society suffered a serious shock, which strained its most honoured institutions. The great monasteries never recovered their position and influence as centres of cultivated and devout life[2]; the supply of clergy for the parish churches became quite inadequate. The scandals, which became more frequent and patent, were subsequently dealt with in some lands by the Council of Trent, while they were made the occasion for religious revolution in other countries.   The Church not only suffered from an insufficient supply of men, but came to be more exposed to another attack, after the Black Death.   Since a large proportion of the population had died, and the conditions of life and labour had changed for the worse, the amount of wealth devoted to religious objects appeared to be excessive and to be quite disproportionate to the requirements of each state.   The jealousy of needy potentates was roused and their avarice was quickened; they were eager to take advantage of any chance that offered for diverting the grants that had been made by pious benefactors.   Much of the contemporary testimony as to the corruption of the Church comes from tainted sources and is untrustworthy, and it is a thankless task to try to sift the evidence in detail; we can see that apart altogether from any religious or moral causes which contributed to the downfall of the ecclesiastical system, the Latin Church must have lost its predominance, so soon as society was able to dispense with the support it had formerly afforded.   The Truce of God had ceased to be a useful guarantee for the opportunity of pursuing peaceful avocations, since the royal authority was better able to enforce the law,

[1] Cunningham, *Growth of English Industry and Commerce*, I. 331.

[2] Gasquet, *The Great Pestilence*, pp. 205, 214.

and to secure that the intermission of war and pillage should not be exceptional and occasional, but general and permanent. There were trained civilians who could administer the affairs of the realm, so that rulers were able to dispense with the services of the clergy in many capacities which ecclesiastics had at one time filled to advantage. In earlier times the monks had improved the art of agriculture, and aided in the development of commerce; but in the fifteenth century the abbey estates were no longer models of good management, and trade was cared for by the merchant oligarchies of the towns. The Church had ceased to be a leader in the arts of practical life, while her inability to utilise privileges and possessions to the best advantage under changed conditions, was fatal to her position as the dominating influence over secular life in all its aspects.

The general disorganisation of European society and decreased respect for the spiritual head of Christendom reacted on the finances of the Roman Court, and rendered it necessary for the Popes to devise new methods for obtaining revenue[1]. The temper of the times was such that a systematic attempt to increase papal taxation would have been a dangerous expedient in any case; but murmured criticism gave place to active resentment as the full effects of the Renaissance[2] movement began to be felt. The conscious imitation of ancient models at the court of Rome was a cause of scandal; and the scheme for the erection of a magnificent ecclesiastical edifice which should be a centre for the world's worship brought matters to a crisis; an attempt was made to

[1] Gottlob, *Aus der Camera*, 188.

[2] The Humanists were repelled by mediaeval ideals and did not a little to undermine mediaeval institutions. They valued art and letters; and regarded them as objects well worth living for on their own account. The Humanists refused to look on life in this world as a mere discipline and preparation for another sphere; and thus they contributed to the process of secularisation, but they had little direct influence on economic progress, for they merely reverted to ancient ideals which were already discredited by the logic of events.

meet the expense of the building of S. Peter's by the sale of indulgences in Germany; this roused the indignation of Luther, whose protest served as a wedge, that was driven farther and farther home, till Christendom was severed to pieces.

110. The malign effects of the Black Death and the social disintegration it induced were more obvious and long continued than might have been the case if the ecclesiastical institutions had retained their pristine vigour; but they were no longer able to cope with the fresh difficulties that arose. From this time onwards some important matters which had hitherto been attended to as pious duties were disregarded; churchmen lacked either the will or the power to bestir themselves; and when men tried to remedy this neglect in the sixteenth century, the work was taken up by the civil and not by the ecclesiastical authorities.

The Beginnings of Reconstruction. Territorial Economic Policy.

Internal trade could only be carried on with difficulty in countries where it had previously flourished, for all the facilities for intercommunication had suffered severely. This had been specially the case in France, where the devastation caused by the Hundred Years' War had aggravated the mischief due to mere neglect[1]. Even in England many of the bridges had broken down[2], and there was no one with sufficient public spirit to attend to them properly.

Throughout the Middle Ages it seems as if the repair of roads was rather a piece of Christian philanthropy than anything else. The rendering of assistance to travellers was a form of active benevolence, and the story of the building of Barnstaple bridge[3] shows how much this work was required for the public safety. We find that such repairs were a frequent subject of pious benefaction; the great ecclesiastics and monastic corporations are said to have devoted a considerable amount of

[1] Levasseur, *op. cit.* 421—9.
[2] Jusserand, *English Wayfaring Life*, 64.
[3] Leland, *Itinerary* (1744), II. 75, f. 66.

wealth to this purpose[1]; at all events as their vigour declined they were less ready to take an active part in the matter. The statute of 1555 A.D., which provides for the appointment of road surveyors[2], embodies the modern view of the nature of the obligation; it was a public improvement to which great attention was given by Henry IV of France[3].

There was also a process of secularisation in the arrangements which were made for the relief of the indigent. The distresses of the fourteenth and fifteenth centuries appear to have given new prominence to the question of pauperism, and the need of making provision for the poor was very imperfectly met by the monasteries at that time. This may have been partly due to the diminution of their wealth, and partly to increased carelessness of the wants of the poor; but it should also be remembered that the mediaeval methods of charity were thoroughly unsatisfactory. Doles of food, if occasional, can do little towards aiding the poor effectively; if regularly perpetuated, they tend to create an idle and pauperised class. Many experiments were tried by the founding of hospitals and other charitable institutions for the local maintenance of the poor; in many towns efforts were made to promote discriminating almsgiving and the organisation of charitable help; and the task came to be fulfilled as a matter of civic or municipal expediency[4]. There was some doubt as to how far this way of viewing it was in accord with the Christian maxims of neighbourliness; and the point was discussed at some length by the doctors of the Sorbonne[5]. They gave the sanction of

[1] Thorold Rogers, *Agriculture and Prices*, I. 139. Jusserand, *op. cit.* 45. A. Law, *English Towns and Roads in* XIII *Century* in *Economic Review*, VII. 300.

[2] 2 and 3 Philip and Mary, c. 8.

[3] Fagniez, *L'économie sociale de la France sous Henri IV*, 180.

[4] A. S. Green, *English Town Life*, I. 41, n. 2. E. Leonard, *Poor Relief*, 7.

[5] Ashley, *Introduction to English Economic History*, I. ii. 348.

their authority to methods of undertaking the duty[1] which
had little in common with the traditional Christian practice
of indiscriminate almsgiving.

But distressful as the period of transition must necessarily
have been, it was an enormous boon that civil authority was
so far developed as to be able to take in hand the various
forms of social activity for which the ecclesiastical system was
no longer able to provide.   There were in the fifteenth century
two distinct types of secular authority, the monarchies and
the cities ; both were capable of organising departments of
governmental action which had hitherto been relegated to the
Church, and both were making their importance felt as growing
territorial powers.

The kings and the towns of Western Europe had sometimes found a common interest in opposing the great feudatories and curbing their pretensions ; in the fifteenth century
a fair measure of success had been attained, and the noble
families were relatively less independent of the kings and less
important than the wealthy centres of trade.   Feudal society
passed away throughout Western Europe ; but in some countries,
as in Italy and Flanders, the towns had become so strong that
they were able to maintain an economic and political independence.   In others, and especially in France and in England,
the authority of the sovereign was brought to bear effectively
on the whole territory and controlled the affairs of towns and
of rural districts alike.   In this way it was possible in all the
regulation of industry and trade, to keep one supreme object in
view and to attempt to utilise all resources so as to strengthen
the realm as a whole.   This might necessitate the repression
of particularist aims and even the suppression of local privileges, but it helped to bring out an underlying community of
interest among all the citizens, and to give solidarity to the

[1] On the tentative experiments of Tudor times and the growth of the
English systems see E. M. Leonard, *The Early History of English Poor
Relief*, 21.

whole social system. When a wise economic policy was adopted for any nation there was abundant opportunity for the healthy interaction of rural, urban and commercial life upon each other.

In Italy and Flanders, and to some extent in Germany, many of the towns acquired additional territory; and each was inclined to organise a definite economic system which should suit its own circumstances; monarchic and civic policy have this feature in common[1]. In fifteenth century municipal regulation there is less exclusive attention to the prosperity of the powerful merchants, and there are signs of a readiness to take account of both landed and civic interests in the development of territorial resources. There would be immense interest in tracing the history of particular towns; in seeing how physical circumstances affected the beginnings of their trade; and in noticing the precise fashion in which the commerce of any one reacted on its internal life, and favoured the local development of special branches of industry. Few things could be more instructive to the economist than to examine the precise mercantile policy which was pursued by different city-states in the Middle Ages[2], and to consider how far it tended to their success or brought about their failure. But it may be doubted if any one continental city directly contributed by its experience to the formulating of the schemes for national prosperity that were tentatively devised in the fourteenth and fifteenth centuries and that were systematically pursued in the sixteenth and seventeenth. The course of industrial progress had been directed by the great cities of Italy and Germany; but after the age of discovery it was forced into new channels, and even those towns like Florence[3], which were most ready to

[1] Compare Schmoller, *Mercantile System*, on the whole subject.

[2] Naudé, *Die Getreidehandelspolitik der Europäischen Staaten*, p. 17. In Brandenburg and other parts of Germany the expansion of town regulations to include considerable territories is specially noticeable. Schmoller, *op. cit.* 33.

[3] For Florence see Pöhlmann, *Die Wirthschaftspolitik der Florentiner Renaissance*, p. 140.

adapt their institutions, were being left on one side. Mediaeval civic life is of less interest in its bearing on the
future than in its relation to the past; in the story of the
great towns of the Middle Ages we may see how closely
history sometimes repeats itself[1]; for many purposes, their
glory and their decay serve to illustrate the description that
has been already given of the city-states of ancient Greece;
and there was little in mediaeval town life that was a really
new contribution[2] to the economic progress of the world. The
rivalries of different cities and the ineffectiveness of experiments in confederation were causes of weakness in Germany
and Italy as they had been in the Greek lands. In the fifteenth
century the two former countries were far ahead of the rest
of Western Europe industrially and commercially, and both
had declined relatively, and perhaps absolutely, at the opening
of the nineteenth. They had retained the old political form
of the city-state, and this was not well adapted to guide and
control new experiments in trade; all their economic institutions were devised with the object of giving each merchant a
fair share of the opportunities afforded by a well-known and
limited market, and not with the view of obtaining access to
new regions and ousting rivals by successful competition.
Industrial progress had been restricted to suit the traditional
policy of exclusive communities, and had not such free scope
as it enjoyed in territories where the course of development was
determined by the larger ambitions and the systematic policy
of kings and their advisers. As we look back we may see
that its ability to attain to national unity was the question of

[1] Since history never repeats itself exactly, there is no law of uniformity
in history as there is in physical nature, and generalisations can never be
stated in a rigid form. Where there is a strong similarity, however,
between the institutions in two distinct periods or places, the comparison of
the minor differences throws much light on the special character of each.

[2] The high development of the gild system in mediaeval towns as
compared with those of ancient Greece in their best days, is an important
difference.

supreme importance in the fifteenth century[1], so far as the immediate economic future of each country was concerned. By a curious irony those very countries, where the most noticeable mercantile success had been secured on the old lines were least ready to adapt themselves to the new conditions; and the very greatness and independence of the cities of Germany and Italy were obstacles to further progress.

III. · The welding of different areas of Christendom into large countries, each of which was a single eco- nomic whole, was a consummation of the highest importance; it would be most interesting in this connection to try to trace out the various in- fluences which led to the consolidation of peoples and the rise of nationalities[2]. Military necessities were often an important factor. In some cases, as in Spain, the growth of national unity seems to have been principally due to the pressure of a common enemy; the conquest of Granada added to the prestige of Ferdinand and Isabella, and strengthened the ties by which Castile and Aragon were held together. The seven provinces of Holland were forced into union under similar pressure, and common dangers have sufficed to fuse the varied population of Switzerland into a republican nation. In France the Crown proved to be the centre round which the patriotic sentiment, which resented the English domination, was able to rally. But besides these conscious antagonisms there were other factors which served to strengthen the monarchs who were beginning to exercise a large measure of independent power in their several territories and to mould the separate

The Rise of Nationalities— the Influence of Roman Law.

[1] Ehrenberg, *Hamburg und England*, pp. 12, 35.

[2] The insular position and physical conditions of England, and the administrative ability of her kings, had enabled her to attain to national unity at a very early time. Though her industry was far behind that of the other countries of Europe in the fifteenth century, she had developed national political institutions which enabled her to take full advantage of the opportunities that eventually came within her reach. Cunningham and MacArthur, *Outlines of English Industrial History*, p. 23.

portions of Christendom into well-administered polities. No constructive influence was more important than that which was due to the revived study of Roman Law, for this helped to determine the character of the new civil authority that was absorbing those duties of government which ecclesiastical institutions could no longer successfully discharge. Roman jurisprudence was the characteristic product of the Roman mind; its influence on the economic life of the modern world is the debt we owe to Rome herself, as distinguished from other civilisations of the past.

The revival of the study of Roman Law in the thirteenth century had an extraordinary influence on the political and consequently on the economic growth of modern Europe. Civil law proved an important destructive agent, so far as the organisation of mediaeval Christendom was concerned, for its introduction aided in the process of secularisation by calling forth a class of civilians and temporal lawyers who could supersede the canonists[1]. The canonists had practically acknowledged the supremacy of the *corpus juris civilis* from which so much of their doctrine was borrowed[2]; and justice could be better administered in the civil than in the ecclesiastical courts in those cases in which there were competing claims to jurisdiction. Throughout the greater part of Europe its triumph over badly codified customs was complete; and Civil Law exercised an extraordinary influence in the moulding of thoughts and habits during the period of transition when the mediaeval was giving place to the modern.

The re-introduction of Civil Law not only cleared the ground but distinctly told in favour of economic progress. The Church had established respect for property in barbarous times, and had thus laid the foundation on which all civilised society

[1] The increase of the towns in wealth supplied social conditions in which the pursuit of this study became possible and advantageous. Savigny, *Geschichte des römischen Rechts im Mittelalter* (1834), III. 84.

[2] Adams, *Civilisation in Middle Ages*, 36.

rests ; and the Roman Law with its distinctions facilitated the
discussion and decision of titles to property, and provided the
means of defining and enforcing contracts. In some cases
where the principles of the two systems were in conflict, there
was a distinct advantage in the eventual triumph of the older
code ; for its conceptions[1] were in accordance with the money
economy which was coming into vogue, and gave the means of
thinking clearly about the new problems which the introduction
of capitalism into industry and commerce was bringing to the
front. The Law Merchant of the Middle Ages had been
almost entirely derived from Roman sources ; and as the
sphere of ecclesiastical jurisdiction became more restricted,
the tone of commercial morality embodied in the Civil Code
came to be more generally adopted. Canon Law had condemned usury in a fashion that found little support in the
legislation of Justinian ; the influence of the Christian system
had doubtless been most beneficial during the transition from
natural to money economy[2], but the restrictions which ecclesiastical jurisprudence imposed on the conduct of business
between wealthy merchants appeared to have no real justification, and a little ingenuity served to set them aside[3]. The
ordinary conscience of the plain man was clear that the
lending of money at moderate interest was often fair and
convenient to all parties in the mercantile community, and
that only excessive gains were to be condemned as extortionate. This was the attitude of the Civil Code upon the
subject, and the fact that merchants and financiers could
appeal to such an authority in defence of their conduct must
have done much to remove the ancient prejudice against

[1] Lamprecht, *Zum Verständniss der wirthschaftlichen und socialen
Wandlungen in Deutschland vom 14. zum 16. Jahrhundert*, in *Z. f. Social-
und Wirthschaftsgeschichte*, I. 247.
[2] See below, p. 167.
[3] Ashley on the Contractus Trinus, *Introduction to Economic History*,
I. ii. 440.

traders as a class, and to enable them to maintain their status and dignity as men who were engaged in an honourable calling.

Even more important with regard to subsequent progress than these direct effects on economic life was the influence of Roman Law on the growth of monarchies. Such a maxim as *Quod principi placuit legis habet vigorem* tended to render the rising civil powers the "centre and source of the whole institutional life of the state[1]," as the Emperor had been in ancient Rome. It implied an absolutist ideal; and the administrators who were steeped in its influence, consciously or unconsciously, brought their ideas to bear in curtailing old privileges and in shaping new institutions. There is no country in Western Europe where the legal system was unaffected by the Civil Law; but its influence on the political life of a nation is most clearly seen in France, where it helped to build up a typical example of magnificent kingly power and state. The effects of Roman jurisprudence may be traced in the characteristic weakness as well as in the unique greatness of the *ancien régime*.

112. When the Hundred Years' War had come to an end, and France had rest for a time from the troubles that distracted her, strong and wise government was greatly needed for the sake of restoring social order and encouraging the agricultural, industrial and commercial activities which seemed to be almost extinct. France was fortunate in coming under the rule of kings who threw themselves energetically into the task. Charles VII and Louis XI were able to bring back comparative prosperity to France as a whole. They called her into being as a nation with an economic life directed and inspired by the monarch and his advisers; the congeries of separate cities and provinces was, for many commercial purposes, welded together into one country. On the other hand, the success of these monarchs in creating material prosperity

The French Monarchy and Bourgeois Interests.

---

[1] Adams, *Civilisation*, 326.

anew, reacted on the position of the Crown; the institution of a permanent *taille*[1] supplied a regular revenue which enabled the kings to maintain a well-disciplined standing army and freed France from frequent pillage by unpaid mercenaries.   This greatly augmented the royal power; and it also brought home to the kings the direct gain which accrued to them personally from fostering the material prosperity of the trading classes in the community and thus providing an ample fund from which taxation could be drawn.

In reorganising finance Charles VII was fortunate to be able to rely on the service of Jacques Coeur, a man who had a remarkable genius for making the most of the opportunities that were left to his unhappy country.   The district round Bourges, of which he was a native, had suffered less than the rest of France from the wars; and he was able to give new life to its struggling woollen manufactures.   At the same time he succeeded in taking up the threads of the old trading connections on the Mediterranean; Montpellier[2] became the principal centre of his operations, and attained to great importance till it was superseded by Marseilles. Jacques Coeur had visited the principal marts of the East; he obtained papal permission to trade with Mohammedans, and he was able to settle his factors in the towns of Syria and Egypt[3].   His achievements were astonishing, even though his success was short lived; as the concessions he enjoyed were personal to himself the trade he had established seems to have declined at his death.   He forms, however, an interesting link between the earlier prosperity of Septimania and the later commercial ambitions of the French monarchy.

When viewed, not as a trader but as a financier, Jacques Coeur may be regarded as typical of a class of native merchants who assisted European monarchs in fiscal organisation;

---

[1] De Nervo, *Les Finances françaises*, I. 93.

[2] Germain, *Histoire du commerce de Montpellier*, II. 25.

[3] Pigeonneau, *op. cit.*, I. p. 373.

the advances he made enabled Charles VII to recover Normandy[1], Gascony, and Guienne. The transition to money economy in affairs of state had become complete; and the merchants had silver in their chests with which they could trade, but which they might be prevailed on to lend; they were the men whose knowledge of business enabled them to suggest expedients for raising money, to superintend the process of collecting it, and to make temporary loans to their royal masters. The practical alliance of the crowned heads of Europe and their wealthy subjects was profitable to both; the kings were furnished with the resources they needed without being forced to accumulate treasure and keep money lying idle; while the capitalists obtained trading privileges or mining concessions. Jacques Coeur was the most eminent of the merchant princes of his day; the rapidity of his rise and the extraordinary wealth which he accumulated seem to have aroused the jealousy of less faithful servants of the Crown, and he was treated with base ingratitude by his master[2]. He was the most prominent figure in the finance of the times; and since his day the political power of the banking interest has been constantly felt. The city of Lyons seems to have been for a time the principal scene of their operations[3]; and the great capitalists of Augsburg and the Hanse towns were able to exercise an important influence on the political action of the princes from the fact that they could come to the royal support at critical moments[4].

The revival of French prosperity began in the time of Charles VII, when a great deal was done to improve internal

---

[1] Clément, *Jacques Coeur et Charles VII*, 131.

[2] It is interesting to compare and to contrast the career of the great English merchant-prince of the century—William Canynges of Bristol. Pryce, *The Canynges Family*.

[3] Endemann, *Studien in der Romanisch-Kanonistischen Wirthschafts- und Rechtslehre*, I. 158, and Ehrenberg, *Das Zeitalter der Fugger*, II. 72.

[4] Compare the Fuggers and Charles V, Ehrenberg, *op. cit.* I. 142, 152. The Hansards and Edward IV, R. Pauli in *Hansische Geschichtsblätter* (1875), 75 fol.

communications; he freed the country from brigandage and abolished the exorbitant tolls which had been exacted on the rivers. The work thus begun was carried on by his son Louis XI, who selected his counsellors largely from the commercial classes, and incurred much unpopularity with the noblesse by the attention which he gave to bourgeois interests[1]. Not that he was altogether popular with those whom he befriended; local privileges—like those of the companies of merchants of Paris and Rouen on the Seine—might have to be set aside in the interest of the monarchy as a whole. In the industrial corporations the king claimed the right of nominating members on special conditions[2]; and thus these bodies, which had assumed a new importance with the revival of trade, were brought into direct subjection to royal authority. The organisation of a customs' department was necessary as a fiscal measure; but it caused considerable annoyance to traders. In spite of these difficulties, Louis XI succeeded in developing industrial activities and in consolidating the realm, so that it enjoyed a rapid increase in material prosperity during the peaceful days of Anne of France and Charles VIII. Thus the foundations of the French monarchy—as a centralised economic whole—were laid in the fifteenth century, though there was to be bitter humiliation and disastrous internal strife before Henry IV obtained the reins of power, and Sully and Colbert were able to continue the systematic development of the country.

113. The disruption of Christendom had proceeded some way before the Reformation and the struggle which Luther inaugurated by his defiance of the Pope. The practical proof of the breaking up of the old system lies in the appearance of new polities in its place. As early as the fourteenth and

The Nation as the Unit of Economic Organisation.

---

[1] Pigeonneau, *op. cit.* I. 397.

[2] Levasseur, I. 438. On the corresponding movement for nationalising the municipal gilds in England, compare *Growth of Industry*, I. 436.

fifteenth centuries we see traces of the rise of nationalities, and this change is of unique importance ; we now find something that is characteristic of the modern as distinguished from the ancient world, something that is economically new. The social forms of the household and the city have been found in all ages, since the days of Greek colonisation. Though there had been great states such as the military empires of Alexander and Augustus these were merely held together by force of arms, and the civilisation of these territories was concentrated in the various cities which had been preserved within their limits and survived their fall. The era of industrial prosperity that opened with the Crusades still took the old forms, and Christendom was planted with new and flourishing cities ; but modern times were to witness the relative decay of city institutions. Material welfare was henceforward to be sought for and organised with reference to wider territories, and account was to be taken of the development of the resources and the industry of each country as a whole ; we have come upon a new unit of economic organisation.

A country has been defined for economic purposes as a territory through which there is a free flow of labour and capital ; and this will at least serve to point the contrast between the city life of the Middle Ages, with its effort to maintain the exclusive privileges of each locality, and the broader life of modern times in which industry and commerce are organised, not for the profit of a particular place, but with a view to developing the resources of the whole country and promoting national progress. The definition helps us to note the material conditions which were necessary for carrying out a national economic policy ; unless a considerable amount of capital was available, it was impossible to develop the industrial capabilities of large areas ; and so long as natural economy held good in rural districts there could not be a free flow of labour.

The mediaeval and ancient worlds have been compared and

contrasted above [1]; there were similar types of industrial and commercial organisation in each, but there was a difference of spirit and a difference of moral character between the two. The contrast of the ancient or the mediaeval with the modern world is somewhat different, since the latter is characterised by the prevalence of a new basis of economic regulation and as a consequence by a broader commercial policy directed to national and not merely to civic purposes. The nation was not, of course, an entirely new creation in the later Middle Ages, but it was a most important variant of an old political form ; the terms 'state' and 'polity' may be applied to cities as well as to nations, but the requirements and opportunities of the larger communities are very different, and the process of taking over and applying to the wider areas the best that had been developed in the experience of city life was no small undertaking. The fourteenth and fifteenth centuries were a period of increasing secular activity, and during this time old institutions and administrative machinery were being utilised for national objects. The nationalising of civic regulation is the new economic departure of the fifteenth and sixteenth centuries.

The Roman Empire had preserved for a time the great municipalities as integral elements ; in its declining days they were ruthlessly exploited in the interests of the imperial government ; the wealth of the richest citizens was the object of deliberate attacks. Modern governments have not shown the same jealousy of the well-to-do ; since rulers began to realise that their own power could be increased through the wealth of the people. The Crown was consciously dependent for occasional supplies on the great merchants ; it was not unnatural for princes to consult the opinion of financiers as to national welfare, and to give effect to their views as to the best economic policy for the country as a whole. Money was essential for the glory of the monarch, and he gradually

[1] See above, p. 7.

learned that he could not obtain it regularly and permanently unless it flowed steadily into the coffers of the people[1]. Commerce thus came to be a recognised object, not only of local but of national importance; and attention to public resources was also nationalised. The food supply had been a mere matter of civic[2] and municipal interest in ancient times, while in the modern world the development of agriculture has been taken up in a broader spirit as a national interest. The regulation of industry both in France and in England underwent a similar revolution; what had been special to privileged towns and locally established in particular districts, was organised as a general policy; gild regulations became embodied in Acts of Parliament which applied to all places alike; the resources and requirements of the whole realm were carefully considered with the view of introducing new industries. In the ancient world we have seen the planting of towns, and subsequently the despoiling of towns in military and imperial interests; but the development of the modern world has not been so much confined to urban communities on the one hand, nor has it taken place at the expense of towns on the other; it has been guided by the larger conception of national wealth.

In the succeeding chapters we shall be chiefly concerned with the growth and working of national economic policy, and national economic rivalries. This new economic type came into being partly at least as a result of the religious and political changes which brought about the disruption of Christendom and gave rise to national polities. As we look back on the destruction of the old system and the consolidation of modern realms, it is not easy to analyse all the elements that have contributed to the new social form. Community of race is usually the foundation of nationality, and the structure

---

[1] *Discourse of Commonweal*, edited by E. Lamond, p. 35.

[2] The difficulty that was felt was that of catering for Athens or Rome, there was no question of the food supply of Greece or Italy as a whole.

may be compacted by the use of a common language, and experience of a common history, though men of diverse blood have been knit together by the influence of one government enforcing the same fiscal system and administering one code of laws. Another unifying element which was of primary importance in the sixteenth century was that of similar religion; the princes, as sovereigns, sought to enforce a uniformity of religious belief and practice within the realms over which they ruled. So far as the economic side of national life is concerned, nothing has been so important as the existence of a natural boundary to mark out a common country, with the consequent interaction of the different material interests which may cooperate so as to develop the resources and power of the whole polity. Each of these separate factors had played its part in the growth of national life and institutions; and at the beginning of the sixteenth century the geographical discoveries opened up vast fields for national rivalry and political ambition. The rising nationalities were brought face to face as conscious antagonists; the East Indies and America disclosed to the monarchs of Europe a vision of new worlds to conquer. The social system of Christendom was falling to pieces, but European civilisation was not decaying, it was only being transformed. Fresh ideals were taking the place of old ones and were proving attractive, at a time when there were new facilities and opportunities for realising them; the vigorous life which was thus springing up was able to supersede merely local interests, and gave rise to powerful and far-reaching commercial institutions.

CHAPTER II.

THE INTERVENTION OF CAPITAL.

114. THE breaking up of a complex civilisation like that

Capital and its necessary Conditions.

of mediaeval Christendom and the transition to the modern world involved so many and such great changes, that we can only appreciate their character and importance when we look in turn at different aspects of this revolution. From the religious standpoint, we have seen an increasing secularisation; from the political point of view, we have noted the beginnings of the rise of nationalities; and the economic factors which were at work in connection with both of these movements have been indicated. It is important, however, to look more closely at the special economic feature of this period of transition, and to note the gradual and increasing intervention of capital. In dealing with the Christendom of earlier ages we have found it unnecessary to take account of capital, for—as we understand the term in modern times,—it hardly existed at all. In the fourteenth and fifteenth centuries we may notice it emerging from obscurity, and beginning to occupy one point of vantage after another, until it came to be a great political power in the State. It served too, as an instrument for facilitating the development of commerce, of industry and of agriculture in the territories of European nations, and also for effecting the colonisation of the newly discovered lands. When we come to trace the later developments of modern industry, we shall see the enormous power which it has eventually secured.

We cannot attempt to give accurate dates or even assign definite limits to such changes as the progress of secularisation, and the rise of nationalities; it has only been possible to explain in part why corresponding political movements occurred at different times in different countries. It would be still more hopeless to try to treat the intervention of capital as an event which happened at a particular epoch, or a stride which was taken within a given period. It is a tendency which has been spreading with more or less rapidity for centuries, first in one trade and then in another, in progressive countries. We cannot date such a transformation even in one land; for though we find traces of capitalism so soon as natural economy was ceasing to be dominant in any department of English life[1], its influence in reorganising the staple industry of this country was still being strenuously opposed at the beginning of the present century[2]. The revolution— for this has been a real revolution—which came about so gradually in our own island, has run a different course in other lands; there has been no regular series of steps in the march of capitalistic progress. We may, however, hope to get some clear ideas of the nature of the fundamental changes which have been brought about by the intervention of capital, if we are content to note some of the most striking manifestations of this force, as it affected national policy and aided in the development of national economic life.

[1] The collection of the revenue was being organised on a money basis in the Norman and Angevin reigns, and there was scope for the operation of capitalists in farming the revenue and lending money to those who were not ready to meet the calls made upon them.

[2] The agitation of the Yorkshire weavers against the abolition of compulsory apprenticeship was due to conscious hostility to the capitalist organisation of the weaving industry. *Growth of English Industry*, II. 455.

We have already noticed the partial persistence of natural economy in the later Middle Ages; with the era of the Crusades, however, there was a rapid extension of money economy, and therefore a general introduction of those con-ditions under which the formation of capital and the em-ployment of credit became possible. Under natural economy they cannot exist; there may, of course, be accumulations of wealth, stores of many kinds and stock for carrying on industry; but capital, properly so-called, implies the existence of a fund of money[1] which can be utilised in any direction and transported with comparative ease from place to place. In modern business parlance, 'capital' is regarded as es-sentially fluid[2]; and but for the existence of money, wealth could not have this character. Similarly, commercial credit only comes into being when men have wealth that can be readily realised in money, so that they can be trusted to have the means of meeting their liabilities at a definite date[3]. 'Capital' and 'credit' have their analogues under a natural economy in stock in trade, and the reputation of being rich; but these terms are essentially, as we know them in modern times, 'historical categories,' since they only become applicable in so far as money economy has asserted itself as the order of the day.

So far as town life is concerned, we cannot go back to any period when money economy was not dominant, and we find signs of capitalism and its influence in the cities from very early times. Merchants who carried on active trade appear to have been provided with ready money for their transactions. Though a great part of the industrial population consisted of independent workmen organised in craft gilds, the principal companies of many towns in the fourteenth century were

[1] *Modern Civilisation*, 125.

[2] Capital may of course be 'sunk' in land or 'fixed' in other forms; the statement in the text refers to its nature rather than its applications.

[3] *Modern Civilisation*, 44.

composed of capitalists; both in Strassburg[1] and in Florence[2] the manufacture of cloth was organised on capitalist lines by great captains of industry in the fourteenth century. Even in the most advanced towns, however, there were considerable hindrances which interfered with the free play of capitalist enterprise; each merchant was restricted to one special trade, and was prevented from encroaching on the callings of his fellow-townsmen; there was little opportunity for the transference of capital from one employment to another. Most of the industrial arts, too, were organised with regard to the requirements of the city market by small independent masters, who each hoped to get a fair share of existing trade rather than to extend it; the regulations of their craft gilds were not favourable to the formation or application of capital. Similar obstacles existed in the rural districts, though they were gradually breaking down on all sides, so that there were steadily increasing opportunities for the investment of capital during the fourteenth and fifteenth centuries.

115. Capital was not, of course, a wholly new thing, since it had been familiar enough in the ancient world; but many of its applications were being introduced afresh into Christendom. The Mediterranean lands had undergone the transition from natural to money economy and had come under the dominance of capital in ancient times. We have seen something of the oppression which was exercised by moneyed men under the Roman Republic, and of the grievances to

Favourable Conditions for Minimising its possible Evils.

[1] Schmoller, *Die Strassburger Tucher u. Weberzünfte*, p. 500.
[2] The *Arte di Calimala* was engaged in importing and dressing and dyeing foreign cloth—a business which obviously required capital. The *Arte della Lana* arose later; its prosperity dates from the settlement of the religious order—the Umiliati—who had acquired the art in Flanders and prosecuted it with great success. In 1338 there were 200 shops in Florence, employing 30,000 workmen: so that this industry was apparently also organised on capitalist lines. E. Dixon, *Florentine Wool Trade* in *Transactions of Royal Hist. Soc.* XII. 169.

which they were subjected under the Empire. We should never shut our eyes to the dangers which are inherent in money economy and the capitalistic organisatior of society; but it is important to notice that at the time when this system was beginning to reappear in Western Europe there were tendencies at work which served to set limits to its influence and to minimise the evils it involved.

Powerful as capital is, and great as are the advantages which it has to offer, the conditions of life in the fourteenth and fifteenth centuries were so unfavourable to it as to delay its introduction and to check its operations. The whole social system stood in its way; for the organisation of much of the labour in the towns was so rigid as to admit of little modification, while in the rural districts the survival of villeinage presented still greater obstacles to the enterprise of moneyed men. Astriction to one place is perfectly congruent with natural economy; the mediaeval landowner was satisfied to employ, as best he could, the labour which he found available, and was able to retain it under his control. With the capitalist, the case is different; he possesses wealth which he can direct to any profitable undertaking that opens up, and he has the means of compelling or attracting labour to follow in the direction where his enterprise sees the probability of reward. So long as slavery was in vogue, the transference of labour could be effected in the most ruthless fashion by the purchase and export of slaves; but this was no longer possible at the epoch when capital began to take part in the industrial development of mediaeval Europe; slavery had ceased to exist[1]; labour tended to follow capital because it was attracted, not because it was forced. In the fourteenth century the labourer had obtained such freedom that he was able to bargain for higher wages, and to insist on obtaining them. The craft gilds conferred a recognised status on skilled artisans[2]

[1] For some exceptions see above, p. 136.

[2] Lamprecht, *Deutsche Geschichte*, IV. 189.

and defined a standard of comfort which helped to determine the workman's demands; they also set an example for the occasional or permanent organisations by which the labourers of lower grades tried to give effect to their ideas[1]. That capital, when unfettered, could be quite as oppressive as in the old days, was shown by the reappearance of slave industry in the New World, and at a later date by the degradation of labour under the stress of the Industrial Revolution. But on the whole it is true that the labourer had attained to such a status in Christendom that the organisation of agriculture and industry on a capitalistic basis could proceed on sound lines, and did not prove unfavourable to the material and social well-being of the working class. Capital has been a disintegrating force and has broken down the astriction of the serf to the soil, and the restriction of the artisan to the narrow limits imposed by the gild, but its action was restrained until they were capable of facing the new conditions. Capital has not crushed the individual workman as a man, or forced him into the degraded and helpless position of the labourer in the old world.

Whilst the organisation of labour both in town and country limited the field for the application of capital to industry, the current sentiment on usury laid down practical restrictions which favoured the development of a healthy system of borrowing. In all ages of the world's history, there has been a temptation for the moneyed man to take advantage of the occasional necessities of his poorer neighbours and to lend money on exorbitant terms; in every period of transition from natural to money economy there is especial danger that this evil may arise, as it has commonly done[2] in connection with the collection of a money revenue. Christian sentiment had set itself against the extortion of usurers, for this had been

---

[1] On journeymen's gilds on the Continent see Schanz, *Zur Geschichte der deutschen Gesellen-Verbände*, 26; in England, Webb, *History of Trades Unionism*, 2—11.

[2] Vol. I. 47, 128, 187.

one of the most blatant evils of the later Empire, but it had recognised as legitimate two distinct methods—apart from partnerships in commercial business[1]—in which capital might be temporarily transferred to a borrower. No objection was taken to the conduct of those who tried to buy a *rent-charge*, and thus to secure an income in perpetuity by sinking money in a definite estate. The return of the principal thus invested could only be obtained by reselling the rent-charge; the man who entered into this agreement parted with his capital and obtained the right to enjoy a regular income. It was also regarded as permissible to lend capital for a definite time on a pledge, such as the Crown jewels, or the anticipated receipts from a tax; this secured the repayment of the principal at the date assigned, but was only supposed to ensure the return of the exact sum lent. Doubtless there was much evasion of the prohibitions against usury in actual life, but the fact remains that borrowing was chiefly done by wealthy bodies like towns, or by princes, for public purposes, and not by the cultivators of the soil. The peasantry continued to pay their quotas of taxation in kind or in service; while the princes had recourse to moneyed men to advance current coin which should enable them to anticipate or to realise their wealth. It was not the poor taxpayers so much as the authority who levied the tax, that had recourse to the money-lenders. The sale of rents or pledging of property gave a town[2] or a prince the temporary command of a large sum of money; and the system which was developed for public convenience came, as capital grew more abundant, to be gradually introduced into private affairs as well. At all events the chief economic contrast between the later Empire and the later Middle Ages may almost be

[1] It was always permissible to enter into partnership in risks and profits, but the opportunities of doing so were rare. Ashley, *Introduction to English Economic History and Theory*, I. i. 155.

[2] Schönberg, *Finanzverhältnisse der Stadt Basel im xiv. und xv. Jahrhundert*, 90.

summed up in the fact, that the Byzantine statesmen devised expedients for despoiling the wealthy, while modern potentates were reduced to borrowing from them.

The fact that capitalistic intervention in finance took this less oppressive form, was not only important so far as the peasantry[1] were concerned, but it also had a most favourable bearing on other monetary conditions. The gold paid by the industrial and mercantile classes to the Roman emperors was sunk in buildings or expended in wars on distant frontiers ; it was usually withdrawn from circulation in the district where it had been collected. On the other hand the money borrowed by princes from mediaeval bankers had to be repaid ; it was not wholly sunk, and it was not merely dissipated ; it was returned after a time into circulation and might be used as capital in industry or commerce. Hence the princely expenditure of the later Middle Ages did not prove as exhausting as that of the later Empire had been. In the fourth century the State was the oppressor of the men of enterprise and resource ; in the fourteenth it was becoming apparent that the interests of the monarchy and the moneyed men were the same in the long run ; government had on the whole to be conducted on principles that had the approval of financiers, and kings were learning that honesty in the repayment of loans was the best policy.

Beneficial changes of many kinds resulted from this practical alliance between the princes and the capitalists and from the pressure which moneyed men could bring to bear on government. Their influence was felt most advantageously in connection with the circulating medium. The kings of Europe, like the emperors of Rome, had yielded to the temptation to snatch a temporary gain by debasing the coinage ; and it was not always possible to demonstrate the dishonesty and inexpediency of the step in a convincing fashion. But the real

---

[1] That the *incidence* of taxation in France was such as to burden the peasantry specially, is another matter.

inconvenience became apparent when it was necessary to repay large loans, especially if these loans had been negotiated by foreign capitalists who had stipulated as to the coin they would receive. The difficulty of contracting new loans, had a similarly educative effect; it convinced the monarchs of the fifteenth century that it was wise to pay their debts and thus to maintain their credit.

The evils of the transition were thus minimised, owing to the restricted and gradual manner in which the power of capital, with its influence on social organisation, was brought into play; and it must be borne in mind that the introduction of the new system under proper limitations was advantageous to society and to individuals of every class. In Athens, the existence of money economy had rendered true political life possible, by conferring on the individual, freedom in the management of his *time*. In the modern world the prevalence of money and capital has encouraged and facilitated freedom of movement from *place to place*; it has thereby had a disintegrating effect on many institutions, but it has tended to promote a form of personal liberty which is highly prized in the present day. The feudal system implied the existence of local restrictions and responsibilities, and the feudal armies were based on local obligations, till capitalists were able to relieve the pressure of military obligations by providing better armies of soldiers habituated to constant fighting and drawn from distant regions. Industry had been controlled by local organisations, with exclusive privileges and special powers of supervision; but at length capitalists were able to introduce new methods and processes under more effective supervision; and the localised gilds became an anachronism. The thoroughgoing introduction of money economy once again rendered personal freedom possible; and the change in later mediaeval times was not confined to the privileged citizens of great towns but also affected the peasantry and inhabitants of rural districts.

116.   The intervention of capital eventually brought about an entire reconstruction of the social system of Western Europe.   The conditions under which this occurred have been described in the preceding paragraphs and the character of the new order has been indicated in general terms.   It is worth while, however, to consider some aspects of the matter in greater detail, and to examine the new administrative and financial machinery which these fresh activities shaped for themselves as they gradually entered into political life.

The new finance in its bearing on Military and Political Organisation.

The military system of the early Middle Ages was organised on the lines that have been already described[1] in connection with the Empire of Charles.   Each political magnate maintained his own troops, and was responsible for bringing them into the field properly equipped and provisioned.   The commissariat was irregular or non-existent, and it might be hardly possible to retain an army in the field, or to continue siege operations at the critical moment in a campaign.   The slightness of the political ties between the feudatories and the Crown rendered it difficult to get soldiers together, and they were likely to disband so soon as the specified time for which they were bound to serve had elapsed.   Military operations carried on under such conditions were not only very ineffective but also extraordinarily expensive.   The withdrawal of the industrial population and the yeomen from their work must have been a serious interruption to the ordinary processes of production, while the undisciplined hosts were only too likely to provide for their necessities by plundering the country in which they were quartered or through which they passed[2].   The intervention of capitalists, who provided the means of hiring mercenary troops, and later of forming disciplined armies, rendered a better military organisation

---

[1] See above, p. 51.
[2] Cunningham, *Growth of English Industry and Commerce*, I. 455, n. 8; Levasseur, *Histoire des classes ouvrières*, I. 421.

possible and reduced the indirect evils caused by war so as to make it far less costly. In so far as any king became possessed of money, so that he could hire mercenary troops, he had a more efficient fighting instrument at command, and one on which he could rely so long as his money lasted. The Flemish[1], and later the Swiss mercenaries[2], were finer troops than the feudal levies, for they were habituated to constant fighting; not only were they better soldiers, but they were also more completely under control, so that the strategy of a campaign had a greater chance of being carried out as planned. These were military advantages, and the economic benefits to a country were quite as great; the mercenaries could be paid in money at a definite and known date; the raising of a feudal army had involved the disorganisation of ordinary industrial life, and an indefinite charge on the resources of the realm.

The benefits which accrued from the intervention of capital were apparent, not only during the conduct of a campaign, but in all the preparations that might be necessary for a war; capitalists rendered the collection of revenue, in so far as it was taken in money, more 'convenient' and less 'expensive[3].' The sale of offices, ecclesiastical and civil, is a cumbrous mode of obtaining supplies; the payment of the large sums which were occasionally demanded as feudal aids must have been very oppressive. The voting of parliamentary supplies introduced comparative 'certainty' into the system of taxation, as it enabled the landowners and merchants to know beforehand what they would have to pay. The action of the

[1] Cunningham, *Alien Immigrants*, 25; Oman, *A History of the Art of War* (*Middle Ages*) (1898), 374.

[2] The French frequently relied on Swiss help, and Lyons was found a convenient monetary centre for making the necessary payments to them. Ehrenberg, *Das Zeitalter der Fugger*, II. 72.

[3] Compare Adam Smith's maxims of taxation, *Wealth of Nations*, V. Chap. II. pt. 2.

great bankers rendered this practice convenient, not only to the taxpayers, but to the Crown. Financiers were ready to advance money on the security of supplies that were actually voted, and thus to provide the Crown with the use of large sums at short notice, and long before it would have been possible to collect the money.

When the advantages of the new method of military administration were once understood, no prince could afford to disregard them; all monarchs were compelled to rely on money as the sinews of war[1], and had frequent occasion to borrow in order to meet the exigencies of a campaign. The importance of a hoard of bullion had been recognised from time immemorial[2]; and the possession of the royal treasure, at any time of disputed succession, meant nine-tenths of the title to the Crown[3]. These hoards, like other forms of wealth, were subject to vicissitudes, however, and the accumulations of years might be rapidly dissipated or lost; the princes were compelled in such emergencies to turn to the Jews, Lombards, or others who afforded the means of replenishing the royal treasury at times when money was urgently needed. Great monarchs had not been particularly scrupulous in keeping faith with these creditors[4]; but in the fifteenth century they were forced to be more careful in regard to their engagements. An inter-civic money-market had been developed. The great city communities of the Middle Ages were frequent borrowers[5],

[1] Macchiavelli argued on the other side, that war could be rendered profitable, and should be pursued as the best means of obtaining treasure. There have been many cases where it has been successfully conducted on this principle; but it is none the less true that the accumulation of treasure is a necessary preparation for successful war. Ehrenberg, *op. cit.* I. 6—9.

[2] The Goths and other Teutonic peoples accumulated large treasures, but they seem to have employed it to gratify a taste for barbaric display, rather than as the basis of military power.

[3] The case of Henry I of England furnishes an illustration.

[4] Peruzzi, *Storia del Commercio e dei Banchieri di Firenze*, 461.

[5] Ehrenberg, *op. cit.* I. 19.

since they had need of money both for civic improvements, such as the repair of their walls[1], and also for military operations. As the security they offered was excellent, the terms on which they could obtain money were comparatively moderate. The monarchs of the day were forced to offer good security, too[2], in order to borrow at all; and they were compelled to repay the loans, if they wished to maintain their credit and be able to borrow again. The monarchies of Europe outstripped the civic communities as political powers, but the civic communities had forced the monarchs to accept mercantile methods and standards in the management of their finance.

As the rulers of Europe ceased to be primarily dependent on landed estates for their revenue, some interesting constitutional changes followed. In Spain, the government monopolies of commercial or mining rights tended to increase the wealth of the Crown without enriching the subjects, and afforded the firmest basis for an absolutism[3]. The establishment of a permanent *taille* in France gave the Crown an independent income, and rendered absolutism possible in that country as well. As the income of the Crown was derived from the taxation of the agricultural and industrial classes, it was essential that the people as well as the prince should be prosperous; hence the tendency of the French monarchy to the paternal regulation of industry with the view of rendering the country rich. In England the Crown's necessities continued to be the people's opportunities, and all attempts to exercise rule in disregard of the popular will were destined to failure. Not merely did the people as taxpayers succeed in enforcing their demands but there is reason to believe that the intermediaries who negotiated loans were also able to exercise

[1] Lamprecht, *Deutsche Geschichte*, IV. 212.

[2] Towns occasionally made themselves jointly responsible with the kings for royal debts. Ehrenberg, *op. cit.* I. 25.

[3] For this principle of state-craft compare Knies on *Macchiavelli als volkswirthschaftlicher Schriftsteller* in the *Zeitschrift f. d. gesammte Staatswissenschaft* (1852), 272.

considerable influence from time to time. The Fuggers, who supplied resources to Charles V, were in general sympathy with his aims; they were forced by their own embarrassments to refuse him further advances at a critical moment and to ruin his hopes, but they seem to have made no attempt to control his policy. In England, on the other hand, the great London financiers and other royal creditors appear to have aimed at directing the economic policy of the realm and to have been fairly successful in forcing their views upon the Crown. Large sums of money were borrowed from towns in their corporate capacity, and their representatives could make their wishes known in Parliament; from the time of Richard II onwards we can trace the existence in Parliament of a moneyed interest which gradually increased in influence till it at last succeeded in overbalancing the power of the landed gentry.

117. The financial magnates of the fifteenth and six-teenth centuries carried on business in a double capacity, as they not only engaged in lending money to the Crown, but were merchants as well. Their practice in this respect was of great importance, for it rendered their money-lending legitimate from the stand-point of the canonists. Christian moralists considered it fair that any man should be reimbursed for actual sacrifices incurred in making a loan; to take so much as this in return was not to extort money from another, but to guard oneself against a definite loss. Men like Jacques Coeur or William Canynges or the Fuggers and Welsers[1] would not let their money lie idle; and it was perfectly true that in lending it to the king they were depriving themselves of the opportunity of making commercial gain. It therefore came to be recognised that a lender might legitimately charge for *lucrum*

---

[1] These Augsburg capitalists speculated in all sorts of undertakings: silver mining in the Tyrol, copper in Hungary, quicksilver in Spain, colonisation in Venezuela, estate management in Spain, and commercial ventures. Häbler, *Geschichte der Fuggerschen Handlung in Spanien.*

cessans or *damnum emergens ;* and no serious effort could be made to prevent such capitalists from entering on transactions which were practically advancing money on interest. In older days it had been possible for canon lawyers to distinguish oppressive from fair bargains by the mere form of the contract, and to limit the transference of capital, from one business to another, to those cases where a temporary partnership was formed, and risks and losses were shared alike. When it came to be generally assumed that a man would usually get some gain by investing his money, and was therefore entitled to be compensated for merely refraining from using it himself, the old prohibitions ceased to apply and the negociation of loans came to be an everyday feature of commercial life.

In popular opinion, however, those merchants who devoted themselves to foreign banking and financial business, as contrasted with the commercial export and import of goods, were generally regarded as somewhat unscrupulous. It is difficult to tell how far the common accusations were justified, either in the case of the Italians, who were the foreign bankers of the fourteenth century, or of the magnates of Antwerp and Amsterdam in the sixteenth and seventeenth. Possibly these capitalists were strong enough to manipulate the exchanges in their own interests, but there was at any rate a semblance of competition which seems inconsistent with the existence of monopoly rates; even in the fourteenth century there were occasional concourses of merchants when the rates for foreign payments were settled by bargaining in a market. Organised money-markets were held at the great fairs of Champagne[1], Geneva[2], and Lyons[3]; and bills from many distant towns were drawn for a definite date on bankers at these fairs. The coin

[1] F. Bourquelot, *Études sur les foires de Champagne* in *Mémoires présentés à l'Académie des Inscriptions*, 2ᵐᵒ Série, v. (1865), Vol. II. p. 102.

[2] Borel, *Les foires de Genève*, p. 131—142.

[3] Huvelin, *Droit des Marchés et des Foires*, p. 564.

of each country was rated in terms of a standard unit (*scudi de marche*[1]), and money was bought or sold at this price. In so far as this represented the difference in the fineness of the coins respectively, the work of exchangers was of course recognised as necessary and useful business, which had to be attended to in the interests of the currency[2]. There must have been times, however, when the rates were affected by the supply and demand for bills on a particular country, and by the purchasing power of money in that country. From the standpoint of the mediaeval moralists there was much suspicion, to put it no more strongly, attaching to all such transactions; they held that silver was silver, and that for anyone to get advantage by exchanging silver for silver must somehow be unfair. Still these occasional money-markets existed; and though much unfair gain may have been made by unscrupulous men, the gradual development of regular markets and constant competition circumscribed the opportunities for exacting exorbitant rates in performing a real service. As a result of these changes in opinion, the most powerful restrictions which had checked the fluidity of capital were broken down; in the fifteenth century it had at last become possible to obtain the means of developing any promising undertaking.

118.   During the latter part of the fifteenth century many favourable openings at home and abroad were beginning to offer themselves to enterprising men; the exclusive privileges of aliens had been curtailed, and the active trade of France and of Holland[3], of Scandinavia and England[4], was

The influence of Capital in recasting commercial and industrial practice.

---

[1] Endemann, *op. cit.* I. 214.

[2] Cunningham, *Growth of English Industry and Commerce*, I. 362.

[3] Van Bruyssell, *Histoire du Commerce en Belgique*, II. 63.

[4] The importance of the English moneyed men is seen in the number of capitalist companies which were found towards the close of the fourteenth century; as well as in the assessments of merchants and the large loans advanced by the towns. Cunningham, *op. cit.* I. 381.

attracting native energy. The profits on successful ventures were large[1], and every new prospect of profit constituted a demand for capital. And the supply was forthcoming; hitherto prudent persons had been content to hoard their wealth[2]; so soon as they were persuaded to invest it in economical undertakings for the sake of gain, they were treating it as capital.

The best opportunities, of course, lay with those who had the good fortune to live on any of the lines of the world's trade. The Venetians enjoyed a supremacy in the Adriatic[3], and a leading position in the trade with the East by the Red Sea route; the German merchants, who crossed the passes and distributed the spices and other products of the East in the land beyond the Alps, found the connection most advantageous. The Genoese were able to carry on their trade with Constantinople and the Black Sea with little interruption, and the Florentines did a large business with the north coast of Africa. But all this commerce was dwarfed by the ocean voyages which became possible after the discovery of the Cape of Good Hope and of America; Lisbon superseded Venice, and the Netherland merchants, who had found the fishing trade a remunerative industry[4] and a good apprenticeship for seamen, took up the carrying trade between the Spanish Peninsula and Antwerp. This city, as a northern depot for Eastern produce, as well as the centre of a large trade in fish and in cereals, entered on a career of extraordinary prosperity in the sixteenth century.

The rate of mercantile profit was doubtless very large, but expenses were heavy too; many of the fairs, where traders of all nations had had unusual facilities for free intercourse, had declined before the close of the fourteenth

---

[1] The profits of Spanish merchants in the American trade are said to have been 300 or 400 per cent. Beer, *Geschichte des Welthandels*, II. 147.

[2] E. Dudley, *Tree of the Commonweal*, 52.

[3] Lenel, *Die Entstehung der Vorherrschaft Venedigs*, p. 82.

[4] Van Bruyssell, II. 119.

century¹, and business was gravitating more and more to towns which served as permanent, and not occasional, centres of trade. But to trade regularly in any town it was necessary to pay the requisite dues and obtain a definite status; the cost of obtaining such a standing was only lightened in the case of companies of merchants, like the merchants of the Hanse League, who had establishments of their own in London², Bruges³, Bergen⁴, Novgorod⁵, Venice⁶, and elsewhere, and who made rules which enabled them to share the advantages and the expense of maintaining their factories. The discipline was very strict, and their regulations were framed so as to ensure that no one man should monopolise the commerce, or encroach unduly on the trades of other people⁷.

This system, depending, as it did, on the maintenance of exclusive privileges, was inconsistent with that freedom for enterprise in pushing trade which is the life of modern commerce. Antwerp proved attractive to capitalists, not only because of its situation and connections, but because it permitted almost as much liberty to the men of all nations as they could have enjoyed in any fair. There were practically no special concessions, and hence it was possible for any merchant to trade there; but besides this, no objection was made at Antwerp to the practice of dealing on commission⁸. The freemen and privileged merchants of any

¹ Cunningham, *Alien Immigrants*, 91. Huvelin, *op. cit.* 278.
² Lappenberg, *Geschichte des Hansischen Stahlhofes zu London*, p. 6.
³ Stein, *Die Genossenschaft der deutschen Kaufleute zu Brügge*, p. 14.
⁴ Worms, *La ligue hanséatique*, 163.
⁵ Daenell, *Geschichte der deutschen Hanse*, 45.
⁶ Stieda, *Hansisch-Venetianische Handelsbeziehungen im 15 Jahrhundert*; see also Simonsfeld, *Der Fondaco dei Tedeschi in Venedig und die deutsch-venetianischen Handelsbeziehungen*, II. 69, 71. This establishment was chiefly frequented by South German merchants.
⁷ An excellent illustration of the policy is given by the Stint of the English Merchant Adventurers. Cunningham, *Growth of English Industry and Commerce*, I. 416.
⁸ Ehrenberg, *op. cit.* II. 6.

12—2

mediaeval city had been peculiarly careful to retain their exclusive advantages, and to prevent any broker from acting on behalf of an unfree trader ; each merchant dealt personally or through his own factors. But at Antwerp there was no reason for maintaining such limitations, and forms of business agency, which have become universal in the modern world, were first introduced in the city on the Scheldt. The great South German bankers fixed their principal establishments at this centre; they were attracted by the openings it offered and they helped to promote its prosperity. Merchants enjoyed far greater facilities for obtaining loans at low rates of interest, and for any period that might be desired, in the Antwerp money-market, than had been at all usual even in the fairs of Champagne and Lyons. Bruges[1] with its long-established reputation was unable to shake off the old commercial traditions, and was rapidly superseded by Antwerp, where business was conducted on the lines that were most convenient to enterprising capitalists.

As commercial intercourse revived and increased during the fourteenth and fifteenth centuries, it tended more and more to bring about a revolution in industrial life. Groups of small masters, each of whom was working on his own account though they were associated together for mutual supervision, were neither able nor willing to adapt themselves to new conditions[2]; and they were gradually superseded in the more important callings by capitalists who employed large numbers of journeymen. One craft after another was affected by the opportunities which the expansion of trade afforded, and artisans began, under the direction of merchants, to manufacture,

[1] Van Bruyssell, II. 232.

[2] Holland appears to offer an interesting exception, as the small independent masters held their own in all the old industries during the seventeenth century though newly-planted trades were organised on capitalist lines. Pringsheim, *Beiträge zur wirthschaftlichen Entwickelung der vereinigten Niederlande*, in Schmoller's *Forschungen*, X. iii, p. 30.

not merely with reference to the requirements of their neighbours and the demand in the city market, but with a view
to the possibilities of sale in distant places.   There were
some trades—such as the silk trade in Italy in the fifteenth
century—which were forced to rely on commercial intercourse
for a supply of the materials they employed; but whenever,
and from whatever reason any industry was drawn into the
circle of distant trading interests, there was a tendency in
favour of the introduction of capitalistic organisation.   Capitalist merchants were required as intermediaries to purchase
materials or to sell goods, and they easily slipped into the
position of capitalist employers who directed their workmen
and controlled the conditions and terms of labour.

The views of a capitalist employer of labour and those
of small independent masters would often differ as to
the rules which were beneficial in any trade.   The capitalist
would wish to be free to employ as many journeymen as he
liked, with such division of labour as was convenient, while
the small masters would object to an establishment which was
so organised as to engross a great part of the trade.   There
might also be differences about the training of apprentices
and the numbers in which they should be employed; the
capitalist policy diverged from that which was traditional in
the craft gilds.   In some cases, where the difficulty arose, the
wealthy members appear to have been strong enough to take
the control of the gild affairs into their own hands, and to
modify the institution till it became an oligarchical association
of capitalist employers; many of the *corps de métiers* in France
appear to have been thus transformed[1]; and bodies which had
been originally associations of small masters came to be practically identical in character with such a capitalist company

[1] H. Hauser, *Ouvriers du temps passé*, p. 119 fol.   Compare also for
Germany, Lamprecht, *Deutsche Geschichte*, v. 64.   A similar change of
character can be traced in the tailors of Bristol.   Fox, *Merchant Tailors of
Bristol*, 32, 86.

as the Arte di Calimala at Florence[1]. In other cases the
small masters were able to maintain the traditional policy,
and the capitalist employers preferred to migrate beyond the
range of gild authority. The restrictive regulations which the
crafts imposed on journeymen forced them to withdraw from
such old centres of trade as Worcester[2] and York to districts
where moneyed men were free to offer them better terms ;
particular towns were impoverished but the national industries
were fully maintained, and capitalists and wage-earners alike
benefited by the changes.

In this way it appears that capital afforded facilities for
inducing labourers to migrate, and thus helped to transplant
the arts of life and to open up undeveloped regions. In the
earlier times labour had been practically restricted to one
city or to one estate, and there had been great difficulty
in transferring it to places where it could be more advantageously employed. But capital solved this difficulty ; it gave
the means of introducing bodies of labourers and setting
them on work, so as to plant a new industry or to open up mines
and develop unused resources. Capital supplied the material
means of fostering the national wealth of any country, and of
thus giving effect to a progressive economic policy.

[1] See above, p. 94.
[2] Cunningham, *Growth of Industry*, I. 512, 518.

CHAPTER III.

RIVAL COMMERCIAL EMPIRES.

119. THE peoples of Western Europe at last secured direct access to the East through the persistent enterprise of the Portuguese; but this is only a small part of the debt we owe them. Their undaunted energy and heroic sacrifices overcame extraordinary difficulties and rendered it possible for European traders to establish a footing in the Indies, and to open up regular commercial communications with lands that had hitherto been inaccessible. *The Portuguese secure a footing in the East.*

The object of the Portuguese Crown in promoting the voyages of discovery had been clear enough; it was desirable to obtain a share in the Eastern commerce which enriched the Venetians through their trading allies, who monopolised the Red Sea route and the Persian Gulf. The active commerce of these seas was entirely in the hands of Arabs; they had settlements in many towns, and there was a considerable Mohammedan population at some of the ports[1]. The Arab merchants, whom Vasco de Gama and the other Portuguese captains encountered in Indian waters, were not inclined to brook any interference with their profitable monopoly. This mercantile and seafaring race were little more than aliens on the coasts of the Indian peninsula; but as they were long-established aliens they were able to rouse the Zamorin of Calicut into hostility

[1] Rowlandson, *Tohfut-ul-Mujahideen* (Oriental Translation Fund), 70.

towards the Frankish intruders.   The Portuguese had not attempted to found a factory there on their first visit (1498 A.D.), and when the experiment was made on their second voyage (1500 A.D.), it proved a disastrous failure ; for their representative and his associates were murdered as soon as the ships had left.   This was an offence which the Portuguese could not overlook, and it led to their first rupture with a native prince.

They thus learned that it was impossible for them to share in the trade of the Arabs, or to have factories side by side with Mohammedan merchants in the same port ; they could also count on a cordial reception in places where they were not thwarted by these commercial rivals.   The Nestorian Christians[1] were a considerable body, whose influence was favourable to men of their own faith ; and the Hindu princes were glad to find any power that could stay the progress of the Mohammedan races, which were encroaching by conquest on the north and carried on an exclusive commerce on the south.   Favoured by these circumstances, and by the divisions in the Mohammedan world[2] which prevented any united attack upon them till they were well established[3], the Portuguese were able to found commercial factories at Cochin (1501 A.D.) and Cannanore (1502 A.D.) on the Malabar coast.   They quickly attained such maritime superiority as to monopolise the trade of these towns, and vessels which were not protected by Portuguese permits[4] were destroyed.   Portugal thus began to enforce an effective sovereignty in the Indian Ocean.

In order, however, to control the spice trade with Europe, and to transfer this business from the Arabs and Venetians

[1] Beazely, *Portuguese Colonial Empire* in *Royal Hist. Trans.* (1894), VIII. 115, 116.

[2] H. Morse Stephens, *Albuquerque*, 77.

[3] Suliman organised such an attack soon after his accession in 1520. See Morse Stephens, *op. cit.* 177.

[4] Rowlandson, *Tohfut-ul-Mujahideen*, 90.

into Portuguese hands, it was necessary to obtain the command of the gates through which trade passed at Aden and the Persian Gulf. This had been a favourite scheme with King Emmanuel; and more than once the establishment and consolidation of the settlements in the East were sacrificed to fruitless efforts at closing the Red Sea route from Suez to the East[1]. The Portuguese first established themselves on Socotra (1507 A.D.), and eventually secured possession of Aden for a time (1517—1538 A.D.); but Albuquerque, with all his genius, had never been able to give full effect to his master's purpose. Still he was so far successful in hampering the Arabs in their Red Sea trade as to cause a serious diminution of the customs which passed into the hands of the Sultan of Egypt.

The Portuguese were more fortunate in their attempts to control the navigation of the Persian Gulf, through which access could be obtained to the Euphrates valley and the caravan routes to the Levant. They obtained permission to establish a fortress at Ormuz and subsequently got possession of the entire city; they were in consequence able to claim a maritime authority over the whole of the trade of that region; coasting voyages were the usual method of communication, except during the Monsoon, and those who possessed this harbour could command the route[2].

The most simple, and at the same time the most efficacious method of obtaining the desired monopoly was to exercise a control over the spice trade at its source. All the commerce of the Spice Islands, as well as of the Far East, was concentrated at Malacca; and after establishing a factory at this point the Portuguese soon found a pretext for taking possession of the town. They were consequently able to regulate the supply of pepper and nutmeg in their own interests; while this commercial depôt gave them a basis from which they could

[1] H. Morse Stephens, *op. cit.* 94.
[2] Compare Vol. I. p. 63 on the spheres of Greek and Phoenician influence.

push their trading connections in China (1517 A.D.) and Japan (1542 A.D.)[1]. They thus laid the basis for the establishment of direct and regular commercial intercourse between Europe and the principal countries of Asia, and for nearly a century they succeeded in retaining as their own a monopoly of the trade they had wrested from the Arabs.

Almeida and many of the Portuguese would have been content to aim at making their sovereignty of the sea effective by maintaining a strong navy; they believed that this would give adequate security to the commercial factories which were planted at different points of the coast. But Albuquerque, the greatest of the Portuguese governors, was convinced that this policy was impracticable; he set himself to obtain so much land as would enable him to maintain self-sufficing stations which might serve as a basis for the operations of his ships. Without adequate territory it seemed to him impossible to keep up the efficiency of the fleet, so that it should be able to protect the factories from attack by land, and to over-power the naval expeditions that might be expected from Egypt. With this object he forced the hands of the home government, and established, not mere commercial factories, but garrisoned fortresses; he also obtained such concessions of tribute as might render the administration of the new empire self-supporting. The final conquest of Goa, and the organisation of a Portuguese Civil Service to take over the government of the territory, were the fruits of Albuquerque's unwearied efforts to develop the commercial empire of his master on a basis that he believed to be really sound, and to offer a prospect of permanence.

The Portuguese were engaged in a new undertaking; but the commercial intercourse which they established on the new route, very closely resembled that of the Venetians and Arabs whose profitable monopoly was now a thing of the past[2]. It

[1] Saalfeld, *Geschichte des portug. Kolonialwesens*, 104.

[2] Heyd, *op. cit.* II. 517.

was the practice of the Portuguese to send out a fleet to the
Indies once a year; the management of the undertaking was
in the hands of officials, though the merchants who sailed in
the ships were independent traders.   They had to pay customs
to the government, and certain articles were reserved as a
State monopoly[1]; though the organisation of the fleet had a
political and military character, the actual trading was a matter
of private enterprise[2].   In this we have a very close reproduction of the system that regulated the fleets of Venetian
galleys which traded in the Mediterranean[3].   It was also the
deliberate purpose of Albuquerque to substitute a Christian
for the Arab trading population which had carried on active
commerce in the Indian Ocean.   He took their capital Goa,
and used the lands which had belonged to mosques for the
endowment of Christian Churches and monasteries; and by
deliberately encouraging the marriage of Portuguese soldiers
with native women, and the growth of a Eurasian population,
he set himself, like Alexander, to bring about the fusion of
the East and West.   It was a bold line of policy, and one
which later rulers of India have scarcely dared to follow; it
certainly had its dangers; for the corruption of the administrative class, and weakening of the moral fibre of the
Portuguese is commonly associated with their adoption of

[1] Häbler, *Geschichte der Fuggerschen Handlung in Spanien*, 24.

[2] The merchants who travelled by the fleet were not necessarily
Portuguese, and Germans were allowed to fit out ships for the voyage.
F. Kunstmann, *Die Fahrt der ersten Deutschen nach dem portugiesischen
Indien*, p. 5.   Many interesting details will also be found in the *Tagebuch
des Lucas Rem*, edited by Greiff in the *Sechsundzwanzigster Jahres-Bericht
des historischen Kreis-Vereins im Regierungsbezirke von Schwaben und
Neuburg* (Augsburg, 1861), and in J. P. Cassell, *Privilegia und Hand-
lungsfreiheiten welche die Könige von Portugal ehedem den deutschen
Kaufleuten zu Lissabon ertheilet haben*.

[3] On the organisation of the Venetian fleets see Lenel, *op. cit.* 68.   On
the similar organisation of the Flanders galleys compare R. Brown, *State
Papers, Venetian*, I. pref. p. lxii.   For the Portuguese fleets see Saalfeld,
op. cit. 138.

Eastern habits. The attempts which were made by the In-
quisition to prevent the deterioration of Christian principle
by contact with heathen and Mohammedan peoples were
mischievous in other ways. The action of the Holy Office was
disastrous to the ancient Church of India, which was suspected
of heresy, while it was powerless to check the wrongs which
were wrought by greedy and irresponsible officials.

Even in the days of its greatest prosperity the commercial
empire of the Portuguese proved disappointing; it failed to
supply the streams of wealth which had been expected. The
reasons for this are obvious; such efforts had to be exerted to
maintain the political conditions, under which this trade had
become possible, that the energies of Portugal were exhausted,
and the profits of commerce did not repay the outlay. It is
marvellous that a nation of 3,000,000, and an army of 40,000,
should have sufficed to obtain a supremacy over the whole of
the Indian Ocean, and to secure a footing in Africa and in
Brazil as well; but when we read of the frightful loss of life in
each expedition, we cannot be surprised that the effective force
of the country was sapped in the course of such a gigantic
struggle.

It is to be noticed, too, that the enterprise of individual
citizens was diverted from fruitful industrial employments and
even from shipping; the Indian commerce, which centred at
Lisbon, did not react favourably on home industry or internal
trade, and the active work of distributing the Indian products
in Europe was done by alien merchants[1]. All those who

---

[1] "Nowe lett us goe to the good simple Portingall who full hongerly
for spices almost sales yeerely in compasse about 3 quarters of the world,
and when they have brought their spices home are not the riche purses of
Antwerp, the subjects of King Phillip ready to ingrose it into their handes
and oftentimes give money for it aforehand." *Epistle to the most noble
and illustrious Lordes Edzart and John, Earles of Estfrizland, Lordes of
Emden* (1564), f. 7. *Sloane MS.* 818, British Museum. The Hollanders
and Zeelanders did most of the shipping, especially after the fall of

wished to better their fortune sought for administrative posts, and many of the officials were tempted to try to advance their personal interests more quickly by a resort to unfair means. Eventually the administration became exceedingly corrupt and therefore very expensive; but even in its best days, the political outlay which was necessary for developing the trade absorbed all the profit to which the Portuguese rulers had so confidently looked forward.

It is also true that the economic policy of the Portuguese was not commercially sound; it depended to a large extent on their power to oust the Arabs and to secure a monopoly; they had few products or manufactures to export in exchange for Indian spices, and they were reluctant to send silver abroad. They might have succeeded by means of military power in extorting a tribute, but political changes at home upset their whole commercial system. After 1580 A.D. the fortunes of Portugal were linked to those of Spain, and the enemies of Spain attacked the trading factories of the Portuguese; these had no means of effective resistance, since their commerce had not been based on physical advantages but on political superiority.   When the Dutch were strong enough to defy the united forces of the Iberian peninsula they were easily able to direct the trade with the Indies into new channels, and thus they entered into the enjoyment of the possessions which the Portuguese had so hardly won.

Though the fruits of Portuguese enterprise were wrested from them so soon, we cannot but give a tribute of admiration to the men who had the heroism and enthusiasm to win their way against such odds as Albuquerque faced.   They were in a way heirs of the old crusading spirit, at least on its commercial side; they broke the Arab monopoly in the Indian Ocean and rendered it possible for that great peninsula to be brought into contact with Christendom.   They were less successful

Antwerp; though Danzic and the Baltic Hanse towns were keen competitors. Häbler, *op. cit.*, 174.

in Africa, and the Arab trader remains as one of the curses of that benighted land; but India and the Far East have been rescued from his exclusive domination. Though the principal motive was merely commercial, and as such one with which he would have had but little enthusiasm, the hopes of Prince Henry were at last accomplished; the flank of the advancing Crescent was turned, and the Moslem power was threatened at its very heart. Portugal was exhausted for the time[1] by the effort, but the world is a gainer in that she was ready to take the lead.

120.   There is a contrast in every particular between the

The Spaniards and Treasure.

history of the rise of the Spanish Colonial Empire and that of its neighbour in the Iberian Peninsula. The Portuguese obtained access to a highly civilised country, and sought to bring a profitable trade under their own control; the Spaniards secured a footing among barbarian and half-civilised peoples, who had made but little progress in the arts of life and had no organised trade. The Spaniards encountered no opposition in attempting to colonise southern and central America; they were perfectly free to deal with the country they had conquered as they pleased, and were able to give effect to their views as to the wisest use to make of their power and the best methods for utilising the resources of their new possessions. The decline and fall of their influence in these countries has demonstrated that the economic policy which the Spanish king and his advisers pursued was completely mistaken.

The mineral wealth of the new world seemed to open up

---

[1] The revival of the Portuguese power under the House of Braganza in the seventeenth century was undertaken on other lines. The colonising of Brazil had been deliberately neglected in the period of Portugal's greatest prosperity, and the efforts of the Marquis of Pombal to develop native industry in the eighteenth century may be regarded as an imitation of Henry IV and Colbert, or as an attempt to shake off the influence of England by copying English methods.

the prospect of accumulating such a vast treasure, that it
would enable the Spanish monarch to determine the destinies
of Europe. The realm which had been consolidated by the
marriage of Ferdinand and Isabella and the conquest of
Granada had ample resources of its own; in some parts the
soil was admirably cultivated, while there were also large areas
devoted to pasturage, and the native wool supplied ample
materials for an extensive manufacture of cloth. The long
wars against the Saracens seem, however, to have had disastrous effects both on the country and on the population; the
land had been rendered less fit for tillage[1], and the military
ardour of the people[2] distracted them from the drudgery
and comparative indignity of agricultural or industrial pursuits.
The conquest of the new world with its mineral treasures
was congenial to the national temperament. It was a task
calling for military prowess; and the rapid success of the
Spaniards raised the expectation that they would be able to
accumulate such masses of treasure that they would be irre-
sistible. Severe prohibitions were enacted to prevent the export of gold or silver from Spain, in the hope that other
nations, which were possible political rivals, might be precluded
from having a share in the mineral wealth that was annually
imported to Seville. This was the staple port where the India
House was established and all the trade was concentrated[3];
the galleons were loaded at Seville in August and September,
and then dropped down to Cadiz, where they waited for a
favourable wind; one armada accompanied the fleet, and
another cruised the seas, as far as the Azores, on the look-
out for pirates. On the return voyage the fleets bringing the
silver plate from Mexico and Peru were combined at Havana,

---

[1] Naudé, *Die Getreidehandelspolitik der europäischen Staaten*, 181.

[2] *Ib.* 182.

[3] J. de Veitia Linage, *Spanish Rule of Trade*, translated by Stevens,
p. 84. In later times goods intended for consumption in Spain might be
landed at any port where the vessel touched.

and sailed together for Spain about the month of June[1]. Masses of bullion were brought to Spain, especially in the eleven years from 1545 A.D. onwards, during which the mines of Potosi yielded annually, at the lowest computation, 2,215,000 *pesos*[2]. The government obtained a large revenue from customs, and was at pains not only to protect the plate-fleet by sea, but to prevent the export of the bullion that was safely landed at Seville. But the policy thus pursued proved a disastrous failure: the Crown never enjoyed a period of repose when saving was possible; the wars of Charles V were too costly to permit the formation of a hoard; the India House was crippled by the loss of the Armada, and Philip II died deeply in debt[3]. The Spaniards had sacrificed everything else to the attempt to build up political power by the mere accumulation of bullion; their want of success in the main object of their policy left them so impoverished as to demonstrate that the means by which they pursued it had been grossly mistaken.

Spanish colonial policy was at fault, as little attention was given to the cultivation of the soil, or to the planting of any industry. The colonists exported such natural products[4] as could be obtained with little labour, and devoted all their energies to mining operations; the working of the mines was not a government monopoly, but was carried on by private enterprise. Large as were the total returns, it does not seem to have been a profitable speculation in all cases[5]; and at

[1] J. de Veitia Linage, *Spanish Rule of Trade*, 193.

[2] Soetbeer, *Edelmetall-Produktion* (1879), 72. The opening of the mines of Potosi almost synchronised with the discovery of improved processes of reducing the ore with quicksilver.

[3] Beer, *Allgemeine Geschichte des Welthandels*, II. 147. Ehrenberg, *op. cit.* II. 259.

[4] See the list in J. de Veitia Linage, *op. cit.*, Preface.

[5] The determination of the Fuggers in 1531 A.D. to drop their scheme of colonising in S. America after they had succeeded in procuring all the necessary concessions may be taken as indicating their view of the value of colonial investments. Häbler, *Die Geschichte der Fuggerschen Handlung*, 67.

all events it diverted both capital and labour from attempts
to develop the other resources of the colonies. Mining on a
large scale was pursued in a manner that was detrimental to
the native population[1], and rendered it necessary for the under-
takers to procure more stalwart labourers by arranging for the
importation of negroes. The regular business of supplying 4000
to 5000 negroes per annum was contracted for in turn by the
Portuguese and the Genoese; the Spaniards, with all their
faults, had a rooted dislike to taking part personally in the
traffic[2], and in the eighteenth century it came to be absorbed
by the English merchants, who outbid the French. There was
little labour available for other occupations than mining, and
as a consequence the colonists were dependent on the mother
country for supplies of all kinds, not merely for textiles and
manufactured articles, but for cereals as well[3]. They had of
course the means of purchasing these goods easily with the
silver of the mines, but the Spanish colonies would have been
far stronger if more vigorous attempts had been made to
develop their general resources.

The colonial market for Spanish foodstuffs was large,
and it might have afforded a great stimulus to tillage in the
Peninsula, where there were doubtless regions which were
able to respond to the increased demand[4]. But in many
parts of Spain natural economy still held good, while other
districts had not recovered from the devastation and depopu-
lation caused by the war. The colonial requirements were so
considerable that they caused a rapid rise of rates in the home

---

[1] Leroy Beaulieu contends that the oppression of the Indians in connection with mining has been much exaggerated. *De la Colonisation chez
les peuples modernes*, p. 14.

[2] J. de Veitia Linage, *op. cit.* 159.

[3] Martin Hume, *Spain*, 1479—1788, 84.

[4] Charles V made considerable improvements in Aragon which rendered large tracts of territory available for tillage. Martin Hume, *op.
cit.* 85.

markets; considerable purchases of growing crops[1] were made
by merchants who wished to export them, and the government
endeavoured by legislation to prevent the rise of prices.
Again and again the Cortes were compelled to raise the
maximum tariff of permissible rates[2], but these imperfectly
successful efforts to keep prices low rendered agriculture less
profitable. There were other difficulties to which tillage was
exposed; the *mesta*, a great organisation of sheep farmers with
ancient privileges, not only objected to the increase of tillage
at the expense of pasture[3], but exercised their rights in the
driving of their flocks so as to injure the arable farms through
which they passed on their great migrations[4]. Altogether the
legislation of the Cortes was so unfavourable to agriculture
that the Spanish corn-growers derived little advantage from
the great colonial demand.

The depressed condition of tillage, and the fact that
food continued to be scarce and dear, was one of the main
reasons for the failure of the Spaniards to reap the benefit of
the large colonial market for textiles and other manufactured
goods. For a time indeed there was a rapid expansion;
German capitalists settled in the country[5], and manufacturing
was conducted on a considerable scale; Cuenza and Seville
were the centres of the cloth trade, Valladolid of the silk
industry, Cordova of leather manufacture, and Toledo of the
production of arms[6]. Foreign labour followed in the wake of

---

[1] Bernays, *Zur inneren Entwickelung Castiliens* in Quidde, *Deutsche Z.
f. Geschichtswissenschaft* (1889), 1. 404.

[2] Naudé, *Getreidehandelspolitik*, 184.

[3] In 1552, Church and corporation lands which had been broken up for
tillage were thrown back into pasture. Martin Hume, *op. cit.* p. 85.

[4] Naudé, *op. cit.* 201.

[5] They hoped for liberal concessions from Charles V. Lamprecht,
Deutsche Geschichte, v. 479.

[6] Beer, II. 144. Häbler, *Die wirthschaftliche Blüte Spaniens.* The
subject has given rise to much controversy, but it appears that there has
been a tendency to exaggerate the duration of the prosperity of Spain.

foreign capital, but the new development of industry was not heartily welcomed; the increased population it had attracted seemed to be to blame for the scarcity and dearness of food; while the gilds of small masters were opposed to the capitalist organisation of industry that had sprung up so rapidly[1]. The traditional policy of the country was that of legislating on behalf of consumers, and the newly-developed industries had to contend with unfavourable conditions. The Spanish markets were flooded with goods produced in countries where the range of prices was lower[2]; while a prohibition of export[3], along with sumptuary laws[4], seriously limited the demand for native manufactures. There are indications that the short-lived industrial prosperity of Spain was waning as early as the time of Charles V. The Spanish policy of maintaining privileges and favouring the consumer was as disadvantageous to the capitalist manufacturers as it had been to agriculture. The wealthy foreigners were blamed by the *hidalgos* for all the difficulties that arose in connection with the rise of prices; native pride and prejudice formed an alliance with native poverty; the expulsion of the Moriscos was only one instance of a continual attack upon alien elements[5], till the disabilities to which they were exposed—either as capitalists or labourers—forced them to withdraw. The Spaniards had been unable, in spite of the stimulus of the colonial demand, to develop great manufactures, and they would not allow the Germans or Italians to do it in their stead.

In these circumstances there is little difficulty in accounting for the complete failure of the bullionist policy of Spain: even if the ruling dynasty had enjoyed a perpetual peace, it would have been impossible under the existing

---

[1] Martin Hume, *op. cit.* p. 84.
[2] *Ib.* p. 87.
[3] Beer, *op. cit.* II. 145.
[4] Martin Hume, *Year after the Armada*, p. 220.
[5] Martin Hume, *Spain*, 1479—1788, p. 213.

economic conditions to retain the silver in the Peninsula and to prevent it from passing out in the course of commerce. The prohibition of the export of bullion had never been absolutely enforced, as some of the German and Italian capitalists had enjoyed permits[1] which allowed a limited export; and the balance of trade was so heavily against Spain, that the temptation to smuggle silver out of the country must have been great. The mass of the treasure of the new world did not find its way to the Spanish mint, but came into the hands of men who desired to use it as capital, and who succeeded in transferring it to Antwerp, Genoa and other centres where they could invest it at a profit. The Spaniards, by their harsh legislation in the interest of consumers at home, interfered to prevent the colonial demand from stimulating the development of agricultural and industrial resources in the Peninsula. There were ever-increasing difficulties about maintaining their shipping and equipping their armies; as their commerce declined, it became obvious that they had missed the opportunity of attaining to great material prosperity. The bullionist policy had proved impracticable, it entirely failed to buttress the military power of Spain, and the colonial empire which Spain had created became the prey of peoples with a keener commercial spirit.

121. In the earlier part of the seventeenth century there
seemed to be every prospect that Holland would
The Dutch   soon attain an undisputed position as the predo-
and Shipping.   minant power, not only in European waters, but
in the East and West Indies as well. She had great wealth; her ports formed the chief European emporium both for fish and corn; and the trade in these necessaries of life gave employment to an enormous mercantile marine, which far exceeded the fleets of the Mediterranean cities in their most prosperous days. The United Provinces had means at their disposal not

---

[1] Bonn, *Spaniens Niedergang*, 182. Ehrenberg, *op. cit.* II. 223.

only to secure their own independence, but also to break the power of Spain in the East Indies and in America.

The foundations of their commercial prosperity were deeply laid, since the Netherlanders had been carefully endeavouring for centuries to make the most of their resources and of their opportunities for trade. From the earliest times of its known history Flanders had been famed for its industry and particularly its woollen manufacture, which centred round Bruges and Ghent. In the fourteenth century the towns of Brabant, especially Louvain, also excelled in this art; and though Dordrecht and Amsterdam were chiefly given to maritime employments and engaged in the import of wool from England, they gradually took to manufacturing and attained considerable success in the making of cloth. It was in the fifteenth century, however, that the Netherlands made most rapid progress; and owing to its varied maritime and industrial advantages, this territory enjoyed under the Burgundian family a period of extraordinary material prosperity. Most of the wealth of the northern provinces was due to the herring fishery. The art of curing fish had been much improved at Biervliet[1] in the earlier half of the fifteenth century; and the Dutch threw a great deal of energy into the prosecution of the fishing trade, so that their fleets reaped the richest harvest of the sea, not only near their own coasts, but off the shores of England and Denmark and in the Baltic. Thus they obtained a large supply of an article of common consumption throughout Christendom, and were able to do a profitable trade with Germany by the Rhine, and with France, Spain and Portugal by sea. Though the greater part of their country was little adapted for corn growing, it had admirable facilities for pasture, and not only enabled them to provide wool, but large quantities of dairy products for export. Their commerce was thus firmly based on the excellence of their manufactures,

---

[1] J. de Witt, *Political Maxims of the State of Holland* (1743), p. 22.

198 Western Civilisation. [BOOK V.

and the abundance of the products of land and sea. The
men of Amsterdam were able to take advantage of the position
of their city to make it the centre of the maritime trade
between the Baltic lands and the rest of Europe. The Netherlanders were forced to import corn from Prussia, Poland and
Russia for their own requirements, and they succeeded in
organising a great carrying trade for supplying the deficiencies
of countries on the Mediterranean. This transport of corn
between the districts which were then the granary of Europe
and the southern lands which raised other products, came to
be of far greater importance than all the rest of the Dutch
trade put together; the Hollanders competed successfully with
the Hanse towns in the sixteenth century, and after the fall of
Antwerp they had only occasional cause to fear the interruption of this traffic[1]. It continued throughout the seventeenth
and the greater part of the eighteenth century to be the back-
bone of the Dutch commercial system: so long as this trade
with neighbouring lands was left to them, they could afford to
regard the distant commerce of the world and the maintenance
of colonies and factories in America and the East Indies with
comparative indifference[2].

The Dutch monopoly of the Spice Islands, which moved
the jealousy of other nations in the seventeenth century, was
not the foundation of the prosperity of the United Provinces,
but was a mere excrescence, which was added incidentally and

[1] Considerable alarm was felt in 1611, when Christian IV of Denmark
increased the toll on vessels passing through the Sound. The Dutch trade
was also threatened in 1622, when the Spaniards endeavoured to revive
their connection with the Hanse towns on the Baltic; but the Dutch suffered
no lasting injury. The most serious difficulties were caused by Gustavus
Adolphus, when he established Swedish power on the Baltic in 1630, and
diverted the corn from Poland for the commissariat of his armies. Naudé,
op. cit. 348, 354, 360.

[2] It is interesting to compare Adam Smith's chapter on the different
employments of capital with the Dutch practice. *Wealth of Nations*,
II. v.

under the pressure of their great struggle with Spain.   The
severities of the Spanish rule in the sixteenth century and the
cruelties inflicted during the War of Independence had seriously
interfered with the commerce, and with much of the industry
of Flanders and Brabant.   Refugees from these districts migrated northwards, and Amsterdam gained immensely by the
fall of Antwerp.   That city had been the chief emporium for
the distribution of the spices and other valuable products
which were imported into Spain and Portugal; and despite all
efforts to force this trade into other channels, it continued to
enrich the merchants of the United Provinces.   They were
able to avail themselves of opportunities which the Spaniards
had failed to appreciate; and the linen manufacture of Holland
received a considerable impetus from the market that was
opened up in the Spanish colonies.   Just as Napoleon's armies
were supplied with English manufactures, so was Spain forced
to purchase goods from the nation of traders[1] which she was
endeavouring to coerce.   Still, this illicit trade though highly
profitable was extremely uncertain; and Philip, by seizing
fifty Dutch ships in Lisbon harbour[2], forced the merchants of
Amsterdam to adopt a bolder line, if they were not to lose
this branch of business altogether.   They determined to attempt to penetrate to the sources of the spice trade for themselves, and to organise expeditions to the East, instead of
confining their energies to European trade.

For some little time they prosecuted the attempt to open
up an independent line of communication by the Arctic Seas[3],
though the first voyage (1594 A.D) had showed that the difficulties were very great; but in 1595 A.D. they adopted the
southern route and sent out a fleet by the Cape, so that they

---

[1] Rogers, *Holland*, 162.
[2] Saalfeld, *Geschichte des holländ. Kolonialwesens*, I. 10.
[3] Rogers, *op. cit.* 173. This had been already attempted by the English;
it gave access to the silk trade with Persia, but not directly to a spice
trade.

entered into direct competition in waters where the Portuguese had established their supremacy. The four Dutch vessels which formed their first East Indian fleet (1595 A.D.) sailed by way of Madagascar to Java; and though one ship had to be abandoned and many lives were lost, the adventure was so far successful that a larger fleet started in 1598 A.D.[1], and a permanent factory was established at Bantam in 1602 A.D. Several partnerships were formed and fleets were sent to the East, with the result that the market for spices was glutted, and some of these associations were ruined by the fall of prices[2]; but in 1602 A.D. the various partnerships were united into one company which was privileged to carry on the trade as a monopoly. In the first half of the seventeenth century it had a very large measure of success; the factories which the Portuguese had established were incapable of defending themselves against the Dutch[3], and the latter were able to put serious hindrances in the way of the development of the East Indian trade of England, which promised to become a formidable rival. The Dutch came to be heirs of the monopoly in the Spice Islands, and of the Portuguese trading connections with China and Japan; while the linen manufacture of Holland[4] enabled her traders to export cargoes for which there was a ready sale in the East[5].

The Dutch were less willing than either the Portuguese or English to assume the cares of an Eastern Empire; but not even they were able to avoid it altogether. Political responsibility had been forced on the Portuguese by the need of a firm basis from which to resist the Arabs; and though

[1] Bonnassieux, *Grandes Compagnies de Commerce*, 44.

[2] Beer, II. 180.

[3] Amboyna fell in 1605. Saalfeld, *op. cit.* I. 38.

[4] Negapatam was the staple for this after 1606. Beer, II. 181.

[5] Neither the Portuguese nor the English manufactured commodities which commanded a good sale when offered in exchange for the goods they procured from the Indies.

the Dutch were content on the whole to avoid continental possessions, and to try to secure commercial privileges by treaty with native rulers, they were impelled to exercise a strict territorial supervision over the particular islands where the spices were produced. They paid pensions of about £3300[1] to native rulers to exterminate the clove and nutmeg in other islands, and concentrated the cultivation in Amboyna, where they were able to control it themselves. So far as their East Indian trade was concerned, they were not eager to de-velop it, but preferred to keep it within such limits that they might secure a high rate of profit[2].

While we are inclined to blame this restrictive policy, we ought not to shut our eyes to the fact that it proved, in some ways at least, a wise one. Holland was never exhausted as Portugal had been by the attractions of eastern traffic and command. On the contrary, the great gains accruing from this exclusive trade were capitalised and advantageously employed other mercantile and industrial undertakings, both in their own and in neighbouring lands. The Baltic trade in corn and furs showed a steady improvement; the Hanse towns were completely superseded, and the Dutch enjoyed a very large share of the active commerce of Sweden and Russia. They also entered the Mediterranean and took up much of the business formerly done by Italians. The Venetian shipping continued to decline, and the Dutch commenced to carry on a considerable trade with Smyrna and the Levant. In all these directions they out-distanced the English merchants, and, as it appeared, chiefly because there was an abundance of money in Holland which could always be obtained for new enterprises that offered the prospect of a moderate return on the capital invested.

While her trading relations were thus extending on all

---

[1] Raynal, *Voyages*, I. 186.
[2] Saalfeld, *op. cit.* I. 274. On the policy pursued in limiting the production of coffee, sugar, etc., see *Ib.* I. 236. Also on the restrictive policy at the Cape, Leroy Beaulieu, *Colonisation*, 89.

sides, the original sources of the wealth of Holland were not neglected. Fishery was actively carried on, and attention was given to sealing and whaling, which were pursued at first with the aid of Biscayan harpooners[1]. The industries which migrated from Flanders, from Germany, and later from France, were prosecuted with success in Holland, where they were organised on capitalised lines[2], so that the country became more noted for the excellence and variety of its manufactures. Besides this, unremitting attention was given to farming; root crops and artificial grasses were introduced so as to afford winter fodder, and though Dutch horticulture was in some ways an extravagant hobby, it none the less gave a stimulus to a remunerative business. The reaction of Dutch commerce on the industry of Holland led to a remarkable development of native resources of every kind.

There had been a strange fatality about the conduct of Spanish affairs, especially in the way in which the action of the government played into the hands of the provinces that were defying them. The low import duties on goods entering Spain had been highly advantageous to the Dutch; they had also gained by the immigration of protestants expelled from Spanish dominions; and there was another way in which the policy of Spain worked for the ultimate benefit of Holland. In November 1596 A.D.[3], Philip repudiated his debts and resumed possession of the lands which he had mortgaged; he thus destroyed his own credit, while he also ruined the Italian and German financiers from whom he had borrowed, and left the Dutch without rivals in this lucrative business. The monetary world of Florence had received a blow from which

[1] Beer, II. 203.

[2] Pringsheim, *Beiträge zur wirtschaftlichen Entwickelung der vereinigten Niederlande im* 17. *und* 18. *Jahrhundert* in Schmoller's *Forschungen*, X. iii. (1890), p. 33. The old-established industries of Holland continued to-be carried on as domestic crafts, and the gild regulations were strictly enforced. *Ib.* 40.

[3] Rogers, *op. cit.* 187.

it did not easily recover when Edward III and Robert of Sicily failed to keep faith with the Peruzzi; and Philip's bankruptcy destroyed the financial supremacy of the Fuggers of Antwerp and Augsburg. Amsterdam became the new monetary centre of Europe; the business of foreign banking was increasingly concentrated there.

This succession of great opportunities, which occurred during the first half of the seventeenth century, enabled the Dutch to attain the highest pitch of prosperity in every department of economic life. They reached the zenith of their prosperity about 1649 A.D.; from that time onwards, though the Baltic trade which was the main source of their wealth continued to flourish, they began to lose the lead in the race; and rivals, who imitated their methods, became successful competitors. The French under Colbert developed industries of their own, so that a valuable neighbouring market was closed to Dutch manufactures; the Scandinavians, like the English, were jealous of the intrusion of Dutch fishermen in their waters, and the practical monopoly of the Dutch was at length completely broken down by the opening of the Sound. The English Navigation Act of 1651 A.D. had been partly dictated by political considerations and by a desire to sever the West Indian colonies from intercourse with royalist sympathisers, but it also struck a severe blow at the carrying trade of the Dutch and weakened their hold upon North America. They even failed to maintain their interest in the Peninsula; for in the middle of the seventeenth century, when the Portuguese power was revived under the house of Braganza (1640 A.D.), considerable advantage accrued to England and but little to Holland. The struggle of the Dutch West India Company for the possession of Brazil[1] was useless so far as Holland was concerned, while the alliance of Charles II with the royal house of Portugal restored an ancient friendship and gave substantial advantages to the growing maritime power of England.

---

[1] Bonnassieux, *op. cit.* 74.

The revival of Portugal and of the Portuguese colonies was profitable to English capitalists[1], and was controlled to a certain extent in the interests of English industry; the Methuen treaty marked the success of English merchants in their contest with the Dutch for the carrying trade of Portugal and her dependencies.

The inability of the Dutch to secure and to maintain a predominant position and to exercise a world-wide influence, was not due to any economic weakness, but rather to their political temperament and character. The Dutch had not attained to a true national life; it is hardly an exaggeration to say that "the Netherlander before 1795 A.D. recognised no fatherland, but only a father-town[2]." The strength of their civic as compared with their national patriotism prevented them from making the most of their opportunities in the seventeenth century; they did not fail from lack of means, so much as from want of will; they had no ambition to develop a colonial empire. In no other country did the strictly economic motives count for so much in the determination of policy. Even their struggle for independence had been greatly influenced by a desire to escape the centralised government and the taxation which the House of Austria had imposed on their commerce[3]. John de Wit, the leader of the merchant princes, explicitly advocated " Peace at any price[4]," as the aim at which their diplomacy should be directed, since any war was likely to injure their shipping and its interests. They had no positive ideal towards which their pursuit of material wealth was subordinated; with the Dutch, as with

[1] Beer, II. 119, 133. At the earthquake at Lisbon the loss of capital to English merchants is said to have been very large. *Ibid.* 121 note.

[2] J. Blok, *Eene hollandsche stad in de middeleeuwen.* 1883. Preface.

[3] Pringsheim, *op. cit.* p. 1. On the struggle over the *Congiegeld* which was revived by Charles V in 1540, to the serious disadvantage of the corn trade, see Naudé, *op. cit.* 319.

[4] Naudé, *op. cit.* 436.

the Phoenicians in the old world, commerce was not so much a means to an end as an end in itself.

Had Holland been ambitious of retaining her position as a world power she had ample resources at her command, and she might have made an effective bid for the leadership among the representatives of Western Civilisation. But she did not rise to the responsibility; while other nations advanced and expanded, she concentrated her energies more and more on the trade that lay easily within her reach. The wealth and prosperity of Holland continued till the latter half of the eighteenth century, when improvements in the cultivation of England[1], together with the opening up of Odessa[2] as a new port and of fresh sources of supply in America, revolutionised the corn trade. But long before statistics showed any signs of the decline of her wealth or her maritime importance, she had lost all pretensions to rule the destinies of any large area of territory. Indeed her system of government rendered it impossible for her to undertake such a task with success; the seven United Provinces had been drawn together by the requirements of common defence, but they did not succeed in organising a workable administrative system. Though the Dutch were willing to make vast sacrifices at some moment of dire necessity, they were unable to make steady and regular preparation for possible exigencies[3], and had not the means of repairing their losses and retrieving their disasters. The particularist interest of different towns and districts was strong enough to paralyse the action of the Admiralty and to render the central government inefficient and corrupt[4]; and the cumbrous

[1] Naudé, *op. cit.* 379.

[2] *Ib.* 440.

[3] A. T. Mahan, *The Influence of Sea Power upon History*, 68.

[4] Pringsheim, *op. cit.* 2, 3. An enquiry in 1685 proved that the officials of the Admiralty allowed whole cargoes to be smuggled without interfering, as they dared not offend the various town authorities who were interested in these ventures. The most important posts were sold for money to incapable people; in times of crisis the officials were often not to be found,

system of management which was adopted for the East Indian and other companies[1] was incompatible with the maintenance of an effective rule over distant dependencies. The Portuguese continued to retain something of the missionary aspirations of the Crusaders in the organisation of their colonial empire, and the Spaniards had an insatiable desire for power; the Dutch deliberately confined their energies within a very restricted sphere; and because they would not progress, they were unable to retain what they possessed. It is impossible to win a victory over energetic rivals by always remaining on the defensive, and the Dutch were forced to relinquish piecemeal the advantages they had once secured[2].

122.   The politicians in the latter part of the seventeenth

The French and Internal Development. century, who indulged in forecasts of the future of the civilised world, were very apprehensive of the dangers to which other nations were exposed from the growth of France. The military resources of Louis XIV inspired his contemporaries with awe, and the palace which he erected at Versailles impresses succeeding generations with some idea of his magnificence. Powerful at home, the French monarchy seemed able to establish its

the book-keeping was careless and the accounts were in disorder. There was no question of anything like a unified customs regulation. The central government had as a rule no officials of its own to carry out its decrees, the execution of which was left to the provincial or town officials, who thought it their duty to put the interest of their province or town before that of the general interest of the country. On the management of the companies' affairs abroad compare Stavorinus, *Voyages to the East Indies*, I. 278, also III. 475.

[1] Wilcocke's notes to his Translation of Stavorinus, *op. cit.* I. 89. Leroy Beaulieu, *De la Colonisation chez les peuples modernes*, 79.

[2] The parallel between England and Holland is of much interest, especially in connection with the history of experiments in Free Trade. It is to be noted, however, that the English imperial sentiment and eagerness to expand are wanting among the Dutch. Further, English trade is not based on advantages secured by treaty, and has not the exclusive character which made that of the Dutch an object of jealousy.

influence at any moment in the most distant parts of the globe;
for it had secured a footing in India and had commenced to
found a series of settlements in the Antilles and along the great
rivers of North America—the Mississippi and St Lawrence.
Till the middle of the eighteenth century it appeared likely
that France would ultimately inherit the territories which had
been opened up to Europeans in the age of discovery. But
these expectations were mistaken; France has never obtained a
great colonial empire, and as we look back we may be able to
see some of the reasons why, with all her great resources
and eager national ambition, she failed to make the most of
her opportunities in the seventeenth century.

It is easy, but somewhat unmeaning, to say that the
French have no genius for colonisation; as we review the
work of such pioneers as Cartier or Champlain, or read of
the enterprise of Breton fishermen and Normandy merchants[1],
we feel that there were abundant elements for founding and
maintaining vigorous settlements in distant lands. The religious orders in the West, and military leaders like Dupleix in
the East, showed a capacity for dealing with native populations
such as few Englishmen have ever displayed; and the prosperity of the French colonies in the Tropics—in the Antilles
and at Mauritius—proves that there was no inherent incapacity
on the part of the nation for carrying out such undertakings
with success.

The defect did not lie in the genius of the people, so
much as in the habits of political and economic life that had
been formed in the course of many years. The revival of
French industry and commerce under Charles VII and
Louis XI had been brought about by royal and governmental
action; under these monarchs the French learned to rely on
kingly direction and encouragement instead of personal effort;
and Francis I seems to have been responsible in no small
degree for giving a mistaken turn to the national ambition.

[1] Gaffarel, *Les Colonies françaises*, p. 80.

His eyes were fixed on Italy; he was eager to obtain Italian possessions, and his ideas were all coloured by reminiscences of Italian glories. The new world was being opened up; the sailors of Rouen and Dieppe[1] were competing with the Portuguese on the African coast and with the Spaniards in America; but Francis I would have none of it. He stimulated and revivified the moribund Levantine commerce of the southern ports[2], and during his reign the town of Lyons became the centre of an enormous trade in articles of luxury[3]. Immense palaces, surpassing those of Florence and Venice, were built in Paris and throughout the country, both by the king and by the nobles who imitated him; France began to take the lead, which she has never lost, in matters of fashion and taste. Though the interests of the importers and those of the native artisan were somewhat in conflict, there was a frequent effort from the time of Francis I onwards to plant the manufactures of cloth-of-gold, glass, silk, and tapestry, so that the king and court might be supplied by home producers, and not by importation from abroad. France was by nature self-sufficing and independent of foreign countries for the necessaries of life; it was the policy of the king to make her independent with regard to artistic productions also[4]; and on the whole, subsequent rulers have continued to encourage those branches of industry which were first developed under the impulse they received from Francis I.

In the sanguinary struggle of the wars of the League, France was once more devastated as she had been in the Hundred Years' War; and the statesmen of the time were therefore compelled to concentrate all their energies on repairing the ravages of that sanguinary struggle; they could not attempt to take up the work of colonisation seriously or to compete for a commercial empire while there was such terrible social disintegration at home. Henry IV was a king who threw

[1] Pigeonneau, II. 45.   [2] *Ib.* II. 126.
[3] *Ib.* II. 28.   [4] *Ib.* II. 58.

himself heartily into the task of reviving internal prosperity, and once again the economic life of France was restored by royal initiative. In Sully the Crown had a financial adviser of conspicuous ability, who introduced reforms into the fiscal system of the country and greatly reduced the burden to the taxpayers; at the same time he provided such a revenue that Henry could introduce some new industrial experiments, and undertake important public works. In all these matters the Crown could rely on the assistance of Olivier de Serres and Laffemas, who were authorities in regard to scientific agriculture and commercial and industrial development respectively. Henry IV, during the few years when he was undisputed master, did not give complete adherence to the views of either of the competing doctrinaires, but he laid down the lines of that systematic development of internal resources by which the French monarchy was to attain to its greatest glory.

His most important work was that of developing internal commerce[1] by improving the rivers and constructing canals; he spent immense sums on the repair of roads and the building of bridges so as to facilitate the transport of grain; he also did much to reduce the provincial restrictions which had hitherto fettered the trade in corn. This in itself gave a decided impulse to agriculture; every effort was made to encourage the nobility to settle as residents on their estates, and the *Théâtre d'Agriculture* of Olivier de Serres gave them the fullest instruction as to the best methods to pursue in the management of their land. There were, however, many obstacles in the way of change for the better; it was hopeless to expect that the peasantry would adopt improved methods of their own accord; and hence it seemed wise to maintain a certain amount of natural economy—in the *metayer* system[2]—so that the influence of the proprietor as an interested partner might

---

[1] Fagniez, *L'économie sociale de la France sous Henri IV*, 182.
[2] J. S. Mill, *Political Economy*, bk. II. c. viii.

be directly brought to bear on the mode of cultivation[1]. The homestead system, which has proved a practical barrier to capitalist farming, was retained in France; but the seignorial powers failed to exercise an educative influence on the peasants or to set an example by introducing new methods of cultivation and other agricultural improvements.

The conditions of industrial life in the sixteenth century gave rise to a great deal of complaint, and powerful forces were at work which demanded the regulation of the crafts in Lyons[2] and other towns on the model of the *corps de métiers* at Paris. Henry IV, in accordance with the principles of Laffemas, organised the industrial system of the whole country on very definite lines. The exceptions which were allowed were due to the direct exercise of royal authority and the creation in the various crafts of masters who had not served an apprenticeship; the Crown also exerted its powers by granting special patents for inventors, by the appointment of artisans to the Court, and by the establishment of large numbers of workmen in the Louvre where they were free from interference by the *corps de métiers*[3]. These interferences with the rigidity of the system were unpopular and were of doubtful advantage; but the general tendency was to strengthen the hands of the wealthy oligarchies in each trade[4], and thus, while mediaeval forms were preserved, to facilitate the introduction of capitalistic organisation in industry. However unsatisfactory the system may seem in the retrospect, it proved, with the assistance of protective laws, to be the means of greatly

[1] The alternative would have been to allow the peasantry to rent land for money, but the introduction of this system would have tended to widen the severance between the two classes who were concerned with the land, and the numbers both of non-resident proprietors and of unenlightened cultivators would have been increased.

[2] Hauser, *Ouvriers du temps passé*, 129.

[3] Hauser, *op. cit.* 135—140.

[4] The wealthy oligarchies had been chiefly instrumental in securing increased regulation. Hauser, *op. cit.* 127.

developing the native trades; while considerable pains were also taken by Henry IV to plant the silk manufacture[1] in new regions and to introduce a fustian manufacture as well[2].

The extent to which the material prosperity of France was actually dependent on royal authority became apparent when Henry IV was removed by the dagger of Ravaillac. Under the government of Marie de Medicis much of the old disorder returned; but when Richelieu assumed the reins of power he reinforced with fresh vigour the industrial policy of Henry IV.[3] He also had such faith in the resources of the country that he consciously aimed at developing a naval and mercantile marine[4], so that France might hope to compete with Holland and England for commercial supremacy and colonial empire. In neither case did he obtain the success he anticipated; great commercial companies were organised, in imitation of those of Holland[5]; but the financiers who subscribed the capital could not furnish the practical business ability[6] which was necessary to render these undertakings a commercial success in the Baltic or other fields where Dutch traders were already established[7]; the French Crown conferred privileges and powers, but the fostering care which had regulated actual industry could not call a non-existent commerce into being[8]. The comparative failure of French efforts at colonisation was partly owing to maladministration and partly to other causes. The pioneers

[1] Fagniez, *op. cit.* 105 fol.   [2] *Ib.* 142.
[3] Levasseur, *op. cit.* II. 151.
[4] D'Avenel, *Richelieu et la Monarchie absolue*, III. 167.
[5] Bonnassieux, *Les grandes compagnies de commerce*, 166.
[6] The practical merchants were too deeply attached to the trade of particular cities, Rouen, St Malo or Rochelle, to throw their energies into schemes that concerned the nation as a whole. Pigeonneau, II. 346.
[7] Sargent, *The Economic Policy of Colbert*, 82.
[8] "Un gouvernement peut utiliser et diriger un courant national; il ne peut ni le créer, ni l'arrêter." D'Avenel, *op. cit.* III. 217. Compare also P. Masson, *Histoire du commerce français dans le Levant au xviime siècle*, p. 523.

had, unlike the Dutch, a very keen sense of a national mission and destiny, they had ample privileges granted them by the Crown, and the men of Normandy[1] were enterprising sailors, but the people generally hung back from the effort to transplant French civilisation into distant lands. Much of the success of the English colonies was due to those who were, from one cause or another, dissatisfied with the conditions of life at home. Puritans and Roman Catholics and Quakers were alike concerned in the founding of settlements which proved to be places of refuge for Englishmen to whom their native land was uncongenial. But the Frenchman, who was dissatisfied with the social system at home, would have found no place for him in New France[2]; and others, who would have been welcomed there, saw little to attract them to emigrate. Pioneers had begun to establish themselves at Montreal before Richelieu came into power; but though he took up the matter in earnest and entered into one scheme after another, he failed to attract a regular stream of emigrants. The companies of New France[3] and of the Antilles[4] were called into existence, and thus late in the day the first serious efforts were made to found a French colonial empire; when the attempt was once begun it was carried out on an extensive scale, for encouragement was given to the trading intercourse which the Norman sailors had established with Senegal[5], and possession was formally taken of Madagascar[6]. Some of these schemes were hampered for want of capital, and others suffered from the insufficiency of the French marine and the inadequate communication between the colonies and the mother

[1] Pigeonneau, *op. cit.* II. 442.

[2] Coligny attempted to found Huguenot colonies both in Brazil and Florida, but neither attempt attained much success. Pigeonneau, *op. cit.* II. 329.

[3] Bonnassieux, *op. cit.* 350.

[4] Gaffarel, *Les Colonies françaises*, 206.

[5] *Ib.* 20. Bonnassieux, *op. cit.* 223.

[6] Gaffarel, *op. cit.* 142.

country[1]. The establishment charges were also very heavy, and the Court favourites[2] who were willing to expatriate themselves for a time, were not always the men who were fitted to preside over the destinies of a struggling colony.

Richelieu, with his unbounded belief in the resources of France[3], had given his approval to ambitious schemes which he had no sufficient means of carrying into effect. Fortunately for his country he was succeeded by a man of more restricted ambitions who was a great master of detail. When Colbert was entrusted with the charge of the finances of the realm he proved to be an admirable administrator ; and his reforms in the levying of taxation were most successful. But he had an undue belief in the power of administrative machinery to exercise a beneficial effect on industry and commerce ; in some cases there was an absurd waste from his efforts to introduce model manufactures ; in others there was much disturbance from his drastic attempts to improve those that already existed. Over-regulation and over-organisation affected every branch of industrial life[4], and seriously hampered the development of commercial enterprise ; while his measures for agriculture gave it no chance to revive[5] after the disad-

---

[1] D'Avenel, *op. cit.* III. 225.

[2] *Séances et travaux de l'Acad. des Sciences Morales*, CXXII. (1884), p. 482.   [3] Pigeonneau, *op. cit.* II. 379.

[4] " Unfortunately for the progress of industry in France, state aid and patronage, especially under despotic rule, inevitably implies state interference. Judging from the character of Colbert, we should expect such interference to be pushed to its furthest limit under his *régime*; that such was the case his letters amply prove. Here is his view on the subject: ' On this matter I would have you know that the only means of rendering our manufactures perfect and of establishing a good system in our commerce is to render them all uniform. The way to accomplish this is to insist on the practical execution of the general regulations of 1669; the more so that obedience is easy, and that in the end the workmen will find in it their real profit.' " Sargent, *Economic Policy of Colbert*, 50.

[5] The general policy of Colbert involved the subordination of agricultural to industrial interests, since he aimed at procuring a large supply of

vantages to which it had been exposed from the fiscal burdens imposed by Richelieu. Colbert's efforts to foster industry in the way it should go proved a failure; an economic despot had need to be omniscient, and Colbert was not wise enough to play the part of Providence with success.

Hardly any economic system would have had a fair trial in the circumstances of the day; political ambition left no scope for steady and systematic attention to economic development. The policy of Louis XIV would have drained the magnificent resources of France at any time; to the artificial scheme which Colbert had built up it was positively ruinous. The strain of foreign war was exhausting on one side; while the internal policy that was pursued in regard to the Huguenots struck a serious blow at some of the principal seats of French manufactures, and destroyed the industries to which so much attention had been given. Europe continued to tremble before the projects of Louis XIV; but the break-down of Colbert's system had left the great monarch powerless to carry them into effect. In every aspect the governmental initiative and administrative organisation proved baleful for France; with a fixed ambition to rule the destinies of Europe, her monarchs neglected the opportunity of securing a firm footing in the New World, and gave but little support to the enterprising men who were cherishing wider ideals for their native land. Her very wealth tempted her statesmen to be content with a self-centred economic policy; by protectionist measures against outsiders they sought to encourage a large home supply of manufactures of every sort; but they saw no occasion to attend to the permanent well-being of the agriculturists, though this was essential for the maintenance of a food supply, and also for nurturing a population adapted for colonisation.

food at low rates for the manufacturing population. There was a constant change of regulations in regard to the corn trade, according to the varying circumstances of different provinces in different seasons. Naudé, *Getreide-handelspolitik*, 39—58.

Colbert's system hardly had a fair chance, but its utter collapse is none the less a renewed demonstration of the economic difficulties which attend even the far-seeing absolute ruler.

123. Two hundred years after the establishment of direct communications with the East Indies and the discovery of the New World, there was still much uncertainty as to the precise form in which Western Civilisation would be brought to bear upon them. *The English Mercantile System.* During the eighteenth century this question was settled for our age at any rate; England ousted France from her strong position both in the East and in the West, and came to be the principal heir of competitors who had each shown in turn their inability to retain their hold over these distant lands. In the East the Portuguese had succumbed to the Dutch; the Dutch had proved incapable of rising to the situation; and the French missed the opportunity of supplanting them. It was the good fortune of England that she was able to take advantage of the openings that were offered her as they occurred, but it is not easy to detect the precise reasons of her success. There were, however, two features which distinguished England from her rivals in the earlier part of the seventeenth century; while there was considerable scope for personal energy, there was also a solidarity of sentiment throughout the English nation, and popular enthusiasm demanded the building up of maritime power; " her subjects were occupied during the greater portion of Elizabeth's reign in teaching their queen the use of a navy[1] "; and the maladministration of this service under James I and Charles I, despite their real interest in it, not only involved the Stuarts in difficulties with their parliaments, but was indirectly decisive as to the issue of the Civil War[2]. The Commonwealth, by its larger and judicious expenditure[3] on the navy, was really giving effect to a widespread popular ambition,

[1] Oppenheim, *A History of the Administration of the Royal Navy 1509—1660*, p. 115.
[2] *Ib.* 240—243.   [3] *Ib.* 303.

to which there was nothing that corresponded either in Holland
or France.   And just as it may be said that the Crown and the
Commonwealth rather followed than directed the national bent
in this political ambition, so does it appear that there was no
need for authority to attempt to call forth commercial or
colonial enterprise among Englishmen.   Trading interest and
the love of personal adventure were widely prevalent in England ; the Government was required at times to control and to
protect, but not to initiate new undertakings.   This vigorous
spirit was hampered by the lack of material means to carry out
its projects ; England in the seventeenth century had neither
such a large mercantile marine[1], nor such abundance of capital
as Holland.   But even as regards pecuniary resources, English
subjects were better provided than the English Crown.   The
great engineering works in France had been started at the
royal expense ; but such public works as the draining of the
Cambridgeshire Fens or of Hatfield Chase were committed in
England to local magnates and private adventurers[2].   The
secret of her ultimate success seems to have lain in the vigorous enterprise of individual Englishmen and the strength of
patriotic feeling.

At all events, it is clear that England did not suffer from

[1] Oppenheim, *op. cit.* 307.

[2] There had been, through the later Middle Ages, considerable scope
for individual enterprise as the craft gilds, which would have been opposed
to it, were carefully kept in hand.   The town authorities had been jealous in
restraining the powers of these gilds, and Parliament in the fifteenth century
pursued a similar course.   In the time of Elizabeth they practically disappeared, as industrial legislation had been nationalised ; and unnecessarily
rigid as the new system seems to us, it was yet comparatively flexible.   The
Commons were inclined to resent any attempt on the part of the Stuart
kings to exercise an effective control over particular branches of industry by
the appointment of patentees.   Freedom for individual enterprise, both
personal and associated, was consonant with the habits and institutions of
the people; they would not be coerced into adopting one particular model,
and there was, under the circumstances, little encouragement to attempt
the introduction of cumbrous administration into the English colonies.

the special political weakness which affected the Dutch; the particularism of the various cities and provinces rendered effective administration impossible[1], and prevented the growth of such patriotic sentiments as actuated all classes of Englishmen. The first settlers in Virginia were eager to extend the range of English influence and to Anglicise a portion of the New World[2], and English seamen were proud to try to hold their own against hereditary enemies like the Spaniards and the French. Dutch enterprise was purely commercial in its inception; the merchants of Holland had no ambition to rule other lands, they were merely concerned with their business interests. But though commercial gain was a main motive in English colonial activity, it was not kept in view so exclusively as to limit the hopes and ideals of the leaders in the movement.

There was also a great difference between the manner of determining on the economic policy of the country in France and in England respectively. The highly centralised system of regulation which prevailed in France enabled the kings and their advisers to exercise an extraordinary influence; and the tastes and ambitions of the French monarchs gave a special and not very fortunate direction to industrial development, but the English Government was much more ready to follow the guidance and advice of English merchants. The requirements of the Court diverted French energies into the manufacture of costly luxuries; though the English Court might admire French taste and indulge in French goods during the Restoration period, it did little to direct industrial energy into these channels in preference to other trades. In England the national ambition, which one monarch after another adopted as his own, coincided with the interests of the mercantile

[1] English naval administration was often corrupt, but the Dutch system was so complicated that it was necessarily inefficient. Oppenheim, *op. cit.* I. 305.

[2] John Smith, *Advertisements*, c. 14, in *Works*, p. 957. Hakluyt's *Voyages*, III. 302.

community, while the kings became more reluctant to offend the moneyed men to whom they were forced to look for occasional supplies; thus a close alliance between the monarchy and the traders was gradually compacted. Under these circumstances a scheme of economic policy was devised, which in its main outlines dominated English legislation and administration for more than two centuries. It was clear that alike for purposes of defence and offence the success of England in rivalry with other nations must be achieved with the help of naval skill; while the available revenue of the Crown was largely dependent on taxation, and the Government was compelled for its own sake to attend not only to the development of shipping, but to the improvement of agriculture as well. The policy, which had been thought out for England, was applied on a larger scale as new areas were added to her dominion and could be dealt with as part of her territory.

The lines of this economic policy, which was maintained through the seventeenth century and most of the eighteenth, are clearly discernible in the Elizabethan period, before England had any pretensions to be a colonial power at all. Every effort was made by Burleigh to develop the maritime power of England; the seafaring population and the subsidiary industries which are necessary for the provision of naval stores had his constant thought. A stringent navigation policy might have created a fleet for a time, but his object was to increase the resources from which maritime equipment might be steadily drawn in the future. Among all the governmental changes from the Tudors to the Hanoverians, there was no period when the necessity of maintaining the maritime efficiency of the country was left out of sight, but the exigencies of the revenue system prevented any sacrifice of agricultural to commercial interests. After the time of Henry VIII the Crown was very dependent on parliamentary grants for the ordinary expenses of government, and the taxation was chiefly levied upon the

landed proprietors; it was a matter of immediate interest to
the administration that the country gentlemen should be in
receipt of large rents from which taxation might be paid; and
this could only be satisfactorily attained[1] if agriculture was
profitable. Fiscal considerations gave greater cogency to the
arguments of those who were alarmed at any movement which
was prejudicial to the rural population. Efforts were made
to give encouragement to arable farming and to compel the
gentry to settle on their own estates, and schemes were approved for banking out the sea and the rivers which flooded
low-lying land, so as to increase the food-producing area of
the country.

The English colonies in North America were habitually
spoken of as 'plantations,' and this word seems to carry the
implication that they were regarded as extensions of England[2];
they were not to be treated as separate entities but as parts
of one whole, to which the familiar principles of economic
policy should be made to apply. The territory which Cabot
discovered and the stretch of coast which was claimed by
England did not offer attractive facilities either for commercial
stations or for mining; but the land afforded admirable opportunities for farming, and the seas for fishing; so that the
design of developing rural and maritime wealth could be
carried on in this new field. The actual progress made under
Elizabeth and James was exceedingly slow, and the several
settlements that were established in the seventeenth century
differed in their legal and political character. But economically
they were founded on very similar principles. They were

[1] In the Elizabethan statute of apprentices the interests of agriculture
and of employments subsidiary to agriculture had a distinct preference as
compared with the industry of the towns. This distinguishes English policy
very clearly from that of Colbert. The development of sheep-farming
at the expense of tillage was always regarded as a political danger,
and favour was shown to the interest of tillage by the Corn Bounties Act of
1689. Naudé, *op. cit.* 111, 121.

[2] Cunningham, *Growth of English Industry and Commerce*, II. 144.

emphatically a new England, which was to be treated in such a fashion that the total maritime and territorial resources of the realm might be increased and that the Anglo-Saxon race might hold its own in the struggle with other world powers.

The disabilities to which the colonists were exposed in the eighteenth century were very real grievances, and many people find it difficult to appreciate the true character of the underlying principles on which the growing empire was regulated in the seventeenth century. The English colonies were not exploited in the interests of the mother country; they were territories to which Englishmen came in order to establish their homes and to make the most of the region where they settled. The restrictions imposed on them were connected with one fundamental maxim, which is hardly on the face of it unreasonable, and the colonies were prevented from engaging in hostile competition with the mother country[1]. So long as they paid little or nothing to the expense of defending the realm of which they formed a part it seemed reasonable that they should be precluded from developing on lines which tended to diminish the resources of the mother country. Subject to this principle of restriction, their progress was encouraged, and it was felt that their prosperity was an added strength to the realm[2]. The effort to form a plantation was arduous; and more than one expedition suffered severely before the preliminary difficulties were overcome, and the settlers became independent of imported supplies of food. But the motive of English colonisation was not that of conquering a territory and obtaining access to its mineral wealth, as the Spaniards had done, but of expanding the area which was peopled by Englishmen.

[1] See opinions quoted by G. L. Beer, *The Commercial Policy of England towards the American Colonies* in *Columbia College Studies*, III. 366, also Cunningham, *op. cit.* II. 153.

[2] E. Lord, *Industrial Experiments in Colonial America* in *John Hopkins University Studies* (1898), p. 86.

Like other European nations in the East Indies, the English aimed at commerce rather than at colonisation; there are, however, striking contrasts between the policy they pursued and that of their predecessors. The English East India Company was in a way a monopoly; it had special territorial and judicial privileges, and it showed itself jealous of the interference of interlopers, but it did not pursue the Dutch policy and deliberately limit the trade. The directors in London were persistent in their efforts to induce their agents abroad to make a large investment in Indian commodities for sale in Europe, and many of their servants were keenly interested in promoting internal trade in India[1]. The Dutch hoped to gain by artificial restrictions, while the English Company on the contrary conceived that the best way to make a profit lay in the direction of an expanding rather than of a limited trade. In course of time, too, the English merchants departed farther from the Dutch system, since they were led to adopt the policy which Albuquerque had sketched for his compatriots. They gradually and hesitatingly accepted a larger and larger measure of territorial power as the best means of securing their commercial footing without extravagant expenditure in the defence of their trade[2].

It has been pointed out in a preceding paragraph that the extended commerce of the Dutch reacted favourably on the industries of the United Provinces; and considerable pains were taken by the English to reap similar advantages: the traditional scheme for promoting the welfare of the country was carried out under a fresh stimulus and with increasing success. The necessity of keeping up maritime communications with distant lands gave remunerative employment for English shipping, and the plantations afforded a new market

---

[1] Cunningham, *op. cit.* II. 274.

[2] In early times the English appear to have been even more careful than their predecessors to preserve peace. Penny, *Fort S. George, Madras,* p. 34.

for English manufactures. There were symptoms, too, of a tendency to study the methods of Colbert and to imitate the policy he pursued; the efforts in which Parliament engaged to protect and to promote native industry and to introduce new employments, which might enable us to supply our own requirements instead of purchasing goods from abroad, do not differ in principle from the schemes which were adopted in France, though they often took a distinct form. The great industrial gain to England at the close of the seventeenth century came about by the action of and at the expense of France. The expulsion of the Huguenots drove to our shores some of the workmen whom Colbert would gladly have retained; and the arts which they practised were transferred with them from French to English soil. In setting aside local jealousies and welcoming these alien refugees, Englishmen showed that they were willing to copy the policy by which Holland had been so much enriched.

The commercial scheme which England had adopted, so far as the East India Company was concerned, would hardly have been carried out persistently if Englishmen had not deliberately discarded the bullionist system which Spain pursued[1]; they adopted instead a new view as to the means by which a mass of the precious metals—the sinews of war—might be best obtained. England did not contain mines of gold or silver and her colonies had no precious metals; hence it was only by traffic that she could procure treasure, and her wool trade had enabled her to obtain an ample supply of silver in the early Middle Ages. Statesmen began to realise that commerce might be so regulated as to induce a constant influx of silver; they endeavoured to promote the export of English commodities to countries that had few goods to offer in return, in the confident expectation that a payment for these exports would be made in bullion; the mercantilists agreed that when the " balance of trade " was favourable, treasure must flow into

---

[1] Cunningham, *op. cit.* II. 211.

the country. A hearty reliance on this principle enabled Englishmen to lay aside the policy of rigidly restricting the export of the precious metals which had wrought so much mischief in Spain; they were not bullionist but mercantilist. We have to some extent outlived the aim they set before them, and no longer attach the importance they did to the possession of treasure; but it is important to notice that the means they adopted for pursuing this object were perfectly compatible with the constant expansion of commerce, and that they were wonderfully successful in attaining what they had in view.

Working steadily and slowly for the development of maritime resources and natural advantages and appropriate industry, England reached a high degree of material prosperity, and obtained the sinews of naval and military power. The possession of great wealth of many kinds enabled her to attract considerable quantities of treasure in the course of trade. In the seventeenth century England was a profitable field for the investment of foreign capital; but with the increase of her trade the formation of capital went on more and more rapidly; the moneyed men began to overbalance the landed interest, and England abounded not only in wealth but in treasure. The foundation of the *Bank of England* gave a great impulse to the growth of a healthy credit system[1], so that, when the financial importance of Amsterdam began to decline, London was ready to take its place as the monetary centre of the world. At the time when England secured a great opportunity of guiding the destinies of India and America,

[1] This proved one of the greatest of the advantages which England had in the struggle with France. The system of Law appears to have involved a confusion between currency and capital (Levasseur, *Système de Law*, p. 26); but the multiplication and forced circulation of paper money altogether failed to realise his expectations and reinvigorate the economic life of France. The relations of Law's bank with the French Government were much closer than those which subsisted between the Bank and the Government in England; the failure of his system directly increased the embarrassment of the French Crown.

she also had command of the material means of bringing her influence to bear.

The success of England becomes less astonishing when we see how closely it was connected with the political conditions and economic system which had determined the aims of the Government and the habits of the people. The English overtook and surpassed their competitors, not because they had any special genius for the work, still less because they were the mere favourites of fortune, but because they were true to themselves, and eager to learn from their neighbours. They were ready to be guided by the experience of others ; to imitate their successes and to profit by the lessons of their failure. England secured an empire in the East, such as Albuquerque had desired for Portugal; while her commerce abroad reacted on her internal development so as to encourage the pursuit of agriculture as a profitable calling by resident gentry and to promote the manufacture of the products of the realm. This practical wisdom, combined with the soundness of the economic policy which was adopted, conspired to place this country in the front rank of European nations. The French had been the representative of Mediaeval Christendom in its struggle with Mohammedanism in the East; but in the eighteenth century England took the lead among the rising nationalities, and it is by means of the influence of English-speaking people that Western Civilisation has spread throughout the world in modern times.

BOOK VI.

THE EXPANSION OF WESTERN CIVILISATION.

CHAPTER I.

I. THE INDUSTRIAL REVOLUTION.

124. In the latter part of the eighteenth century there was a burst of inventive genius in Great Britain. Many improvements were rapidly introduced, and the useful arts, as practised from time immemorial, were revolutionised in a few years. This was no mere accident, but was at least partly due to the fact that the conditions of economic life had become more favourable to such change than they had ever been before. The age of geographical discovery had paved the way for the age of invention; England had succeeded in surpassing each of the rivals who during a century and a half had striven with her for the commercial supremacy of the world; her predominance afforded the English inventors of the eighteenth century unexampled opportunities for turning their talents to account.

Holland, which had been the leading economic power of the seventeenth century, was no longer the carrier of the world,

The age of Invention, and its effects.

and during the first half of the eighteenth century her manufactures had declined in importance. The over-centralisa-
tion of authority in France had reacted injuriously on all
branches of industry and agriculture in that country; it had
destroyed the initiative of the people and brought about
the decadence of the realm. English shipping had increased
as the Dutch declined and had opened up distant markets for
the national manufactures, especially for hardware and for
textiles. The East Indies were willing to accept unlimited
supplies of cotton cloth; and the continent of Europe and the
colonies of America were largely dependent on Great Britain
for woollen goods; manufacturing could be conducted on a
larger and larger scale without immediate risk of glutting
the widespread demand by overproduction. So long as commerce had been organised as an intercivic affair, or on the
old regulated lines of exclusive privileges in limited markets[1],
there could not have been any such stimulus to the invention
and introduction of machinery as the world-wide markets
naturally afforded.

But more than this: the mines of the New World and the
successful commerce with the East had given England the material means for the formation of large amounts of capital, which
were now available for employment. There had been much
admirable ingenuity among seventeenth century engineers and
mechanics, but they were hampered by want of capital; their
projects could not be carried out[2]. In the eighteenth century
London had become the monetary centre of the world, and
it was no longer impossible to venture on the long and

---

[1] After the Revolution of 1688 the English trading companies found
it much harder to maintain their restrictive rights. Cunningham, *Growth
of Industry*, II. 282.

[2] Compare the projects for improving the internal communication of
England by water. Even in the latter part of the eighteenth century the
Duke of Bridgewater had the greatest difficulty in procuring the necessary
funds for his first undertaking. Smiles's *Lives of Engineers*, I. 222.

costly experiments that were often needed to render some mechanical improvement a financial success.   We are not detracting from the genius[1] of Watt or Arkwright if we say that they seized and made the most of opportunities, such as no other men had ever had before.   Had they lived under the conditions which were in vogue in preceding centuries, both as to demand for goods and the supply of capital, these great inventors could only have enjoyed the meagre distinction which future generations accord to men who were in advance of their times.

It has been pointed out above, that the great geographical discoveries of the fifteenth century were the result of long-continued and conscious effort, directed to a clearly understood aim ; great expeditions had to be organised to sail on unknown seas and establish friendly relations with distant potentates. Explorers were forced to wait on courtly patronage and royal initiative ; but mechanical invention has run a different course. The coincidence of the two phenomena, a world-wide demand and a large supply of capital, enabled humble and unknown men to push on step by step ; political prestige and elaborate organisation were not so essential as in schemes for colonisation ; mechanical skill and personal ingenuity had at last obtained their chance.   The new industrial era, which the age of invention brought in its train, has offered a free field and given the greatest rewards to individual enterprise.   It is commonly said, that the physical advantage of England in the possession of enormous supplies of coal and iron side by side[2], have enabled her to out-distance her rivals, not only in

[1] See below, Appendix, p. 276.

[2] The advantage England derived from this source of wealth, in her struggle with France, was very great.

Coal had been worked in Roman times, and there was a considerable coal trade with London and with foreign countries in the seventeenth century.   But the cost of carriage rendered it impossible to work the Lancashire, Yorkshire, or Derbyshire coal-fields to any considerable extent till canals were introduced.   When the difficulty of smelting iron with

commerce but in industry; still, the proximity and quantity of coal and iron do not in themselves account for her success completely; in the case of such inventions as Arkwright's they do not account for it at all. The favourable conditions which English manufacturers enjoyed, in the eighteenth century, and the reliance on individual enterprise which had been traditional in Great Britain, were not unimportant factors in rendering this island the workshop of the world.

The Industrial Revolution has nowhere exerted its full influence as yet; we cannot regard it as an era that is in any sense closed even in any one country, while there are many lands that are only beginning to feel its effects. There can be little doubt, however, that the industrial methods which it introduces will sooner or later be adopted with more or less completeness in every part of the globe. In no territory can the rulers afford to hold aloof from the march of material progress; they might do so in times of peace, but they cannot in case of war; the mechanical appliances of modern warfare—including the railway as a means of massing troops,—are indispensable to those who desire to preserve political independence successfully; and the only hope of effectively handling the weapons of war lies in developing native skill. It is impossible even to depend entirely on the supplies of the

coal was solved as a practical thing, so that coal smelting could be a commercial success, there was a great increase in the demand for the fuel, and new fields could be profitably worked. But it was the invention of the steam-engine by Watt that enabled England to take full advantage of her mineral wealth, as she had never previously done. The coal and iron trades developed in combination and with enormous rapidity; both were requisite for the construction of machinery, and coal was needed for providing the power by which it could be continuously worked. It thus came about that the commercial supremacy to which England attained in 1760 reacted on her manufactures and gave a new importance to her mineral wealth. The age of invention and the introduction of steam-power combined to give her not only a commercial, but an industrial supremacy as well.

munitions of war that may be procurable from foreign nations. Modern mechanical skill and modern methods of organising industry are forcing themselves on all the peoples of the world; and this imitation under compulsion is not likely to be checked within any period we can forecast.

The age of invention is having a very deep influence on the thickly populated countries which were brought into contact with Western Civilisation at the epoch of the great discoveries; Asia and Africa had been but little affected by intercourse with Europe till this new movement began. It would have been possible to carry on commerce between England and India for centuries, without bringing any novelty into the social life of the 'changeless East.' But the introduction of modern industrial appliances and organisation is a different matter; the building of railways and the erection and working of other machinery has come about through the intervention of capitalist direction and control; and modern methods of business administration tend to modify the habits of daily life and work of Eastern peoples. No attempt can be made as yet to summarise the precise nature of the changes which have taken place in every part of the world as the result of the age of invention; it must suffice to indicate the general trend of these new economic forces, so far as we can gauge it. To do this intelligently it will be necessary to concentrate attention on the recent history of England, as that is the country where the changes originally began, and where there has been most opportunity for the reaction of the Industrial Revolution on various sides of social and political life. We may thus detect the prominent tendencies that may be looked for in other parts of the globe, though they will of course be greatly modified according to the special circumstances of each country. By examining the results of the age of invention as we may see them in England itself, and as we may trace them in English policy, we can form some idea of the lines on which the slower movements in other lands are likely to proceed.

125. The true character of the Industrial Revolution

The loss of industrial Sta-bility. may be most easily seen if we contrast the conditions of English industry in the middle of the eighteenth century with those that were current in the staple trades of the country about seventy years later[1]. At the earlier date there was an extraordinary *stability* in the economic life of England; manufacture was on a very small scale as compared with the giant production of a later date; but it had a firm footing, and there was little danger of violent fluctuations or of serious competition. By far the most important industry was the weaving of cloth, both woollen and worsted; closely connected with this, were the preparatory processes of carding or combing and spinning, as well as the separate callings of shearmen, cloth-workers, and dyers. This great industry catered for foreign markets, and there were, of course, occasional periods of depression, owing to interruptions of exportation; but on the whole the steadiness of the trade was remarkable, and was due to the fact that England produced her own raw materials, chiefly if not exclusively, and that the reputation of English manufacture stood so high that the goods could almost always be sold at remunerative prices. On the one hand, there was not much risk of a wool famine; and on the other, the demand for so excellent an article was not likely to fall off. Those who were employed in the trade could usually count on doing a regular and steady business; the man who started as a clothier or merchant[2], might have little prospect of making a fortune rapidly, but it was most improbable that he would fail altogether.

In the early part of the present century, the cotton trade had grown from relative insignificance to great importance and had out-distanced the woollen trade. Drapery was no longer

[1] The period between the triumph of the English arms at Plassey and Quebec, and at Waterloo, may be taken as giving the limits. 1759—1815.

[2] The term clothier is ambiguous; it applies to cloth merchants in the West of England, and to weavers in Yorkshire.

the principal article of English export. There was a large market for cotton yarn in Germany, and for cotton cloth in the East; the raw materials in this industry, however, were not of home production. English workers were dependent for a supply on Egypt and later on the Southern States, and the frequent interruptions, to which the trade was liable, rendered cotton-spinning highly speculative. There were sudden changes in the conditions of business; and while many men made large fortunes, there were numerous capitalists who had great diffi-culty in maintaining their commercial existence. The instability of the cotton manufacture was brought into clear light during the war with the United States in 1812[1], and became still more obvious half a century later, during the cotton famine con-sequent on the Civil War between the North and the South. The progress of mechanical invention, and the success of English producers in catering for distant markets, have involved this serious drawback,—that there is far more instability in industry than there used to be in the pre-revolutionary era. The fluctuations are more violent, and there is also much greater probability that some foreign competitor may be success-ful in ousting the English producer from markets which he has hitherto supplied.

The commercial supremacy of Great Britain in the eighteenth century led to rapid industrial growth; and by that develop-ment her textile and hardware trades have become her chief resources; they now constitute the basis of much of her com-merce and the means of purchasing supplies of food. The rela-tive instability of her industry, now that manufactures form such a vital factor in her national economic life, is a serious danger to the continuance of the material prosperity of Great Britain as a political power; and the uncertainty attaching to modern industry also has a very detrimental effect on the condition and

---

[1] The difficulty of procuring raw materials by importation had been one of the causes for the industrial decline of Holland. Pringsheim, *op. cit.* 38.

comfort of thousands of workmen personally.   Fluctuations in trade must mean inconstancy of employment and such variations in the rates of wages that it is almost impossible for the workman to maintain his ordinary standard of comfort.   The industrial changes which have been forced on by the age of invention have deprived the working classes of the means of warding off the mischief which this element of irregularity entails.   In the pre-revolutionary days, there was a very close interconnection between industrial and rural employments.   This was especially true of the staple trade of the country—the manufacture of cloth.   Many of the weavers were small farmers with a little grazing land, while others could eke out their subsistence by occasional labour in the fields during harvest and at other busy seasons.   As weaving came to be more and more attracted to the industrial centres, and to be organised by capitalists who provided weaving sheds in which the hands worked under supervision, there was less opportunity for combining agricultural work with cloth-making.   The introduction of the power-loom drew the industry still more into factories and completed the divorce of the weavers as a class from the soil; they could no longer rely on a rural by-occupation for the means of subsistence, but were forced to be dependent on wages alone, at the very time when wages had come to be very irregular.   In this way, the introduction of machinery accelerated the aggregation of the population in factory towns.   The prejudicial effect of this change is most clearly seen in the case of the Yorkshire weavers, who strove to resist it by all the legal means in their power; but industrial employments of other kinds and in other places were somewhat similarly affected.   Artisans, who had had allotments from which they could procure garden produce, were deprived of this outside source of supplies and were reduced to the position of mere wage-earners, when the expansion of the great towns like Sheffield covered the available space with busy shops[1].   In the pre-revolutionary days the

[1] Cunningham, *Growth of English Industry*, II. 480.

majority of the skilled workmen of the country seem to have had a second string to their bow; in the early part of the present century they appear to have become wage-earners pure and simple.

The concentration of industrial enterprise in large centres has been an inevitable result of the age of invention and has many economic advantages; it gives great facilities for effective supervision[1], while it enables the capitalist to turn natural supplies of power to good account[2]; none the less must it be recognised that the effects on the hands were temporarily injurious from the first, and that the permanent loss to the rural districts has been very great. So long as weaving was widely diffused throughout the country, there was in every district plenty of work for those women and children who liked to betake themselves to the spinning of wool[3]; this served as a by-employment by which a substantial contribution could be made to the family income of rural labourers and of farmers. The concentration of the trade, and still more, the introduction of spinning machinery, deprived the agricultural population of this opportunity of earning a livelihood; the period of transition was tided over by a liberal distribution of poor relief, which had disastrous results in pauperising the rural districts; but the net result, at the close of the Napoleonic War, was similar in rural and urban life,—the labourer was everywhere reduced to the condition of a mere hand, who was wholly dependent on his wages for the means of subsistence, and who had no means of supplementing his earnings from any other source.

126. This serious industrial change occurred at a time

[1] See above (p. 181) on the Gilds and capitalist organisation.

[2] This is especially true in regard to water, which was the motor-power chiefly used in the first phases of the industrial revolution.

[3] Cotton-spinning was a comparatively small affair, and was confined to a small area before Arkwright and Hargreaves revolutionised it by their inventions.

when English agriculture was also being revolutionised, and
when the general trend of progress in the
management of land was proving disastrous to
the rural labourer.   In many parts of the
country some sort of open field cultivation
continued to be practised in the eighteenth century; the
yeoman farmers had holdings of thirty or forty acres each,
and these consisted of separate strips, intermingled with
those of other cultivators.   All landlords and others who
were interested in promoting agricultural improvements regarded this primitive system of tillage as a serious obstacle
to the changes they contemplated; and the process of enclosure was pushed on rapidly, so that each farmer might
have his own land in severalty, and be able to work it to
the best advantage, according to his own ideas[1].   This
rearrangement might have been beneficial to all parties, but
it was so costly, that the small farmers had difficulty in
paying their share of the expense; and during the period of
transition, a great many of the little holdings appear to have
been consolidated.   The yeoman farmer, whether freeholder or
tenant, who worked the land himself, with only occasional help,
was rapidly superseded by the capitalist farmer, who habitually
employed labourers for wages.   Some of the small farmers probably sank in the social scale to the position of mere labourers,
who as a class, also seem to have suffered by enclosing, at all
events, in cases where they had been permitted to put a little
stock on the common waste.   Generally speaking, the labourers
lost their chance of rising in the world; this had always been
open to them so long as small holdings were available, which
they might sooner or later be able to stock and to work.   The
progress of enclosure deprived the rural labourer of an effective

*The Capita-
listic Organi-
sation of Agri-
culture.*

---

[1] Enclosures had taken place in the fifteenth and sixteenth centuries,
in order to develop sheep-farming and at the expense of tillage, but in the
eighteenth century they were introduced for the sake of improved tillage.

ambition, at the very time when the loss of employment in spinning was pauperising his family.

We may thus see that the changes which followed on the age of invention resulted in the development of similar economic conditions both in town and country. Throughout England we find the triumph of capitalist organisation. The domestic[1] system was passing away so far as the clothing trade was concerned, and the yeoman farmer was rising to a different grade, or was disappearing altogether. Both in town and country life there were capitalist employers, who controlled and supervised the work of labourers; in town and country alike the labourers were strictly dependent on the employer for the means of subsistence, and had no means of supplementing their earnings by applying themselves occasionally to other occupations. The age of invention accelerated the change which had been going on slowly for centuries[2], and brought about the complete reconstruction of society, economically considered, on a capitalistic basis.

127. We have already seen that, at its first introduction, the capitalistic organisation of industry proved to be incompatible with the existence of the gilds and other institutions of mediaeval civic life; in some places they checked the introduction of capitalism, in others they were completely superseded by the new scheme which gave greater scope for the division of labour. The antagonism between the old associations and new methods becomes more obvious when we see the disintegrating influence of the modern system at work on a large scale. Capital, when it learned to employ the new forces which were put at its service by the age of invention,

The Disintegration of National Economic Life.

---

[1] This term as commonly used does not include all those artisans who worked at home, but applies to the economic system, where the weaver worked on material he purchased, and sold the result of his work to the cloth merchant.

[2] See above p. 180.

outgrew the English system of regulation, which had been established in the interest of the nation as an economic whole. During the early part of the present century, the structure which had been consolidated in the age of Elizabeth was discarded bit by bit, until at last all legislative attempts to pursue the special interest of Great Britain, as distinct from and opposed to that of other countries, were definitely abandoned. Economists claimed that national prosperity was best attained by leaving capital absolutely unfettered. In the beginning of the present century, Parliament was inclined to accept this opinion as axiomatic; and it is worth while to notice the effect of this maxim and to trace the successive steps by which the great Elizabethan system of regulation was rapidly undermined.

The first important agitation arose in connection with the cotton trade. This industry, which had previously been pursued on a very small scale, had developed enormously owing to Arkwright's inventions; the cheapness of cotton yarn and cloth had stimulated the demand, and, despite the improvements in the processes of production, there was a much greater demand for labour in connection with the expanded trade than there had been in the old days. The application of machinery to this manufacture had not injured the labourers at all; it had provided an increased and not a diminished field for employment. The fluctuations in the trade, however, which rendered employment irregular and caused frequent changes in the rates of wages, had reduced the workmen to the lowest depths of distress. The men were anxious to introduce greater stability into the conditions under which the industry was carried on, and attempted again and again to secure, by arbitration, a list of the prices which should be adhered to; they recognised, too, that it was practically impossible for the masters generally to abide by the rates of the list, if any single employer began to cut down wages. In the hope of obtaining a remedy for this state of things,

the workmen fell back on the Elizabethan Act for the regulation of wages—a measure which had long before ceased
to be effective, but which seemed to bear directly on the
case, and, at least, gave a legal character to their demand.
They asked that the provisions of the statute should be set in
force[1]; but when the attention of Parliament was called to
this obsolete enactment, the House of Commons took an unex-
pected view of the situation; instead of re-enforcing an existing
law, they swept away the clauses which had been intended to
protect the labouring classes, by providing that wages should
be periodically assessed and the rates fixed according to
the plenty or scarcity of the time.   It is not certain that this
measure had ever been generally enforced ; attempt had been
made to put it in operation in a systematic London[2], though
the system seems to have been allowed to fall into desuetude
during the seventeenth century and Parliament could hardly
have succeeded in re-enforcing it in the nineteenth; but the
repeal of these clauses marks a change in the current view of
the duty of the Government towards the workman.   In the time
of Elizabeth, magistrates were expected to assess fair wages ;
in 1811, this safeguard against the mischief which competition
may do in reducing wages to starvation rates was swept away.

Disputes in the woollen trade were the cause of the
repeal of the apprenticeship clauses of Elizabeth's great labour
code.   Many of the weavers in the West of England had not
complied with the requirements of the Act by serving a seven
years' apprenticeship ; the legal weavers, who had undergone
this long training, demanded that the provisions of the Elizabethan Statute should be enforced against the ' illegal' workmen.
This the capitalist employers of the West of England determined
not to do, as they had no complaint to make of the 'illegal'

---

[1] Cunningham, *Economists as Mischief Makers*, in *Economic Review*,
IV. p. 8.
[2] E. A. McArthur, *Regulation of Wages* in *English Historical Review*
(July 1900), p. 449.

weavers, many of whom were competent workmen; for the long term of apprenticeship was not a good guarantee of real efficiency, at all events so far as weaving was concerned[1]. The legal weavers had started an agitation for enforcing existing, though obsolete, laws; but in the course of the discussion that followed, parliamentary opinion became more and more opposed to their demands. The principal question raised was in regard to apprenticeship; and the House of Commons finally took the extreme step of withdrawing all the legal encouragement which had hitherto been given to this method of industrial training. The advocates of *laissez faire* believed that in those trades where it was working well, the seven years' apprenticeship could hold its own, without legislative support; but later events have proved they were mistaken; the capitalist organisation of industry is not favourable to apprenticeship, and the system has practically disappeared[2]. The Yorkshire weavers, who looked on the binding of apprentices as a barrier to the farther inroads of capitalism on their "domestic system," were perfectly right in their forecast of the results of repealing the measure; the change has been the most drastic of all the innovations caused by the industrial revolution.

The introduction of the factory system and the depletion of the rural districts have also tended to bring about the disintegration of the household as an economic whole. In prerevolutionary days the children had been kept at home and helped in domestic work or outdoor tasks in farm or garden; and so long as apprenticeship lasted there was a natural training at home for the industrial duties of adult life. Each household, moreover, was an economic whole[3], as the

[1] The art could be learned in two years, and the long term was inconvenient to the masters in the case of idle youths, and pressed hardly on the youth who was doing man's work, but not getting man's pay.

[2] On present methods of entering different trades, compare S. and B. Webb. *Industrial Democracy*, II. 454—507.

[3] The contrast between the mediaeval and modern methods of regulation is instructive. The craft-gilds, by exercising a right of search, could bring

various members contributed their quota of work, and obtained support from the common stock. The factory system has changed the character of the family as an economic group; the women and children may go out to earn wages at the factory; domestic employments must necessarily be neglected; and the children, as self-supporting by their own earnings, assume a position of independence which would not have been natural in the old days. As a consequence, parental responsibility for maintenance of the family ceases at an earlier age than was formerly the case[1]; but the sense of duty in this respect was seriously weakened by the action which the guardians of the poor in rural districts felt forced to take during the wool famine of 1793 A.D. At a time when food was scarce and dear the women and children in rural districts were prevented by lack of material from adding to the family income by spinning, as they had been accustomed to do. The guardians in one district after another granted allowances to supplement wages, as a means of tiding over what seemed to be a temporary difficulty; but the industry never revived, and the application of machinery to the spinning of wool killed it off altogether. The action of the poor law authorities in assuming so much of the burden of supporting families was a most serious departure from the principle, which had been assumed from time immemorial, of recognising and enforcing the responsibility of parents for the upbringing of their children.

The last remnants of the regulations which had been

pressure to bear on men working at their homes as to the condition under which work was done, and the payment and treatment of workmen. The factory Acts and factory and mining commissions aim at supplying similar supervision and are probably much more effective; but the household is no longer the unit to be taken into account, and the master of the household is no longer the responsible party. The whole series of factory Acts assumes the existence of new conditions of industry, and helps us to see how complete the disintegration of the household had become.

[1] The evidence before the commission on mines in 1840 A.D. brought out the necessity of protecting children against their parents.

framed with the object of building up a national industrial system, were swept away, as a result of a parliamentary committee[1] which reported in 1824 A.D. In pre-revolutionary times, when nations were engaged in keen industrial rivalry, such as subsisted between France and England, the authorities were particularly careful to prohibit the emigration of skilled artisans, who might carry trade-secrets with them and plant some valuable art in another country. Great efforts had been made to keep English weavers at home, and to stop artisans from emigrating to the colonies[2]. Circumstances had so far changed, however, that it seemed unnecessary to maintain these restrictions; machinery, rather than manual labour, was now the dominating feature in industrial success. The limitations on the employment of workmen abroad caused special inconvenience to engineers, who were practically prevented from erecting machinery in foreign countries, and no serious effort was made to retain the prohibitions in the Statute Book. There seems to have been an impression that England could maintain her superiority in manufacture without any such adventitious aid; but the fact that the rules were allowed to drop, shows how completely the old methods of building up national industry to the exclusion of possible rivals had been discarded.

This particular change was of great importance in another respect; it removed the legislative hindrances which had stood in the way of founding a new colonial empire on sounder principles than those of the eighteenth century. Mr E. G. Wakefield and a group of enthusiasts were eagerly advocating the planting of Australia as an expedient for relieving the plethora of labour and of capital from which, as they believed, England was suffering. He argued that the colonies should be rendered, so far as possible, self-sufficing communities, equipped

---

[1] The most important result of this enquiry was the repeal of the Combination Acts; on these, see below p. 247.

[2] See below p. 277.

with an urban as well as a rural population, and that their prosperity would react favourably on the material wealth of the mother country. He was not able to persuade the Government to interest itself energetically in promoting colonisation ; the public were, for a time, indifferent to the expansion of England, but at all events, they ceased to be jealous of the new settlements. All attempts to subordinate the economic development of the colonies to the interests of the mother country have been long since abandoned. The prohibition of the emigration of artisans was one of the last surviving elements of the national system of industrial regulation, but this was finally swept away by a great repealing measure in 1825[1] A.D., and the field was cleared for building a new colonial empire.

The *laissez faire* principle,—that regulation was not necessary to promote prosperity and that it might often prove injurious,—was at length applied, though not without hesitation, to the mercantile marine, which had been the most important factor in creating England's greatness. The maintenance and improvement of shipping, as the mainstay of the power of a maritime nation, had been the foremost consideration in the economic policy of the country since the time of Burleigh ; but in the first half of the present century, this legislative interference was abandoned ; it seemed to be no longer necessary, and, in any case, it was of doubtful advantage. During the eighteenth century, the development of commercial intercourse had been regarded as of less importance than the fostering of English shipping ; but under the teaching of Adam Smith, public men began to regard intercourse as in itself a good thing, and to hold that the supposed advantage which accrued from stimulating shipping was illusory, especially when the loss due to limiting the opportunities of exchange was taken into account. The first great relaxation in the Navigation Acts was made in 1796 A.D., in favour of the

[1] 5 Geo. IV. c. 95.

United States; and experience seemed to show, that free communication with the independent country was far more advantageous than the restricted and regulated commerce with the colonies had been. A few years later, in 1820 A.D., the London Chamber of Commerce took the matter up as a general principle of policy, and insisted that the interests of trade demanded the fullest freedom of intercourse between countries, rather than the special encouragement of our own mercantile marine. The object which had so long been the corner-stone of British policy was deliberately rejected, and the navigation system was rapidly modified, in accordance with the new views.

The adherents of the old system of national economics took their last stand in regard to the food supply; it had been the traditional practice in England for centuries to foster agriculture, and so to ensure the existence of sufficient corn for the population[1]. This was a line of policy that was peculiarly English; the profitableness of sheep-farming in the fifteenth and sixteenth centuries had seemed to be a national danger, and special pains were taken for the encouragement of tillage in the Tudor times. The fiscal convenience of government in the seventeenth and eighteenth centuries had told in the same direction; it seemed desirable to provide for the welfare of the agricultural interest, since the taxation of the country fell so heavily on the land. There was a strong

---

[1] The teaching of Malthus had caused a singular change in the ordinary attitude of the public towards the increase of population. In the pre-revolutionary period, there had been frequent anxiety about the alleged decline of population, and some discussion as to the means of stimulating its increase. The rapid development of industry had, as Sir James Steuart insisted, brought about this result so effectively, that the popular mind was scared by the dread of over-population. Further consideration shows that both these fears are illusory; the impulse to increase suffices to take advantage of any opportunity offered by the means of subsistence, but it does not necessarily bring about such an increase of population as to lower the standard of comfort of any class. *Modern Civilisation*, 173.

phalanx of traditional opinion and of vested interests which combined to pass the Corn Law of 1815 A.D., in the hope that this measure would maintain the conditions which had come into existence during the war, and had given an unhealthy stimulus to corn-growing in Britain. This protective measure failed to accomplish the object with which it was framed ; it did little to benefit the agricultural interest generally, though it seems to have been beneficial to the landowners as a class : on the other hand, it hampered our commerce and checked the development of our manufactures[1]. The success of the Free Trade movement was inevitable ; and the genius of Cobden secured a very rapid triumph for the principles he had espoused, by the repeal of the Corn Laws in 1846 A.D. The abandonment of the traditional scheme of economic policy in regard to the food supply—the most vital of national interests —was the final blow before which the old system succumbed. At that date, national wealth and prosperity ceased to be a distinct aim towards which national efforts could be wisely directed ; the triumph of individual enterprise, against all forms of restriction and regulation, was at length complete.

The triumph of individualism over nationalism in internal affairs involved a complete change in the economic attitude which Englishmen took towards other countries. The greatest advantage to Great Britain, under the new conditions, lay in having the freest possible intercourse with other countries, so as to obtain access to the largest markets possible, and to procure supplies on the cheapest terms. It was not to her interest to continue to pursue the exclusive commercial policy by which her naval power had been built up ; and her acceptance of a place in a cosmopolitan Economic System was loudly hailed as the harbinger of an era of universal peace. The jubilations of the Free-traders and Peace party have proved premature ; but yet they were not wholly absurd. The desire to pursue an exclusive commerce has been a frequent

[1] Cunningham, *Growth of English Industry*, II. 591.

occasion of war in the past; national economic rivalry and a war of tariffs keep alive a spirit of hostility which may break out unexpectedly and suddenly in actual fighting. The abandonment of her traditional system by the greatest of commercial nations has already diminished the causes of conflict so far as England herself is concerned. Foreign traders generally have little to gain through a loss to England of any of those portions of her Empire where she has been free to carry out her new commercial policy. Free trade has not secured peace, but it has done much to remove occasions of active hostility.

At any rate the discarding of an exclusive economic policy by the country in which nationality was attained at such an early time is noteworthy. It at least raises the question whether nationality gives the final form for the organisation of industry and commerce. It suggests the speculation that frequent intercourse between different parts of the world may so increase, that all countries may come to be more and more interdependent economically; and that larger and larger sections of the community may find that their interests are suffering from the maintenance of national economic schemes, and may desire instead to be free to make the most of their opportunities as members of a Cosmopolitan System.

128. Attention has been called in earlier chapters of this essay to the fact that there have been three main types of social structure, which have formed the basis of economic organisation—the family, the city, and the nation. The self-sufficing households of great landed proprietors were superseded, as the basis of industrial life, by the growth of cities; the city with its exclusive policy, passed away, before the rise of nationalities. The industrial revolution has tended to introduce a thoroughgoing individualism: it makes for the disintegration of the family and it is opposed to nationalism. But it may at least be doubted whether nationalism is a final form in economic development; and the maintenance of English power under new conditions

(side note: Re-adaptation and Re-construction.)

has discredited the perspicuity of the mercantilists who acted on the opinion that the business pursuits of individuals should be habitually subordinated to the interests of national wealth.

Neither the family, the civic, nor the national types of organisation can claim the predominance which each in turn has formerly exercised; they may, however, each have useful economic functions to discharge. There is no immediate prospect that any of them can be dispensed with altogether, for all may contribute effectively to individual well-being. The importance of the family and the home in connection with the upbringing of each new generation, is obvious and need not be dwelt upon; it is recognised by all grades; not only by Trades Unions whose policy shows that they are fully alive to the importance of family life as an element in the well-being of the working classes[1], but also by civic authorities and private philanthropists who are concentrating attention on the problem of so housing the poor, in town and country, that families may be able to live in decent conditions.

The city, too, is the appropriate organ for attending to many requirements, which are of vital significance to the individual citizen; provision for lighting, for the supply of water, for rapid transit, for sanitation, and for opportunities of healthful recreation in public parks, are essential to the well-being and efficiency of the inhabitants as individuals. The vast aggregations of population, which have been brought together since the age of invention opened, have rendered these problems more difficult, and there is an ample field for the activity of municipal governments in dealing with them effectively[2].

The nation also has economic functions to discharge, which cannot be dealt with so satisfactorily by any organ of local government. In so far as it is desirable to secure favourable conditions for labour, it is advisable that there should be a

---

[1] Cunningham, *Politics and Economics*, 100.

[2] *Modern Civilisation*, 182.

similar rule through the whole area in which there is a free flow for labour and capital[1]. The work of factory inspectors and inspectors of mines, has done much to prevent the deterioration of the population. They have been appointed to enforce laws which lay down a minimum of safety and sanitation and a maximum of hours; in this way there has been a gradual amelioration of the conditions in which work is carried on. It is the duty of the Government of a country to look far into the future[2], and to consider the maintenance of national resources, while it is not necessarily the interest of any capitalist, however enterprising, to take account of future generations.

The final result of the Industrial Revolution, so far as it can be traced in England, has been, not the destruction of the fundamental types of social organisation[3], but their adaptation to modern requirements and changed circumstances. At the same time some institutions have arisen that are so distinct from anything that has preceded them, that they may be regarded as wholly new. Of these, the most important are the Trades Unions. The labour organisations of the Middle Ages, at all events in England, were strictly municipal; the modern labour association has no such localised character, but is adapted for creating international federations, and for pursuing cosmopolitan aims. Both in its genesis and in its constitution, the Trades Union is very different from the ancient *collegia* and the mediaeval craft gilds which are its nearest analogues.

[1] See above on the definition of a country, p. 158.

[2] A new economic importance attaches both to the city and the nation, since the system of public borrowing has become so common. Each is able to draw on its probable future, for the sake of immediate requirements, on far easier terms than is possible for any individual.

[3] On the whole, the old civic institutions have been destroyed; but some remain, and considerable efforts are being made to give them a new economic importance. We may notice this tendency in the proposal to utilise the Livery Companies in connection with technical training at the present time.

Trades Unions have arisen tentatively or permanently, as a means of protecting labour from the dangers to which it is exposed, when the action of capitalists is quite unfettered and there are no safeguards against reckless competition; and Unionism has gradually felt its way towards a more positive programme[1]. So long as the State professed to undertake the duties of assessing wages and of providing for the efficient training of workmen, there was some reason for objecting to the action of private individuals, associated together for interference in matters of public concern. But the repeal of the Elizabethan industrial code left the workman exposed to all the uncertainty and misery caused by the introduction of machine industry and the sudden fluctuations and ruinous competition which followed in its train. There had been a traditional suspicion of workmen's combinations, and, during the political scare of 1799 and 1800[2] A.D., another attempt was made to put them down altogether, as they seemed to be possible centres of sedition. The conditions of secrecy, under which the societies were forced to work, contributed to give them a tyrannical and criminal character[3], and placed them at a special disadvantage in any attempts to obtain a legal status. As a matter of fact, however, they were only contending for a more thoroughgoing application of the principle of *laissez faire*; if the individual ought to be free to act in his own interest, he ought also to be free to combine with other individuals for the pursuit of their common interest[4]. In 1825 A.D. the

---

[1] It may now be summarised as the struggle for a Standard Wage and Normal Day, to be secured by legislative action.

[2] Cunningham, *Economists as Mischief Makers*, in *Economic Review*, IV. 12.

[3] Webb, *History of Trades Unionism*, 72. Mrs L. Bankes, *Bond slaves*.

[4] The freedom of combination for all sorts of economic objects, is the last triumph of individualism. In the days of slave labour, combination might mean a servile war. Even among the free labourers of Athens, there seems to have been very little association; while the *collegia* had a chequered existence at Rome. In the Middle Ages the craft gilds, with

Combination Laws were repealed, under the mistaken belief that
it never could be for the real interest of individual workmen to
combine for trade objects, and that they would soon discover
this fact, when once they had perfect freedom of action in
the matter[1].   But the steady increase in the numbers and
power of labour organisations, during the last seventy-five years,
has given another instance to show how completely mistaken
the most skilled observers may be in their forecasts on political
and social affairs.   The Trades Unions have, for the most
part, discarded the restrictive policy which they were inclined
to follow at first[2], and try to pursue a course that is compatible
with the attainment of the highest possible efficiency[3].   In so

all their dignity, were often kept in hand by municipal authority or royal
regulations ; the possibility that they might prove an economic danger
was clearly understood.   In our country and days attempts at suppressing
such organisations have ceased to be possible, even if they were desirable ;
the freedom to form voluntary associations for economic objects has been
won ; but there may still be grave anxiety about the wisdom of the Unions,
and of the policy they pursue.   If these associations concentrate attention
on the special interests of one section or class, and are not ready to
abandon any line of action which is injurious to the public as a whole,
there must be class antagonisms on the largest scale, entailing frightful
economic loss.   If they have self-restraint enough to take the well-being of
the whole community as a principle controlling their action, they will prove
their fitness for a share in government by themselves adopting the principle
which was authoritatively imposed on voluntary associations and combinations in earlier times.

[1] This was the opinion of Francis Place and Joseph Hume, under
whose guidance the House of Commons was induced to include the
Combination Acts in the great Statute of Repeal in 1825.   Wallas, *Life
of F. Place,* 211, 217.

[2] For instances of this action see Webb, *Industrial Democracy,* 392 ; on
the objection to machinery, see *Modern Civilisation,* 126—7, also *Outlines
of English History,* 226.

[3] The Manchester School did not take sufficient account of the fact that
improved conditions for labour may often bring about increased efficiency
of labour, and that under certain circumstances the indirect effect of
shortened hours may be to increase and not to diminish production.   On
the whole, however, they were right in taking the greatest possible amount

far as they keep within these lines, their action is innocuous, while they have introduced some useful correctives to the mischiefs which accompanied the transition to capitalist organisation. They have set themselves to introduce greater stability, so as to diminish the violence of trade fluctuations, with its disastrous result on the lot of the workman ; and they have also endeavoured to maintain the workman's standard of comfort, and to oppose all influences which directly or indirectly tend to diminish his welfare.

It is sometimes asserted that the improved condition of the English working classes is due to the "general progress of Society," and that there would have been similar results if factory Acts and Trades Unions had never existed; the statement is certainly unprovable, and it is, on the face of it, highly improbable. Mere individual competition may tend to the progress of society, but it does not necessarily take account of the probable position of the next generation, or of the prosperity of the wage-earning class generally. The State has stepped in with legislation and inspection, and the artisans have organised themselves to secure important elements of well-being, which individuals, as such, would have hardly had the power to obtain. Despite the miserable circumstances of many of the poor, there is yet reason to believe that the new social conditions introduced by the Industrial Revolution are favourable to the welfare of the working classes, both as regards material surroundings and personal character. It is easy to idealise

of production as a test of the beneficial or the hurtful effects of industrial changes. Any combination, be it of labourers or of capitalists, that by its demands or rules limits the total of production and thus reduces the possibilities of enjoyment is justly suspected of being a public nuisance. There may be adequate grounds for such action, but at least it demands a very full justification, and there is a *primâ facie* case against it. There is also a real danger that, since economic relations and organisations are becoming more and more cosmopolitan, there may be no political power which is capable of dealing effectively in any one district with organisations which have such wide ramifications.

the past, and to paint a picture of the independent and happy weaver, living in a pretty village, working on his own account, and assisted by his wife and family. But the more we examine the details, the more we shall see reason to suspect that the life of the manufacturer in pre-revolutionary days was not one which would rouse the jealousy of the average modern artisan. The standard of comfort was low; and the weaver, who could earn good wages, was content to spend much of his time in mere idleness; in the narrow circle of village life, he could have no intelligent interests in politics or sport, while he was cut off from all opportunities of musical or literary cultivation. We know, from surviving examples, how miserable were the rooms in which he did his work, and there is no reason to believe that his children always found him a just and self-restrained master; the primitive factories adopted the normal arrangements of domestic industry, so far as sanitation and ventilation are concerned. The factory system brought to light the thoroughly unsatisfactory state in which men, women and children were living and working, and made it possible to attempt a remedy. There doubtless has been serious loss to the individual, who has found that he is no longer an independent man, but a hand controlled by the tyranny of the factory bell; but the discipline of regular work and hours, and the training which comes by association in work, have contributed to the formation of an admirable type of character. As we look back to pre-revolutionary days, through all the misery of the transition period, we may doubt if there is any point in which the artisan and his family were better off then than they are to-day. This result has not been due, however, to the blind play of economic forces; so far as these were concerned they only caused social disintegration and individual degradation. It is the machinery which has been devised to control these blind forces which has been mainly instrumental in bringing about this general amelioration, and has rendered it possible to care for the interest of the masses of the population, present and future.

129. Every scheme of nationalist economic policy had
assumed as axiomatic, that there were certain
kinds of material prosperity, which it was desirable to cultivate in the interests of national
strength ; and that it was the duty of the Government to induce the business energy of the people to take those
directions which would be beneficial to the country as a political
power. Under the influence of Adam Smith, this doctrine fell
into disrepute. Since the community is an aggregate of
individuals, it seemed that the general wealth was best attained
by leaving each man to pursue his own affairs ; it was felt too
that if general prosperity were increasing, there would be
facilities for procuring any particular form of wealth that might
be desired. The recognition of nationality as the guiding
principle in all economic organisation had been an important
step in advance, but so soon as the country became doubtful
of the wisdom of controlling all the economic activities of
Englishmen with the aim of fostering the power of the realm,
the whole system of national regulation fell into abeyance.
Enactments to direct the course of industry, to encourage
shipping, and to obtain a sufficient food supply at home,
were, as we have seen, abandoned one after another. Para-
doxical as it may appear, it is yet strictly true to say that
for commercial and industrial purposes, England has ceased
to be a "nation" in the economic sense of the term. The
change has, however, introduced considerable difficulties in
regard to the financial system of the country. From time
immemorial, the chief expenses of government, so far as they
were defrayed by taxation, had been borne by the land ;
customs were comparatively unimportant, so long as the trade
of the country was trivial, and excises were not levied before
the Great Rebellion. The landed proprietors bore the
principal part of the burden of taxation, and after the
Restoration they showed an increasing jealousy of the moneyed
interest, who managed to enjoy great fortunes, while they

(margin: Modifications in English Finance.)

contributed but little to the expenses of the nation.   Fiscal convenience rendered it easy to assess and collect contributions from those who had a fixed stake in the country ; while Locke taught that the burden of taxation must ultimately fall on the landed proprietors, and that it was best and cheapest to levy it upon them directly.

The highly protective Corn Law of 1815 A.D. was in part an attempt to remove the unfairness which was due to the pressure of taxation ; this fell unduly on the landed interest, while agriculturists were also burdened by the obligation to pay tithe, and the necessity of supporting the pauperised population in rural districts.   The Act failed to accomplish its object of rendering the landed interest more able to bear the unfair share with which it was charged.   The cost to certain sections of the community proved so great, that it was impossible for Government to persist in this clumsy expedient for rectifying the injustice of the fiscal system.   Considerable progress has been made, however, in solving the difficulty in a better way ; arrangements have been devised which have proved fairly successful in assessing and collecting revenue from citizens whose wealth does not consist in real estate.   The excise and customs have come to be very large branches of revenue, and they are paid by consumers of every class, rich and poor, rural and urban.   Still more important in its principle is the income tax, which forces the capitalist to contribute from the profits of his business, and the *rentier* to pay a portion of the revenue from his savings.   The machinery for the collection of this branch of Inland Revenue can be used for adjusting the incidence of taxation, to a considerable extent ; though it is not easy to fix on any standard of fairness or unfairness in apportioning public burdens between the landed and the moneyed interests.   There is however one obvious advantage which arises from the existence of the income tax ; it has become possible to discard the nationalist economic policy without serious financial danger.   In days when landed proprietors were the only class that could be reached by the collectors of revenue, it was necessary to safeguard their interests[1]; but the income tax gives the means of deriving revenue for the State from the profits of capital invested abroad; it removes the financial motive which formerly gave rise to jealousy lest colonial progress should interfere with the sources from which national revenue was drawn. So long as moneyed Englishmen continue to prefer their own country and make it their home, it is a matter of comparative indifference to the Government, whether their capital is invested in India, or the colonies, or in this island; it still pays its quota of revenue to the Crown. The re-organisation of our revenue system, which was accepted by the country in 1874 A.D., is compatible with the development of English economic activity, not merely on national, but on cosmopolitan lines.

England has been the pioneer of the age of invention; by herself accepting the results of the industrial revolution, she has been fitted to take a principal part in diffusing these industrial improvements and introducing rapid means of communication in all parts of the globe. The work she has already accomplished, directly and through her great offshoots in America and Australasia, give her a unique importance in the history of the world, while it has forced her to adapt her own economic life to a cosmopolitan environment. A country has been defined for economic purposes as an area within which there is a free flow of labour and capital; but England recognises and imposes no limits of area; she has allowed the emigration of her skilled labourers since 1825 A.D., and has become fiscally indifferent to the fields which may be chosen for the investment of capital. For good or for evil, she has abandoned a national economic policy, alike in commerce and industry, in agriculture and finance.

---

[1] This is particularly noticeable in the treatment which Ireland received in the seventeenth century. Cunningham, *Repression of Woollen Trade*, in *English History Review*, I. 287.

CHAPTER II.

GENERAL TENDENCIES AND PARTICULAR CONDITIONS.

130. THE rapid material progress which began in England
last century is being communicated to the rest of

The inevitable tendency of Economic Forces.
the world. The benefits which the new processes of industry and means of intercourse
offer are so great that peoples, like the Japanese,
who have long remained in an almost stationary condition are
glad to imitate the progressive races of the West, and to
introduce mechanical inventions of every kind. In other
cases, such as that of China, the necessities of military defence
have compelled princes to adopt modern weapons, and to
borrow some assistance from European instructors. Enterprising capitalists are ready to force their way into any part
of the world, where there is a prospect of developing natural
resources, which will yield a profitable return on their ventures.
Mechanical improvements and the capitalist organisation of
industry—with which machine-production is most conveniently
associated—are superseding the primitive industrial arts and
earlier types of economic life in every known region of the
globe.

Some of these changes are inevitable; it may often be a
matter of regret, but the great economic forces, when once
they are allowed to come into operation, will not be gainsaid;
and it is improbable that the movements which begin when a

country is drawn into the circle of trading intercourse, can be arbitrarily arrested at any point. When barriers are once broken down, the substitution of money payments for natural economy, of competition for regulated prices, and of capitalistic supervision for gild organisation, is likely to go on apace ; it is difficult to conceive of any means by which these changes can be checked so that the old social forms and customary usages may be preserved intact. It is easy to denounce the "greed" of prospectors and pioneers who open up some new country ; but their gains are not merely personal, since their enterprise is only rewarded[1] when they succeed in meeting a general demand by catering for the requirements of the inhabitants of the thickly populated European countries. We live in times when claims to exclusive privilege are subjected to careful scrutiny ; civilised peoples are insisting that the resources of the earth shall be utilised to their fullest extent ; they resent the claim of any barbaric or half-civilised people to retain territory when they are careless about turning it to good account. It is in the interest of the race as a whole that the possibilities of life on the globe should be fully enjoyed ; and those who prefer to live as hunters or nomads on land that is suitable for tillage will never be able to hold their own in the struggle for subsistence. If any tribe or community refuses to bring its energy to bear in turning the land to the most profitable use, it is likely to be ousted by others who are ready to undertake the task.

131. There are many persons who believe that these changes are deleterious and who look towards the future with the gloomiest sense of foreboding. They believe that every step of progress means that a larger and larger portion of the population of the globe is drawn into a keener struggle for existence ; that every improvement in the industrial arts conduces to providing a larger food

Pessimism and Anarchism.

---

[1] *Modern Civilisation*, 141. As Mr Booth urges, profit is not so much a motive as a guide. *Life and Labour of the People in London*, IX. 170.

supply, but with severer toil[1]; and that the race is steadily
tending towards a desperate plight when the numbers will be
far greater than at present, and the misery of all more intense.
But this pessimistic view of the future of the race rests on the
assumption that man is the slave of his grosser impulses.
Each advance in material progress in the past has opened up
an opportunity which may be used either for the diffusion of
increased comfort, or for the mere multiplication of numbers
on the existing level of comfort, or partly for one and partly for
the other. There is a current opinion that such advantages are
sure to be misused for the increase of the numbers at the old
standard, but this is not necessary or inevitable; still less is
there any reason to believe that the increase of population will
go on mechanically so as to drive the masses to a lower level of
life[2]. So far as we can judge, the standard of comfort of the
skilled artisan in America and in England is higher than it has
been at any previous period of the world's history; and the
labouring classes possess so much political power in these
countries that the efforts they are making to maintain or to
raise that standard will not be easily thwarted. So long as this
is true of the most advanced communities we need not fear
that material progress must necessarily lead to the increased
misery and degradation of the race.

The mere increase of numbers and the capitalist organisation of modern society are, however, inconsistent with the aims
that many individuals cherish for themselves personally. The
classical economists idealised a condition of affairs in which
every man should be free to pursue his own interest as he conceived it; and they urged that this is advantageous for the community as a whole, since it conduces to the production of the
greatest mass of goods. A more thoroughgoing individualism
insists that in the existing state of society the majority of
the population are deprived of all opportunity of making their

---

[1] On the law of diminishing returns, see *Modern Civilisation*, 77—79.
[2] *Ibid.* 174.

way in life, and are condemned from their birth to toil in a fashion which may be advantageous to others, but is not in their own interests at all. As the line between the employing and the labouring classes becomes more clearly drawn, and as there is increasing difficulty in passing from one grade to the other, together with diminished facilities for rising into the more important positions in the employing class, there is less scope for the individual to carve out a career for himself. Persons of exceptional ability are still able to force their way to the highest rungs on the social ladder, but those with ordinary attainments and abilities can hardly hope ever to advance to the grade above them. There are larger and larger numbers of people who feel that they have never had a chance of improving their position, and who resent the institutions of society which have condemned them and so many of their fellows to a life of drudgery. Anarchism is not a mere inexcusable madness ; it is a very real danger to existing society because it is the logical outcome of certain widely current beliefs as applied by many individuals to their own circumstances. The mass of available wealth is of little account to such men, except in so far as it is available for them to enjoy during their own lives ; they demand freedom for individual self-development, and do not admit that they are called upon to sacrifice themselves personally either for the sake of the existing order or for generations to come.

However excusable this attitude of mind may be, such ultra-individualism is inconsistent with the maintenance and progress of human society ; we must not neglect either the personal or the social side of the matter. It is true that the institutions of any society are to be judged by the effect they have on the character of individuals ; but it is also true that the worth of the individual is to be gauged by his ability and readiness to contribute to the well-being of society present or future. That the sphere for independent action is being narrowed by capitalist organisation is a real hardship to the

individual; but from the social standpoint it is advantageous
because it is disciplinary, and renders the man more efficient
than he would otherwise be. We must remember, too, that
the highest development of character is quite compatible with
consciously accepting a place in the social order and making
the most of it. It is a mistake to assume that the limitation
of opportunity, which is brought about by the increase of
numbers and greater complexity of society, must necessarily
involve personal degradation.

Those who contemplate the greater command over the
means of production which has been placed within our reach
by the age of invention, cannot but feel a sense of dis-
appointment that so little has resulted for the happiness of
the human race. Still, though we can no longer sympathise
with the light-hearted optimism of the classical economist, we
need not fall into the opposite blunder of decrying material
progress as if it were merely mischievous, or necessarily involved serious evils. It does open up the possibility for an
improved standard of comfort, though the occasions it offers
may be neglected or misused; it leaves less scope for individual
independence, but this does not necessarily imply a deterioration of personal character.

132. At the same time, it is to be noticed that the mischiefs and hardships, on which pessimists and
anarchists lay such stress, are real; and they are
deeply to be regretted; but, while the march of
progress moves relentlessly on, it is yet true that
some of the evils, which have often accompanied
it, are not inevitable; for successful attempts have sometimes
been made to prevent their occurrence or to check them where
they have arisen. The best safeguard against some dangers
is to be found in recognising their existence, and in being
prepared to face them; and it is well that we should remember that social distress often attends the introduction of
economic changes. There is need for citizens to be constantly

*Control over
the operation
of economic
forces in
different cir-
cumstances.*

on the alert, so that associated effort and legislative enactment may be steadily directed to counteract any mischiefs that may arise during a period of transition.

This is the principal duty, in regard to economic problems, which rests with the political authorities of the present time. The diffusion of democratic principles and the manner in which political power has passed into the hands of the masses of the population among English-speaking peoples have turned attention to the welfare of manual labourers as a class; and this has come to be a criterion of national prosperity. We are no longer concerned with discussing the methods by which national resources may be most rapidly developed so as to conduce to the increase of national power, or to the largest mass of products; that question is solved. Experience has shown us that material prosperity can be best attained by giving play to the capitalist administration of in-dustry. The modern problem is that of controlling this force so that its disintegrating effects on society and its pressure upon individuals may be kept within due limits; and that advances in material progress may really subserve the moral and intellectual welfare of mankind. This problem is not susceptible of any general solution; it must be dealt with in different fashions, according to the particular circumstances of each community; and peculiarities of physical character, national temperament and political constitution must be taken into account.

New inventions and methods of business organisation have been introduced into countries where the economic conditions are very dissimilar to those in Great Britain. In some places natural economy is still dominant, or prices are practically determined by custom; while other peoples are habituated to money-bargaining and competition. The physical resources which attract capitalists may be different; in one country there are great opportunities for mining, in others for wheat-growing, in others for manufacturing; and the reactions on society generally and on existing industry will be quite distinct in character. The improvement of internal communication by means of railways has dissimilar results in the unoccupied prairies of the West and in a thickly populated country like India. Benefits accrue in both regions ; but just as the advantages are distinct, so the evils that may arise, and that ought to be guarded against, are not the same. In the United States, the railroads have been the pioneers which opened up the country and rendered the settlement and cultivation of distant districts possible ; but there is a danger that these roads may become a giant monopoly that will control all future development in its own interest. In India isolated villages have been brought into contact with the outside world, and have a better market for their products ; but the rapid transition from natural to money economy and the abandonment of village self-sufficiency have tended to render the pressure of taxation more onerous, and to remove some of the old safeguards against times of scarcity and famine. In whatever form the capitalist system is introduced, the mass of the population will be under the necessity of readjusting their ordinary habits of life to new conditions ; but the nature of the strain upon society, and the character of the results will differ according to circumstances. In a country like Great Britain, where the land is owned by large proprietors with great political power, the contest between the landed and the moneyed interests took a special form ; in other areas, both in America, Europe or India, where there are peasant holdings, the corresponding struggle is more likely to arise over the rate of interest[1] than over the legislative protection of farmers. And so with all other changes. The mischiefs due to the

[1] The indebtedness of the cultivators to agricultural banks or to local usurers has become a very serious question in many parts of the world. Very remarkable success has been obtained by the Governments of New Zealand and other Australasian colonies in organising public institutions for granting loans to occupiers of the land.

breaking up of family life will be felt most severely in countries where there is a hard and fast social system, and where labour is divided into distinct castes. In India, for instance, trades are hereditary and highly stereotyped, and the organisation of factories and engineering shops cannot be introduced without a revolution in all the habits of life. The transition from domestic industry must always involve social disintegration, which will be greater according to the rigidity of the system which is being undermined.

It must also be borne in mind that the remedies which can be applied in one country are unsuitable to the circumstances of another ; it may not be possible to transplant the English Factory Inspector or Trades Unions to other climes ; new forms of administrative machinery may be required to undertake the work they are accomplishing. Some peoples by habit and training may be able to organise themselves for self-protection, while others can only look helplessly for State interference in their behalf. The French have been habituated for centuries to depend on administrative initiative to a much greater extent than the English ; such national characteristics must be taken into account, and each country must be considered separately and independently. The method of coping with such problems which has been successful in one land may be quite impracticable in another, but this does not absolve any people or Government from the duty of trying to deal with these difficulties in any form in which they may appear. In no case can it be good policy to let the economic forces work their way without any attempt so to direct them as to reduce the mischief that may arise in the course of the transition.

133. There is, however, one condition which is essential in all countries alike ; if the play of economic forces is to be wisely controlled, so that the evils which accompany industrial changes may be minimised, there must be political power that is strong enough to hold

Nationalism and Cosmo-politanism.

its own and enforce its dictates. There should be an effective authority which can ensure that the true interest of the community as a whole shall not be sacrificed to the immediate gain of any one class. In the civilised states of the old world and the new, such Governments exist; but there is need for the establishment of effective police in many parts of the globe, and it is desirable that this should be exercised not merely in personal or national but in cosmopolitan interests. The areas occupied by half-civilised and barbarous peoples are likely to suffer severely until they are brought under the authority of some power which the white man respects. This is not only desirable in the interests of foreign capitalists, but also essential as the only chance of ensuring that the native population shall receive fair treatment. The energy of pioneers and the enterprise of traders and miners, when uncontrolled, have driven the American Indians and other native populations into desperate straits, and have given rise to outbreaks which occasioned ruthless retaliation. There is great difficulty in allowing uncivilised peoples to retain independence, and attempts at the rapid assimilation of backward races to modern habits of thought and action have often been failures; it is wisest to preserve an artificial isolation in order that the necessary modification may take place gradually, and without causing the best elements in native character and traditions to be subverted. Only under the aegis of a strong political power can territorial 'reservations' be allotted to the primitive tribes and proper steps taken for promoting their gradual amelioration.

The expansion of modern industry and commerce has rendered it most desirable that there should be an extension of the political power of civilised communities, so that one or other of them shall preside over, and be responsible for, the material development of all parts of the globe. It is in the interests of the whole world that security for life and property should be everywhere assured. And this is being brought about. France, Germany, Belgium and England have established distinct spheres of influence in Africa. In the far East a similar process is going on; a great part of Asia is under the control of Russia, and England governs the thickly populated area of India; while the United States aspire to an indefinite protectorate in the New World and the islands of the Pacific. A startling extension of civilised rule has followed as a necessary consequence upon the opening of new and wide fields for economic enterprise. The crucial question for the future is whether this new authority shall be wielded for cosmopolitan welfare or merely directed to particularist and national interests.

This rapid political expansion has certainly not been due to any concerted action for the common good; indeed it can be directly traced to the increased bitterness of national rivalry which has been brought about by the Industrial Revolution. The period which immediately succeeded the Napoleonic war was one of exhaustion and quiet; observers were inclined to believe that civilised men had entered on an industrial era, when the jealousies of nations would be laid aside, and all would vie in the cultivation of the arts of peace and the holding of Universal Exhibitions. But this was an entire mistake; Germany, Italy, and America were only beginning to attain to a consciousness of national existence in the decades when this sentiment was ceasing to be the dominant force in English politics. Events have proved that their industrial development has served to whet the commercial rivalries of rising nationalities. So long as countries traded with each other in their natural products, it was easy to feel that one land was supplementing the requirements of another and that each was profiting by the interchanges; so long even as particular industries depended on hereditary and localised skill, it was not hard to acquiesce in the purchase of manufactures to which some people had a sort of established claim. But since machinery has superseded personal skill, there is no longer the same reason for accepting a position of economic dependence; each country can procure materials and manufacture for itself; each country can therefore aim at supplying its own market, and attaining to a greater measure of economic self-sufficiency.

There have been other ways in which modern inventions have tended to reinvigorate national economic jealousy. As machine industry has been developed in different lands, producers have become ambitious of obtaining access not only to home but to foreign markets. Nations that wished to secure exclusive markets for their goods have engaged in a scramble for territory in Africa and for spheres of influence in the Far East. Giant industry cannot be satisfied with a home market only—even in the United States—but aims at access to wider spheres. Germany with her newly found national unity is the most conspicuous example of this tendency; she is endeavouring to develop her industrial resources and make up for her lost opportunities of expansion and thus to build up an exclusively national economic system as a basis for national power. On the whole it seems that the age of invention has not made for peace; it has given new facilities for organised warfare, while international jealousies and rivalries have become keener, as various countries aim at securing economic independence and vie in obtaining markets for their manufactures.

There is some reason to hope, however, that this recrudescence of national economic jealousy is only a passing phase and not a permanent political condition. England had pursued an exclusive economic system for centuries; she discarded it fifty years ago, not out of mere philanthropy, but because, under changed conditions, it suited her interest to do so. She had more to gain from accepting a position in a cosmopolitan system, and recognising the interdependence between all states, than by striving to maintain a self-sufficing economic life of her own. The difficulty of procuring an adequate food supply forced her to adopt this course; but the benefit which accrues from the new scheme is not confined to England alone; the cosmopolitan policy, which she accepted from sheer necessity, leaves all other nations free to take full advantage of the markets and industrial opportunities afforded by every territory under her government.

The difference between the old nationalism and the new cosmopolitanism, comes out, not merely in the treatment accorded to the Colonies[1], but in the attitude which England takes in her new possessions towards the capital and industry of other civilised nations. English officials are exercising a control in Egypt, with considerable difficulty and under great provocation; while French capitalists reap the advantage of improved conditions, and take a large part in the trading and industrial development of the country. The Nile Valley has recently been opened up at English expense, but no attempt has been made to restrict the economic advantages of this large area to British subjects. The English subjugation of India by Clive was of no direct advantage to the British Colonies in America, but the policy of England in Egypt and on the Nile is beneficial to all civilised nations, since it insures fair play to English, American, French, and German alike. Other nations may not improbably come in time to outgrow the nationalist policy they are pursuing so eagerly at present. They may have it forced upon them by experience that they can obtain access to the largest markets and secure the commodities they require on the best terms, not by maintaining particularist rights but by fostering frequent and general commercial intercourse. Cobden's expectations of the universal adoption of free trade have been woefully disappointed; a nation must be far advanced in its economic life before it finds its greatest advantage in adopting a cosmopolitan policy; but this is a stage of development to which commercial nations are likely sooner or later to attain.

There are important political results which might accrue if

[1] See above, p. 220.

this economic policy were adopted more generally. In so far as any country finds that she is able without detriment to herself to modify or reconstruct her commercial policy on cosmopolitan lines, the occasions for international dispute are likely to be considerably diminished. The cessation of national economic rivalries would do much to remove the most potent of all incentives to war. When we remember how much of the fighting in all ages has been due to efforts to secure or maintain exclusive trading rights, we may feel that the most favourable augury of a coming universal peace lies in the fact that one country has found it desirable to lay aside this policy, and that all nations are allowed to share equally in the commercial advantages of any territory where British rule is established.

While cosmopolitanism in commercial policy encourages us to cherish hopes for an improvement in the relations between nations, it also supplies more favourable conditions than a national economic policy can ever afford, for the internal government of large dependencies. So soon as exclusive national interests are definitely discarded it becomes less difficult for Governments to take fair account of the habits and customs of subject races, and to make their welfare a primary consideration. In the eighteenth century, the welfare of colonists and of the peoples in conquered countries was deliberately subordinated to the prosperity and power of European nations. The policy of civilised states at that time was so self-regarding, that it was hardly ever in accordance with the best tradition of that Roman Empire which, with all its defects and despite its inherent weakness, still sets the type of the grandest polity the world has ever known. It is the lasting glory of that Empire that it retained so many of the noblest elements of earlier civilisations; the Greek cities maintained the traditions of Greek culture; the Goths and other colonies of barbarian soldiers on the frontiers preserved much of their primitive virtue. England in her treatment of Canada and of India has shown herself capable of achieving a similar result, and has avoided any interference with the sentiments or the traditions of her subject populations. The province of Quebec affords a striking example. In 1759 A.D. the most successful of all the French colonies was brought under English rule; but there was no insistence on stamping out what was characteristically French. The language and religion were carefully maintained, and there is no place on the globe where the more wholesome elements of the life of old-world France have been so effectively preserved as in Canada. The French population are loyal to English rule because they are confident that there is no danger of attempts to assimilate them to customs and institutions they dislike. Again, as the administration of India has come more and more under English authority, there has been a scrupulous effort to understand native law and custom, to take account of them and to respect them. Just as Rome rescued Greek literature, art, and institutions when Greek political life was perishing, so English influence is helping to preserve for the world the great heritage of Eastern thought and civilisation.

It is necessary that law and order should be established everywhere, and that there should be an effective police throughout the known world. These are the very foundations of society; but only on the cosmopolitan system is it possible to give security to life and property, and yet to be willing to leave racial habits and national customs comparatively unaffected, and to allow for the perpetuation and diffusion of the best social elements in the countries which are brought under civilised control.

CONCLUSION.

134. THE foregoing sketch has been directed to the

Reciprocal action of Man, and his environment.

elucidation of one particular question ; an attempt has been made to discriminate the specific contribution of each of the great peoples of the past, who have combined to transmit the heritage of Western Civilisation from one era to another. This grand and complex tradition has been shaped and altered, enlarged or embellished a little by each of the hands that have passed it on. The various streamlets have sometimes added to the volume, and sometimes changed the character of the river they helped to form. We have noticed the industrial skill of the Egyptians, the passive trade of Judaea, and the active commerce of the Phoenicians, as the elements of economic life ; we have marked how the Greeks subordinated their regard for material resources to the aim of attaining a worthy human life ; we have seen how the city life of the Greeks was perpetuated and diffused by Alexander the Great and under the Roman Empire ; we have tried to trace the causes which resulted in the ruin of that Empire and the decay of ancient civilisation.

We have also examined the process of reconstructing civilised society, under new authority and sanctions ; the gradual restoration of much that had been lost in the West ; the first steps in the expansion of Christendom ; the influences which brought about its disruption ; the rise of nationalities, with the consequent commercial and colonial rivalries since the age of geographical discovery. Attention has been called to the increased power over nature and the keener jealousies, which have been awakened by the age of invention. We, on the eve of the twentieth century, are debtors to countless generations of men of diverse races and many lands; and common gratitude demands that we should try to understand the nature of our obligations to each.

There is a marked difference in the character of the earlier and of the later contributions. Man is at first "immersed in nature"; physical conditions determine his destiny; the climate and soil fix the arts to which he can devote himself,—hunting, pasturage, tillage, or whatever it may be; and these employments apparently react on character and aptitude. But, as time goes on, and the arts are more developed, and intercommunication diffuses them among the peoples, man comes to have more mastery over nature; he can alter his surroundings; by the acclimatisation of plants and animals, he may do much to subdue the earth, and force it to suit his convenience. The Phoenician, the Greek and the Roman had attained to such dominion over physical environment, as to be able to a considerable extent, to mould it to their will.

Hence in the modern world we have less to do with physical conditions as controlling the character and direction of human development; we see more of human effort deliberately exerted, and of human aims and aspirations as determining the lines of human progress. The course of geographical discovery was not determined by physical pressure or accidental conjunctions of circumstances; it was mainly due to the intelligent and assiduous human energy, consciously directed to this purpose. So too with the progress of invention; this was not the mere outcome of a happy chance, but the work of men who had the wit to meet the requirements of their times.

The growing importance in the later history of civilisation of human activity, as compared with that of physical surroundings, may be seen in another way. The great resources which the age of maritime discovery opened up could not in themselves serve to enrich the peoples who controlled them. Portugal was exhausted by her East Indian commerce, and Spain failed to profit by her American possessions. Opportunities by themselves are of little account; the wisdom to use them is the really important thing. Hence the main contributions of modern nations to the economic progress of the world have lain in their experiments in policy, in the aims they cherished, the means they used in the pursuit of wealth and the success or failure of their attempts.

135. There has, then, been a reciprocal influence between man and his environment; but in the later stages, human activity has been the more potent factor.

Unintentional advance.

It is, however, curious to notice how much of that activity has been unconscious, that is to say, not intentionally directed to the results it produced. We can never understand economic phenomena unless we look outside them to those other sides of human life, which have an indirect bearing upon the course of material progress. It is through the reaction of political life on economic conditions, that the most striking developments have been brought about; or by the reaction of commercial expansion on industry, and of industrial improvement on commerce. Those who built up our free political system, had no conception that they were providing us with the means of securing and developing a colonial empire. Those who devoted themselves to the encouragement of our mercantile marine, had no idea that they were creating the circumstances which rendered an age of invention possible. Nor had the monks and missionaries who laid the foundations of mediaeval society much deliberate aim beyond that of saving their own souls and those of other people. The economic bearing and results of such work are too far off for any human being to foresee or to take them intentionally into account; and thus the whole has grown up to a large extent through human action that was not consciously directed to these objects.

136. Though the growth of Western Civilisation has been brought about with so little conscious human effort, it is difficult to suppose that its course has been wholly fortuitous. Constant change *Progress as real, and not fortuitous.* and decay are characteristic of all organic growth; yet there has been advance on the whole, even though there has been decline here and destruction there all the time. We may take what test we like,—the command over natural forces and the power of obtaining natural products for the use of man,—the facilities for intercourse between all parts of the globe,—the possibilities of maintaining a large population in comfort—and we shall find, that tried by whatever criterion, there has never been an age that could compare with the present. Despite the evils of our time, we may feel that there has been progress in solving some of the most difficult social problems. There never was a time when there were such facilities for organising vast masses of labour, and there never was a period when the individual labourer had more opportunity, not perhaps for choosing his own circumstances, but for pursuing his own self-development. If we compare the work of constructing the Forth Bridge with the traditional accounts respecting the raising of the Great Pyramid, we shall feel that there has not only been progress in the mechanical arts, but in the power of so ordering society that it shall be possible to get the most effective combination of masses of labour, and yet to secure for each individual some opportunities of political power and intellectual interest.

The change in regard to commerce has been even more striking; when we take such beginnings of trade as the 'mutual gifts' and tribute of the Egyptians, the barter of the Phoenicians in Africa and their half piratical expeditions on

the Mediterranean, and contrast them with the commerce of
the present day—the world-wide safety it enjoys, the complicated machinery by which it is carried on, the keenness in
bargaining which prevents its benefits from being monopolised
by one party to the exclusion of others—we are better able to
gauge the extraordinary progress that has been made.   Even if
we feel that the dreams of universal peace are idle, that commerce depends on international security, and security in the
last resort on armaments, we may yet see that an international
organisation of postage, of banking, of traffic, is being gradually
built up, and that arbitration is settling questions which would
in old days have been decided by war ; it is not possible to lay
down limits as to the possible growth of international institutions in the future.   Without indulging in distant speculations,
we may yet recognise the real progress that has been made in
such great departments of social life as industrial efficiency and
organisation, in commercial activity and the safety of international intercourse.   The course of these changes has not
been uninterrupted, but they have seemed to be directed
towards one goal—that of establishing man's dominion over
the earth, and utilising its resources to the fullest extent for the
well-being of the race.

    137.   When we contrast the earliest known beginnings
with the latest developments of human material
progress, the difference is extraordinary ; and yet
it is worth while to remember that each factor
in the great movement has been in itself comparatively trivial.   There have been changes that were startling,
but they were not sudden ; the way had been prepared for
them ; the discovery of the direct route to the East was not a
happy accident ; years of patient enterprise had led up to this
crowning feat ; the work of each individual was superseded,
and forgotten, but it was a necessary step in the advance, and
thus it has had a permanent value and result.   Much has
passed away, but little has been lost ; all forms of human

*Temporary
and permanent
Elements in
Civilisation.*

skill have been surpassed in time, all the various types of economic group have been outgrown; none have been final and lasting.

Nothing has proved of permanent and unchanging value, except the principles which lie at the foundation of all modern society, and which are essential to its progress in the future. The very greatness of our advance in material prosperity may blind us to the truth that human life does not consist in the abundance of the things that man possesses. Great accumulations may cause only jealousy and greed; the mechanical powers and faculty for organisation, which have developed in the present day, may be made to subserve short-sighted and destructive passions. It was the work of the Greeks to set before us a high ideal of the possibilities of human nature, in the individual and in society; and it is a most important Christian duty to strive to maintain an even higher ideal in each generation.

Free play for the individual is the distinguishing feature of our present civilisation, and is alike its glory and its danger. Hence the problem of the age is that of education, which implies not merely the instructing nor even the disciplining of children, but the forming individuals who are capable of self-discipline, and of thus voluntarily rendering themselves useful and effective members of society. Nor has any sounder scheme of self-discipline been devised, than that which is based on truths that were revealed eighteen centuries ago; which rests on the belief in the immortal existence of the human personality, and on the desire to use things material as a preparation for a nobler and worthier life when the temporal shall have passed away. There has been no other teaching which alike enhances the dignity of human nature and brings its most exalted hopes to bear directly and immediately on the routine of ordinary life and the control of mundane affairs. The same principles which served to lay the foundations of a healthier civilisation, when the old seemed to be shattered for ever, will suffice to strengthen the cohesive forces of society and to guard against utter disintegration and anarchy.

In falling back on these principles we may be protected against another danger which threatens us. The expansion of Western Civilisation has brought the various races of the world, with apparently irreconcilable differences of habit, and custom, into the closest contact; there has been much ruthless extermination wherever the civilised and the half-civilised meet, and there are increasing racial jealousies between civilised peoples of distinct races. Deeply ingrained antagonisms cannot be suppressed, but they may be so modified as to cease to be a danger; they do cease to be a danger if we not only recognise that the fitness of different races for different conditions of climate and soil constitutes in itself a right to existence, but also endeavour gradually to raise the lower races to higher ideals of life, so that the introduction of modern machinery and modern organisation may not be in itself a curse. It is only as they and we can take common ground, in accepting the same ideals and striving to realize them, that there can ever be a harmonious development of the activities of all mankind.

APPENDIX.

THE TRANSPLANTATION OF ARTS AND INSTITUTIONS.

THERE are often striking similarities in the arts which are practised and the administrative organs which exist in different parts of the globe. Such a resemblance may be accounted for in various ways. It may be due to the fact that there has been direct descent from a common source along separate and distinct lines ; or it may be explained by independent origination in two different places. There is, however, a third way of explaining the phenomena—by the conscious and deliberate transplantation of arts and institutions from one place to another. The full significance of this third mode of transmission is not obvious at first sight ; but careful consideration brings out the fact that the possibilities of conscious transplantation have been so many and frequent, that it is rarely necessary to assume either *independent descent* or *independent origination* as the most probable explanation of an observed similarity.

An illustration may make the point at issue more clear. Material relics of Roman civilisation are found in many parts of England, and it seems natural at first sight to assume that any of our institutions which are closely analogous to those of the Romans have had a persistent life in this island and are unbroken survivals of the habits and practices of Roman Britain ; alleged instances have been noted both in rural and urban life, in methods of taxation and in conditions of tenure. The more the point is examined, however, the more it becomes probable that the alleged persistence of organised society in Britain through the period of English invasion is incredible, and that the resemblances can be best explained as the work of ecclesiastics and later immigrants who reintroduced into England institutions and terminology that had survived from Roman times in other parts of Europe. Since

18—2

we can account for the facts by the influence of that conscious transplantation which was slowly and steadily at work for centuries, we are not entitled to assume an independent line of descent in this island itself, especially as there is much historical evidence which conflicts with that hypothesis.

There is always a danger of being guilty of anachronism and of taking for granted that social forces which are familiar in our own day must also have been frequently operative in earlier times. The English race, for the last two centuries, has been eagerly engaged in a struggle after progress, and has been consciously endeavouring to devise improvements in all the arts of life. Labour-saving contrivances are invented every day in some branches of industry; we are inclined to attribute a similar fertility of invention to the human race at all stages of development. There is reason to doubt, however, whether the independent origination and introduction of new arts and institutions has been either as easy or as frequent as we might at first sight suppose; the history of inventions shows that it has been extraordinarily difficult for any genius to render a new process a practical success; while it has never been easy to induce peasant farmers to adopt fresh methods of cultivation. The obstacles even to the transplantation of existing industries have been considerable, and there must be still greater hindrances to be overcome by those who create a hitherto unknown art. The probabilities of the independent origination in two distinct places of the same industrial or social habit are comparatively small: but we ought also to remember that this mode of accounting for the phenomena is inherently unsatisfactory, since it is not susceptible of verification[1]. We may often be unable to show from what source some practice was derived, but we can never hope to prove that it was not derived at all. We may be justified in making the negative statement that we cannot account for the phenomena in any other way, but never in asserting independent origination as a fact. It is only allowable to have recourse to this explanation in the last resort, and we ought never to refer any act or institution to independent origination until we have

---

[1] "It appears, then, to be a condition of a genuine scientific hypothesis, that it be not destined always to remain an hypothesis, but be of such a nature as to be either proved or disproved by that comparison with observed facts which is termed verification." Mill, *Logic*, II. 14.

examined all the possibilities of transplantation and have decided against them.

Without attempting an exhaustive classification, we may notice that there are three ways in which the transplantation of arts and institutions may be readily effected ; by personal communication, by the imitation of foreign models, and by literary suggestion.

(*a*) The migration of persons who possess some definite form of skill is the simplest means of transferring an art, and in some cases it is the only possible method by which an industry can be introduced into other lands. There are many matters of *technique* that can only be communicated by personal instruction, especially where manual dexterity is concerned. The invention of machinery not only saves the drudgery of labour, but supersedes many forms of specialised technical skill, and thus enables men to dispense with the effort to acquire aptitudes, which were inseparable from the workmen in all the ages that preceded the industrial revolution. The importation of the necessary machinery is the chief step that is needed now for introducing a new industry, but it was not so in former days. The impossibility of transplanting an art, unless the men skilled in it were transferred as well, has been so generally recognised, that at many periods in the world's history cities or nations have attempted to protect themselves against foreign competition by prohibiting the emigration of artisans[1] with the view of retaining a monopoly of some craft ; while the greatest efforts were made by progressive communities to induce skilled workmen to immigrate. The history of particular industries abounds with illustrations of the manner in which the enterprise and intelligence of some one immigrant, or group of immigrants, have been directly instrumental in planting a craft in places where, though it had not previously existed, it could be advantageously carried on,—the new drapery and the silk trade of England[2], the paper making of Scotland[3], and the linen manu-

---

[1] Vol. I. p. 32. On the other hand, Leo the Isaurian, in attempting to enforce his iconoclastic policy, drove many artists from the Empire, and gave a great stimulus to the pursuit of fine arts in Italy. Labarte, *Histoire des arts industriels*, I. 105. Cunningham, *Growth of English Industry*, II. 348, 361.

[2] Cunningham, *Growth of English Industry*, II. 36.

[3] Cunningham, *Alien Immigrants in England*, p. 242.

facture of Ireland[1] may be adduced as cases in point. For recent centuries, it is comparatively easy to trace the existence of groups of aliens in England and to specify the industrial impulse which they severally communicated. There is every reason to believe that a similar process has gone on in all ages, though the evidence as to the precise links of connection has been lost. When we consider the occasions and the frequency of personal intercommunication which existed in bygone times, we shall see that it is impossible to lay down any limits as to the extent of the influence which may have been exercised in this fashion, even though no information has survived as to the time or the form in which the movement occurred.

In the ancient world, warfare, followed as it often was by the military occupation and the deportation of considerable populations[2], must have played a considerable part in the diffusion of a knowledge of the arts of life ; while the organised slave trade, which existed in the ancient world and lasted through the Dark Ages till mediaeval times, gave immense opportunities for personal migration.

Many facilities for travelling have been introduced within the last century and have rendered touring a pleasure, but we are apt to forget what numbers of persons were compelled in the later middle ages to be constantly facing the dangers and difficulties of the roads. Much of the business which can now be done by letter or even by telegraph could not have been transacted by mediaeval merchants without personally undertaking a journey[3]. The great households of nobles were continually on the move, and many persons went as pilgrims to celebrated shrines in their own or in distant lands. The vast concourse of traders at mediaeval fairs[4] is a sufficient proof that, despite the local restriction which was maintained in many places and for certain classes, there was also a large population which enjoyed considerable freedom of movement. All through the Middle Ages there was abundant opportunity for much personal migration, so that there is no

[1] Cunningham, *Alien Immigrants in England*, p. 240.

[2] Numerous instances occur in the Old Testament, for instance, in the Babylonian captivity of the Jews, and the repeopling of Samaria.

[3] Jusserand, *English Wayfaring Life*, 244.

[4] Bourquelot, *Foires de Champagne*, I. 132.

difficulty in understanding the transmission of any art or practice from one part of Christendom to another.

The possibility of personal migration will frequently suffice to explain the transference not merely of arts but of institutions from one place to another ; we are not compelled to suppose that these last were an independent growth at each new centre. It was a common thing at the period of the Crusades, when town life was reviving, to grant to the citizens of one place all the rights and privileges which were already enjoyed by the citizens of some other borough which was taken as a model[1]. The customs thus conferred may in some cases have been fully committed to writing ; but the practice occasionally involved personal intercourse for the settlement of disputed points. In one recorded instance, too, it seems to have been felt that skill in administering institutions, like the *technique* of some arts, was best learnt from experts who were induced to migrate. When Bishop Robert laid out the town of St. Andrews in Fife he not only borrowed a foreign plan for the streets, but introduced a provost from Berwick[2], who was used to municipal government, and who was capable of organising the institutions of the new town. There is no reason to believe that this case is unique or even exceptional ; it would appear to be highly probable that the *hanse*, or any element which a merchant class contributed to the growth of town life in the backward regions of Europe, was brought from abroad by foreign settlers who had some familiarity with commercial life in more advanced communities.

(*b*) Transplantation may also have taken place at times by the transference of manufactured articles of a new character or design. This may have happened in the course of commerce or through warfare ; and the subsequent imitation of any goods that were much admired would sometimes be comparatively simple. There are many things which are easy to make, when once they are thought of, and the accidental securing of a single specimen might give the necessary suggestion. Such imitation is a very different thing from independent invention. There is considerable resemblance between the chain-armour worn in the East and the *brynja*

---

[1] On the affiliation of burghs, compare Gross, *Gild Merchant*, I. 241.

[2] Scott, *Berwick*, p. 6.

of the Viking[1]; it would not be hard for the Norse workmen to make such protective armour when once the thing or the idea of the thing had been brought under their notice; and the fact of commercial intercourse between the Norsemen and the peoples of the Levant is so far established, that there is no difficulty in accounting for similarities of this kind.

(*c*) There is another method by which a knowledge of arts and institutions may be transmitted not only over considerable distances in space but across long periods of time. Laws and administrative methods, systems of taxation and business practice, may be embodied in writing, and by this means the revival of a long-forgotten usage may be facilitated. The diffusion of Law Merchant, and the influences exercised in the later Middle Ages by the study of Roman Law, may be taken as illustrations. The similar action with regard to wages and prices, which occurred almost simultaneously in many cities and countries after the Black Death, becomes more intelligible when we remember that a tradition may well have survived of attempts which had been made throughout the Roman Empire to meet such dearth by analogous regulations. In more recent times the special character-istics of the Mother of Parliaments were noted by such a keen observer as Montesquieu, and his treatise has not merely had the effect of spreading a knowledge of the British Constitution but has induced nearly every civilised country to adapt its govern-ment, more or less consciously, to this one model as the French writer described it[2].

A knowledge of industrial arts may be conveyed in the same sort of way. The importance of recipes not merely for the cure of diseases, but for such processes as dyeing, and for the decorative arts generally, has been very great. The most cele-brated treasury of such information was the *Diversarum Artium Schedula*, written by Rogkerus, a goldsmith, who was a *Benedictine* monk at Helmershausen[3], in the eleventh or earlier part of the twelfth century. The number and dates of the manuscripts which

---

[1] Du Chaillu, *The Viking Age*, I. 215; II. 99.

[2] The existence of two chambers and the *alleged* severance of the executive and legislative powers were points on which he laid stress.

[3] Ilg, *Theophilus Presbyter* in *Quellenschriften für Kunstgeschichte und Kunsttechnik des Mittelalters*, VII. p. xliii.

survive prove that his book had a very wide and long-continued popularity. In this compendium, according to the author, you will "find out whatever Greece possesses in kinds and mixtures of various colours ; whatever Tuscany knows of in mosaic work, or in variety of enamel ; whatever Arabia shows forth in work of fusion, ductility, or chasing ; whatever Italy ornaments with gold, in diversity of vases, and sculpture of gems or ivory ; whatever France loves in a costly variety of windows ; whatever industrious Germany approves in work of gold, silver, copper and iron, of woods and stones[1]." The generous spirit in which the monk sought to diffuse such technical knowledge contrasts strikingly with the care of the ordinary craftsmen to keep the secrets of the trade to themselves, and in particular to prevent the copying of their recipes. We learn from a case in the glass-industry that the master's daughter did not always sympathise with the parental policy towards apprentices in this matter[2].

When the indefinite possibilities of transmission are once recognised, a large field is opened up for the students of the special history of any one art or institution. The building trades, which have supplied such lasting monuments of the activity of bygone ages, give the most unimpeachable evidence of the growth and diffusion of particular expedients in construction or design. The invention of the arch, the combination of the arch and column, the use of the dome, are important structural improvements; and the districts where early experiments were attempted, as well as the development and diffusion of these architectural features, have been traced with care. The regions within which similar taste in Gothic building was prevalent are well marked ; and the history of architecture in the Isle de France or in England shows not only the regular course of progress in these areas[3], but the occasional introduction of extraneous influences. The visits of workmen from a distance are especially obvious in connection with decorative work, such as carving or the fixing of stained glass ; and the inlaid marbles of the Taj Mahal at Agra show us how far Italian craftsmen might be willing to travel in the seventeenth century[4]. Civil

[1] *Theophilus Rugerus*, Preface (Hendrie's Translation), p. li.
[2] Lobmeyr, *Die Glasindustrie, ihre geschichte*, 73.
[3] E. S. Prior, *A History of Gothic Art in England*, p. 16.
[4] Ferguson, *History of Indian and Eastern Architecture* (1876), 588.

Appendix.

and domestic as well as religious buildings offer frequent examples of the transplanting of particular types of design. We may notice it in the *stoep* of the Dutch house, in the position assigned to the fireplace in New England homes[1], in the method of grouping contiguous houses in streets, as well as in the plans which have been adopted at various times for the laying out of cities[2].

It is in connection with the building and decorative arts, that there is the greatest mass of evidence available for tracing the course of development in any locality and for detecting the introduction of outside influences. But we have reason to suppose that there is a similar story to be told in regard to other arts, if we had but the means of spelling it out. The introduction of the horse into Egypt, with all the influence which it must have exercised on the arts of peace and of war, can be approximately dated[3]; there are probably few lands where ploughing with oxen is indigenous; if we could trace the diffusion of this practice, we might also have the means of following out the introduction of the institutions for collective husbandry with which it seems to be intimately connected[4].

There is also an interesting field for the student of social history in trying to detect the modifications which a transplanted institution may undergo on a new soil. It is curious to notice the changes by which the craft gilds, which were organised in certain English towns under the Angevins to enable colonies of aliens to obtain a political status[5], were adapted in the fourteenth century to serve as a machinery for supervising the quality of manu-

---

[1] Isham and Brown, *Early Rhode Island Houses*, p. 16, *Early Connecticut Houses*, p. 7.

[2] See above, p. 92. In regard to the ground-plans of towns it is at least clear that simplicity of design is not primitive, but has only been attained in advanced civilisations. The American method of laying out cities in blocks was seen to be simple, as soon as it had been introduced in Philadelphia; but it was not natural to the settlers at Montreal or Quebec, at Boston or New York, or to the founders of numberless cities in the old world.

[3] C. A. Piétrement, *Les chevaux dans les temps préhistoriques et historiques* (1883), p. 459 fol.

[4] Cunningham, *Growth of English Industry*, I. 42.

[5] *Ibid.* I. 647.

factures[1], and survive in London in the present day to be the organs of civic munificence. The difference in the course of the development of the corresponding institutions in Scotch towns[2] is very remarkable. Climate and soil, or social atmosphere, may affect a transplanted institution very deeply, and the genius of a particular country is more clearly seen in its real power of adapting what it borrows, than in a fancied facility for independent origination ; that seems to have been a rare occurrence, depending on the conjunction of personal ingenuity and exceptionally favourable circumstances.

It is easy to trace analogies between the development of animal life and of the social organism ; but the student of sociology is often at a loss to secure a sufficient number of independent instances to enable him to formulate well-founded generalisations as to the course of human progress. There certainly appears to be a considerable contrast between the evolution of new forms in the animal world and the course of human history. We do not find an infinite number of experiments in social progress with the survival of the fittest ; there is not such marvellous productivity in the social as in the animal life. Rather does it seem that there is apt to be stagnation and decadence in human institutions, and that progress has on the whole been due to success in cherishing the rare and occasional efforts of human genius.

[1] Cunningham, *Growth of English Industry*, I. 342.
[2] Gross, *Gild Merchant*, I. 199.

INDEX.

Iberian peninsula, 47, 189, 190
Iceland, 3, 110, 113
Immunities, 39, 49, 50, 59
Incidence of Taxation, 76, 169 n., 252
Income-tax, 252
India, 54 n., 66, 183, 187, 190, 221, 223, 229, 253, 260, 261, 265, 266, 267
Indian Ocean, 183, 184, 188, 189
Indiction, 33
Indies, East, 161, 183, 187, 196, 197, 198, 200, 200 n., 215, 221, 226; West, 54 n., 131, 196, 203
Individual initiative, 216, 228, 243
Individualism, 244, 247 n., 256, 273
Indulgences, 146
Industrial arbitration, 236; arts, 6, 7, 36; classes, 169, 174, 247; corporations, 157; depression, 230; revolution, 167, 180 *seq.*, 225 *seq.*, 233 n., 238, 244, 246, 249, 253, 263, 277
Industry, capitalist organisation of, 202, 210, 238, 254, 259; domestic, 250, 261
Ingenuus, 32 n.
Inland Revenue, 252
Innocent III, 121
Interest on loans, 108, 176, 180, 260
Inter-municipal trade, 92, 113, 173, 226
Invention, age of, 225 fol., 232, 245, 253, 258, 264, 269, 270
Ireland, 3, 47, 110, 253 n., 278
Irminon, Abbot, 110 n.
Iron, 113, 227, 227 n., 228
Islam, 49, 116, 118, 130
Isenbert, 98 n.
Isle de France, 281
Isonzo, Battle of, 27
Italian bankers, 67, 86, 89, 176
Italy, 4, 27, 30, 39, 43, 47, 66, 72, 84, 90, 113, 119, 120, 121, 126, 128, 136 n., 139, 148, 149, 150, 151, 160 n., 181, 208, 263, 277 n., 281

Ivory, 121, 281

James I (of England), 215, 219
Japan, 15, 186, 200, 254
Java, 200
Jerusalem, 72, 126
Jews, 26 n., 49, 75, 89, 143, 278 n.
John the Good (King of France), 83
John (King of England), 98 n.
Josiah, 45
Journeyman, 96, 97, 180; gilds, 167 n.
Judæa, 268
Judices, 51, 52
Jumièges, 39
Jumna, 47
Justinian, 12 n., 30, 31, 49, 153

Kind, payments in, 82, 88, 100, 102
Kirkwall, 4

Labour, as Christian discipline, 106; as drudgery, 35; dignity of, 35, 36; division of, 235; free flow of, 158, 246, 253; migration of, 182; of children, 233, 238–9, 239 n., 250; of women, 233, 239, 250; organisation of, 103, 167, 248, 271; regulation of, 16, 237
Laffemas, 209, 210, 238, 241, 247
Lana, arte di, 94 n., 165 n.
Lancashire, 227 n.
Landed interests, 91, 223, 252, 260
Languedoc, 90, 116, 120
Law, John, 223 n.
Law, *see Canon, Civil.*
Law merchant, 3, 91, 95, 153, 280
Law, Salic, 31; sumptuary, 195
Leicester, 110
Leo the Great, 20
Leo the Isaurian, 277 n.
Levant, 108, 185, 201, 280
Levantine trade, 46, 50, 127, 208
Lewis of Bavaria, 142
Liguria, 28

For EU product safety concerns, contact us at Calle de José Abascal, 56–1°, 28003 Madrid, Spain or eugpsr@cambridge.org.

www.ingramcontent.com/pod-product-compliance
Ingram Content Group UK Ltd.
Pitfield, Milton Keynes, MK11 3LW, UK
UKHW042209180425
457623UK00011B/108